PREGNANCY AND POWER

A YAKIMA SQUAW AND HER PAPPOOSE.

RICKIE SOLINGER

PREGNANCY AND POWER

A Short History of Reproductive Politics in America

New York University Press • *New York and London*

Cover images: Mexican mother in California, June 1935 (photograph by Dorothea Lange); pregnant daughter of a migrant family, Imperial Valley, California, February 1939 (photograph by Dorothea Lange); mother of first baby born in Okeechobee migratory labor camp, Belle Glade, Florida, June 1940 (photograph by Marion Wolcott). Images courtesy of the Library of Congress.

About the frontispiece: Yakama woman with her papoose on her back, between ca. 1900 and ca. 1930. Courtesy of the Library of Congress.

First published in paperback in 2007

NEW YORK UNIVERSITY PRESS
New York and London
www.nyupress.org

Library of Congress Cataloging-in-Publication Data
Solinger, Rickie
Pregnancy and power : a short history of reproductive politics
in America / Rickie Solinger.
p. cm.
Includes bibliographical references and index.
ISBN–13: 978–0–8147–9828–7 (pbk. : alk. paper)
ISBN–10: 0–8147–9828–4 (pbk. : alk. paper)
1. Birth control—Political aspects—United States.   2. Abortion—Political
aspects—United States.   3. Human reproduction—Political aspects—
United States.   4. Women's rights—United States.   I. Title.
HQ766.5.U5S67   2005
363.9'6'0973—dc22   2005011937

New York University Press books are printed on acid-free paper,
and their binding materials are chosen for strength and durability.

Manufactured in the United States of America
p 10 9 8 7 6 5 4 3 2

For Nell and Maddy and Sylvie and Nyxi and Ali May and Shiloh and Sasha

who have tolerated my stern eye all of their lives and accepted my love

Contents

Introduction

What Is Reproductive Politics?

LIKE MANY WOMEN, I can summon up that old terror at will: being twenty-one and desperate to locate sensations in my breasts, in my belly, the first stains of blood—signs that my period is coming. I can also remember being twenty-eight and thrilled, my period a week overdue. I must be pregnant! Like many women, I learned early and often that sex-and-pregnancy, what I'll call "reproductive capacity," can carry profoundly different meanings, depending on a lot of variables.

Having learned this personal lesson so well—that a biological event can mean such different things at different times in one's life—and being a person committed to social justice endeavors, I was drawn into a related scholarly journey. My work is about exploring the ways that reproductive capacity, including childbearing and motherhood, has carried a variety of meanings *for* and *about* girls and women in the United States. Pregnancy has carried different meanings depending on the age of a girl or woman and also depending on her race and on whether she is rich or poor or in the middle. The meaning of a pregnancy can also be determined by the historical moment in which it occurs.

Pregnancy and Power is an orientation to reproductive politics in U.S. history. I use the word "orientation" partly as a sign that the book will not cover every important event and development and movement that has shaped the variety of women's reproductive experiences over time. Nor will it cover the ways that each and every demographic group has felt the impact of reproductive laws and policies in the United States. In part because of where the historical sources exist, the experiences of white women and African American women are more fully discussed than those of Latina and Native American women and other women of color.

Here is what *Pregnancy and Power* will do: It will ask, what is reproductive politics? It will build a definition of reproductive politics and use that definition to look at these big questions: How and why have laws and public policies and community attitudes about sex-and-pregnancy changed over time? How have these laws and policies and attitudes shaped the lives of different groups of women differently?

When people have asked me about the book I'm working on, and I've said that it's about reproductive politics in U.S. history, from 1776 to the present, I've almost always been met with: "Reproductive politics in the eighteenth century?? What does *that* mean?" I hope that readers of *Pregnancy and Power* will come away from this book not only understanding how matters of sex-and-pregnancy and power—"reproductive politics"—were key to the development of the United States in the eighteenth century, but also how these matters have continued to shape social and political relationships and the culture of this country throughout its history. I hope that readers will come to the end of the book well equipped to recognize reproductive politics in a newspaper article, on TV, in the doctor's office, wherever it appears. I hope that readers will come away able to construct an informed and reasoned response to the issues involved. To accomplish this task, *Pregnancy and Power* will weave my own research together with the work of many historians and others who have written about reproductive politics.

THE MEANING OF "REPRODUCTIVE POLITICS"

"Reproductive politics" is a late twentieth-century term. Women's rights advocates known as Second Wave feminists devised the term originally to describe late twentieth-century struggles over contraception and abortion, race and sterilization, class and adoption, women and sexuality, and other, related subjects. The term has been useful because it captures the way that questions about power are at the heart of these debates. For example, who has the power to make decisions about keeping or ending a pregnancy? The pregnant woman, a physician, or a state legislator? Who has the power to define a *legitimate* mother, that is, a woman who has the right to raise her own child? A city welfare official, a congressman, an adoption agency, a Supreme Court judge, or the mother herself?

Since about 1970, many public officials and others have used legislatures and courts and the media to define, advocate, and legislate a complex array of public powers over women's reproductive capacity. All this has been partly in response to *Roe v. Wade*, the 1973 Supreme Court decision that legalized abortion and assigned the power of this aspect of reproductive decision making to "the woman and her physician." And in recent decades, millions of girls and women have defined reproductive and motherhood issues as matters of self-determination and human rights, claiming power for themselves. Reproductive politics has been and remains one of the most fiercely contested and most complicated subjects about power in American society.

I understand the term "reproductive politics" to refer most basically to the question, *Who has power over matters of pregnancy and its consequences?* In this book, I'll use this concept to look back across U.S. history and investigate how this kind of power was defined and distributed at various times in the past. We can, for example, look at how lawmakers in South Carolina used their power to assign different values to the pregnancies of women according to their race in the 1830s. We can ask how these racially determined valuations shaped the reproductive and other life experiences of different groups of women differently in that time and place and in others.

We can ask about the power—or lack of power—an enslaved African woman, a Cherokee woman, an unmarried white schoolteacher, the wife of a Philadelphia merchant each possessed in 1850 to make pregnancy a more or less likely consequence of intercourse. Why might each of these women have cared to encourage or discourage pregnancy? What kinds of strategies did various community authorities use to create and maintain control over these matters? What population issues, consumption issues, and labor needs, for example, pressed authorities to exercise what kinds of control over the reproductive lives of the various groups of fertile women in society? What were the consequences for different groups of women of trying to control pregnancies? What were the consequences of becoming pregnant and a mother? How would the answers to these questions be different if we were investigating the experiences of an African American woman, a Cherokee woman, or a white merchant's wife in 1950 instead of 1850? Or in 2005?

These kinds of questions help us see that reproductive politics has been an issue throughout U.S. history. They also help us see that reproductive politics has a history. These are important first recognitions, especially in the United States, where so many people have come to believe that pregnancy and motherhood are simply about a choice, any woman making her own individual choice.

For the rest of this first chapter, I will try to build a definition of—or describe—the *arena* of reproductive politics, looking at six ideas that I hope will help deepen the way we understand what this politics is. In discussing each of these ideas, I will use examples to show how a given aspect of reproductive politics has shaped the lives of girls and women in the United States. Examples, in this chapter and throughout the book, may come from the life of an enslaved woman living in the nineteenth century in the mountains of Tennessee, or a college student in early twenty-first-century Boston; or from the pen of a founding father in the 1780s; or from a speech by a social critic in the middle of the 1900s. Examples will jump out from across time and place. The point of the examples is to ground each of the big, framing ideas in everyday reality, and also to suggest how to recognize the material of reproductive politics, wherever it occurs.

REPRODUCTIVE POLITICS: SOLVING SOCIAL PROBLEMS

Debates about reproductive politics have often been described as discussions about women, their bodies, their reproductive capacity, their social roles, their access—or lack of access—to citizenship rights or human rights, and about their status as mothers. But across the history of the United States, quite often when presidents and senators, social critics, and ordinary people have engaged in discussion about reproductive politics, they did not seem to be talking about women as individual persons or as citizens with personal needs and rights and dignity.

Official discussions about reproductive politics have rarely been women-centered. More often than not, debate and discussion about reproductive politics—*where the power to manage women's reproductive capacity should reside*—have been part of discussions about *how to solve certain large social problems facing the country.* These social or economic or political problems have changed over time. And the fertility of different groups of women has been associated with solutions to different problems. But across time, the social-problem approach to female fertility has prevailed.

Here is a classic and typical example of the social-problem approach, followed by another example, one that flips the first solution on its head. The two examples together show how the content of this approach shifts over time, even while it continues to construct female fertility as a vehicle for solving large social and economic problems.

After the international slave trade was outlawed in 1808 and before the Thirteenth Amendment to the Constitution ended slavery in the United States in 1865, slave owners faced the task of increasing their capital investment in slaves and, at the same time, increasing their labor force. That is, slave owners were very eager to maximize slave reproduction. Owners typically devised "breeding schemes" to achieve their goals, especially during the time of booming cotton profits after 1820. Many owners personally impregnated enslaved girls and women, often through rape. Many also denied enslaved persons the right to choose to live in monogamous marital relationships, demanding instead that enslaved men and women have several or serial sexual partners "to promote the rapid birth of slave children."[1] Thomas Jefferson spoke directly about the benefits to owners of an enslaved and fecund woman: "I consider a woman who brings a child every two years as more profitable than the best man on the farm; what she produces is an addition to capital."[2]

Little more than one hundred years later, in the middle of the twentieth century, the descendants of enslaved women were still the specific targets of "breeding schemes." White people—politicians, policymakers, welfare agency personnel—were now devising and implementing updated schemes, again to solve perceived social problems. In the early 1960s, though, the schemes aimed to limit the number of babies born to African American women. Here is what one African American woman had to say in these years about the way that welfare officials and politicians assessed her life, especially her reproductive capacity and what she should do about it. "They came telling us not to have children," she reported, "and not to have children and sweep up, and all that. . . . They tell you you're bad, and worse than others, and you're lazy, and you don't know how to get along like others do." This woman tried hard to explain to the white social workers visiting her house that her life was difficult and her family's needs were great. She said that she couldn't afford to buy nutritious food. But, she said, the social workers only wanted to talk about "planning—planning, planning that's all they tell you. The worst of it is that they try to get you to plan your kids by the year; except they mean by the ten-year plan. . . . The truth is, they don't want you to have any, if they could help it."[3]

Politicians and others in every region of the country and in Washington, D.C., in the early 1960s proposed scheme after scheme to curtail the reproductive capacity of African American women. They typically argued that the cities were overcrowded and dangerous, that school integration was undesirable, that juvenile delinquency sprang from the slums, that welfare expenditures were too high and were hitting the tax-paying public too hard. Social problems were terrible, the politicians said, and becoming worse. Limiting the fertility of African American and other women of color would solve these problems.

This set of examples highlighting prevailing white attitudes toward the reproductive lives of African American women in the mid-nineteenth and mid-twentieth centuries shows starkly how first slave owners and then social critics, politicians, and people who worked in social services agencies claimed authority and power over the lives of poor, relatively powerless, fertile women through their reproductive capacity. The interveners did not try to improve the lives of these women with, say, offers of dignified employment or education programs or with antidiscrimination laws. Instead, they pressed African American women first to have many children, and then later to use birth control, get sterilized, abstain from sex—all in response to the "needs of society." In both cases, the power holders passed laws to give teeth to the pressure.

In U.S. history, other social problems, such as reproducing a sufficient number of laborers and soldiers, have shaped views of women's reproductive capacity as a national resource. Leaders of the new nation repeatedly expressed their concern about populating the continent while ensuring that the dominant group remained white and "fit." Early national leaders who defined this "need" pressed the case that white women must reproduce in service to the nation. Failure to do so was shameful. Reflecting this longtime orientation to white female fertility, President Theodore Roosevelt worried in 1911 about "race decay," "racial death," and a "vigorous nation" rendered "decrepit" by insufficient breeding of Anglo-Saxon women. He wrote, "Exactly as the measure of our regard for the soldier who does his full duty in battle is the measure of our scorn for the coward who flees, so the measure of our respect for the true wife and mother is the measure of our scorn and contemptuous abhorrence for the wife who refuses to be a mother."[4]

Charlotte Perkins Gilman, an early twentieth-century white feminist, wrote a few years later, "The business of the female is not only the reproduction but the improvement of the species."[5] Roosevelt, Gilman, and others judged Native Americans, Mexican immigrants, and other women of color as incapable of improving the species. They argued that these women threatened white supremacy and the purity of the white race. Theodore Roosevelt and other advocates of racial purity addressed the problem of "tainted" reproductive capacity by enacting selective immigration policies, antimiscegenation laws, and state-enforced sterilization laws. Henry Goddard, an early, prominent twentieth-century psychologist and eugenicist, offered a crude strategic plan for solving the problem of maintaining the United States as a white-dominant country in which the fit reproduced themselves and others did not. Referring to the "others," Goddard wrote, "We need to hunt them out in every possible place and take care of them, and see to it that they do not propagate."[6]

According to these experts, proper deployment of reproductive capacity could strengthen the nation. Just as important, experts counseled that deployment under proper conditions could strengthen the father-headed nuclear family, a key indicator of national well-being but often diagnosed across U.S. history as under assault and weakened. Again, social critics proposed solving this problem by manipulating women's reproductive capacity.

In the middle of the nineteenth century, strenuous efforts to outlaw contraception and abortion took place in a culture where, as one historian put it, "news that [a] woman had made the journey [to an abortionist] threatened all men." For one thing, if a woman knew how to use birth control or abortion to avoid pregnancy, "the man who thought he controlled her"—her husband—"could be cuckolded." More broadly, the American Medical Association (AMA), working to criminalize abortion state by state in the mid-nineteenth century, persuaded men of influence and power in state legislatures that women who sought abortions and not motherhood were immoral and irresponsible. The AMA took the position that abortion represented "a threat to the social order." If women managed their fertility in this way, that would undermine the social arrangements that mandated families in which husbands held power and made all the important decisions.[7]

A hundred years later, Daniel Patrick Moynihan, at the time a domestic policy adviser to President Lyndon Johnson, criticized the reproductive behavior of African American women as threatening to the social order, also because this behavior violated the patriarchal family structure. In a deeply influential report, *The Negro Family: A Case for National Action* (1965), Moynihan stressed what African American women needed to do: get married, stay married, and subordinate themselves in various ways to their husbands during their reproductive and child-rearing years. Only when women behaved in these ways could the Black family escape "the tangle of pathology" and break "the cycle of poverty and deprivation" that afflicted "matriarchal" households in the Black ghettos of America.

In other words, Moynihan did not blame employment, education, and housing discrimination for the poverty of African Americans. Rather, the reproductive (and other) misbehavior of African American women was the core source of the degradation of this people. Adjust that behavior, Moynihan counseled, and African American men could assume their rightful place at the head of the family. When the Black patriarchal family was reconstituted, problems holding back African Americans in the United States would evaporate.[8] Moynihan's work remained influential across the last third of the twentieth century because few Americans were willing to allocate the resources necessary to ensure adequate housing, education, and earnings for minorities or to enforce "equal opportunity" laws.

All these years after *Roe v. Wade* and after a generation of vocal, activist women have worked hard to cement the relationship between women's privacy rights and reproductive dignity, many politicians and others still think of reproductive politics as the arena where social problems can be legislated and cured. If we can end teenage pregnancy . . . If we can stamp out unwed motherhood. . . If we can press poor women to postpone having children until they can afford to give them all the advantages . . . If we can arrange for all unwanted babies to be adopted instead of aborted . . . If we can make abortion illegal again . . . If white women would reproduce at the same rate as Latina women . . . The fulfillment of each of these wishes would bring, according to those who articulate them, a more stable country, a safer country, a fiscally sounder country with lower tax rates, a morally and religiously righteous country.

A generation after *Roe v. Wade*, then, many Americans understand "reproductive politics" as a set of subjects and debates that has little to do with women's lives, their bodies, their needs, their decision-making capacities, their rights, and their human dignity. Rather, reproductive-politics-as-a-way-to-solve-problems reflects a belief that the social, economic, political, and moral problems that beset our country can be solved best if laws and policies and public opinions press women to reproduce or not in ways that are consistent with a particular version of the country's real needs

When social or economic or "values" problems persist, politicians and others claim that this is because women persist in reproductive misbehavior. Welfare reform legislation in the mid-1990s, for example, was built on the proposition that single pregnancy and motherhood is the chief cause of poverty in the United States. Welfare reformers looked past other possible explanations for poverty, such as low wages, scarce and expensive housing, inadequate day care, and lack of medical insurance. Instead, women who made the "wrong" reproductive choices were defined collectively as the engine of national malaise.[9]

REPRODUCTIVE POLITICS:
RESPONDING TO WOMEN'S EVERYDAY PRACTICES

Throughout American history, reproductive politics has involved debates about women's reproductive capacity as a social resource: How should that resource best be managed or expended to respond to society's labor needs, military needs, its need for white citizens or black slaves? Only recently, within the past two generations, have girls and women publicly placed themselves at the center of the arena of reproductive politics. And yet, we can learn a great deal about the behavior of women at any given time—about how women acted in their own behalf—by studying the ways that the government dealt with what political scientist Rosalind Petchesky has called "women's everyday practices and values around fertility."

We can look at the laws and policies and community activities that aimed to regulate what women could and could not do reproductively to find out what women were actually doing to manage their fertility.[10] We can also look at these laws to find out what kinds of behaviors the officials believed should be controlled by law. We can find out what kinds of punishments were considered suitable for women who transgressed.

For example, state legislatures acted one by one in the mid-nineteenth century to criminalize abortion. The historian reads these acts not only as evidence that middle-class white men—state legislators—were determined that pregnant women should remain pregnant for nine months. The new laws were also strong evidence that elite white men were deeply troubled because large numbers of women turned to abortion practitioners to manage their fertility. If women had generally avoided abortionists, no such laws would have been necessary. The history of reproductive laws and policies indicates that these efforts to respond to women's "everyday practices" have sometimes been successful in shaping women's reproductive lives, but never completely successful. Over time, such efforts may change completely or fail altogether.

We can find examples of this dynamic—women's everyday strategies lived out against official rules and policies—throughout U.S. history. During the slavery era, the U.S. Constitution and the nation's legal apparatus protected slave owners' control over the bodies of enslaved men and women, including, especially, their control over the reproductive capacity of female slaves. It was this capacity, of course, that owners exploited to increase and perpetuate their slave property and to mark their domination over enslaved persons. Yet in the face of owners' rights over enslaved women, evidence exists that sometimes women resisted owners' breeding schemes. They used various methods to suppress their own fertility, including herbal contraceptives and abortifacients, infanticide, and resistance to forced sex. Legal historian Peggy Cooper-Davis has pointed out that for many enslaved women, "liberty meant, among other things, the capacity to decline to reproduce."[11]

On the other hand, when an enslaved woman did give birth, she was not only extending the owner's workforce and the size of his holdings in human property. She was also, through the new baby, "ensuring the life of the slave community," extending the history and traditions and human relations within and among enslaved families and persons.[12] In this sense, liberty could mean the capacity to reproduce, even under the horrible conditions of enslavement.

Throughout U.S. history, whenever women have faced systems of reproductive constraint, they have resisted. No matter what the law said during the roughly one hundred years that abortion was a crime in the United States (mid-nineteenth to mid-twentieth century), for example, millions of women looked for and found abortion practitioners to end pregnancies they were unwilling to carry. Women got abortions even in a culture that honored motherhood as women's true destiny. Women got abortion even in a culture that shamed the ones who did not repeatedly fulfill their destiny. In the years just before *Roe v. Wade*, public health and law enforcement experts estimated that as many as 1.2 million women a year resisted pregnancy by means of abortion.[13] Surely we can say that this "everyday practice" shaped reproductive politics in the United States in the years leading up to *Roe* and made the legalization of abortion a public policy inevitability.

The history of reproductive politics will always be in part a record of women controlling their reproductive capacity, no matter what the law says, and by those acts reshaping the law. It is also often a record of women deciding under what conditions to have children, no matter what the social norms regarding proper female conduct prescribe, and by those acts reshaping notions of legitimate motherhood and female conduct.

A government report in 1963 expressed frustration and concern about how hard it was to understand why so many young women defied "the mores of society" by becoming unwed mothers.[14] Thirty years later, legal scholar Martha Fineman defined single motherhood "as a practice resistive to patriarchal ideology, particularly because it represents a 'deliberate choice' in a world with birth control and abortion."[15] For more than a half century politicians, policymakers, clergy, and other authorities have tried to convince and coerce women to marry before having children. Yet one in three births (33.2 percent) in the United States occurs outside of marriage. (The rate for all unmarried women fifteen to forty-four years of age is more than twice the rate in 1960.)[16] Births to unmarried teenagers have been declining, while women in their twenties have the highest rates of childbearing outside of marriage, and these rates continue to rise. Once again, the everyday practices of women are redefining reproductive politics. Contemporary behavior redefines legitimate motherhood. To some extent, women's behavior limits what politicians can effectively condemn and limits the kinds of behavior that other public and private authorities can hope to punish, even as they want to outlaw this behavior.

REPRODUCTIVE POLITICS:
CONTESTING THE MEANING OF WOMANHOOD

Whichever of these everyday practices we focus on—an unwillingly pregnant woman seeking out an abortion in the criminal era, an enslaved woman refusing sex and reproduction, a single woman claiming legitimacy for herself as a mother—we must imagine the dangers these practices involved. Only then can we understand reproductive politics.

A profound source of danger has always rested at the heart of definitions of "real womanhood." These definitions have, as we've seen, changed over time and have been applied to different groups of women differently, depending on their race and class. But when women have acted reproductively against laws, policies, religious dicta, and community attitudes, they have violated the citadel of traditional gender roles. Social and legal rules have historically governed who can be a legitimate mother, under what circumstances, and how women can and cannot legally manage their fertility. These rules have always been linked to traditional assumptions about women's "natural work" as mothers. They have also always been linked to ideas about women's "naturally" subordinate social role and status.[17]

Historically, those who condemned women for making reproductive decisions in violation of female norms stressed this aspect of the violation. Here a doctor, writing for the AMA in 1871, pictures women, implicitly white, who get abortions—and their fate: "She becomes unmindful of the course marked out for her by Providence, she overlooks the duties imposed on her by the marriage contract. She yields to the pleasures—but shrinks from the pains and responsibilities of maternity; and destitute of all delicacy and refinement, resigns herself, body and soul, into the hands of unscrupulous and wicked men. Let not the husband of such a wife flatter himself that he possesses her affection. Nor can she in turn ever merit even the respect of a virtuous husband. She sinks into old age like a withered tree, stripped of its foliage, with the stain of blood upon her soul, she dies without the hand of affection to smooth her pillow."[18]

This doctor associates a woman's impulse to manage fertility with murdering her womanhood: if she will not be a mother, she cannot be a woman. Doctors have historically taken a central role in constructing a woman's reproductive capacity as the site where her womanhood is defined or defiled.

A generation later, in 1908, the U.S. Supreme Court explained how women's reproductive capacity "naturally" affected their capacity as workers. The Court justified laws that limited the number of hours women could work and other conditions of female employment: "That women's physical structure and the performance of maternal functions place her at a disadvantage in the struggle for subsistence is obvious. This is especially true when the burdens of motherhood are upon her. [Yet since] healthy mothers are essential to vigorous offspring the physical well-being of woman becomes an object of public interest and care in order to preserve the strength and vigor of the race."[19] According to this historic Supreme Court decision, woman's capacity to produce babies, to reproduce the "race," justified a gendered division of labor in the workforce. This was a workforce that reflected women's traditional subordination to men, with women occupying lower-status jobs and receiving lower pay than men. Once again, women's reproductive capacity was invoked to define women as naturally subordinate persons and to limit their activities outside of the home and family.

In the middle of the twentieth century, a woman's reproductive capacity still profoundly limited her capacity to earn a living, according to state employment policies. By the early 1950s, every state defined pregnant women as unable to work and as ineligible for unemployment benefits. More than half the states defined every woman looking for a job as ineligible for these benefits for a certain number of weeks before and after she had given birth.[20] These and other state policies "reflected and reinforced social judgments about women's roles" by defining childbearing and motherhood as conditions of economic dependency.[21] Not surprisingly, when the state crafted and justified policies that tied a woman's reproductive capacity to her status as a low-wage worker, then fertile women did become incapable of earning a living wage. These laws and policies made sure that women remained economically dependent because of their reproductive capacity.

In the struggle over who controls women's reproductive capacity, the state has created laws and policies that use female fertility to solve social problems and to sustain traditional roles for women. These laws and policies have often been consistent with other powerful cultural mandates such as religious injunctions against abortion, educational policies excluding pregnant students from the schoolhouse, and medical dicta defining pregnancy as illness. When women have resisted the status of "natural womb" or have claimed control over their fertility, some cultural authorities have raised the specter of science fiction–like scenarios, illustrating what they fear women's reproductive autonomy would lead to. In the 1970s, for example, when authority over reproduction seemed to be slipping into the hands of women, an Indiana obstetrician complained to a congressional committee, "We are aborting all of [these babies] and we are exchanging them for a 'crash program' of 'test tube babies' with artificial placentas—and in time to come, we will not even need the mothers."[22]

REPRODUCTIVE POLITICS:
MAKING "PRIVATE" CHOICES IN PUBLIC CONTEXTS

An orientation to reproductive politics requires moving beyond the idea that pregnancy is always a choice. It also requires moving beyond the idea that women were always in the past victims of their reproductive capacity because they had no choices. In *Pregnancy and Power*, I pay attention to how women in a variety of historical circumstances determined what they had to, or wanted to, or could do reproductively—and how they used the resources they had to manage their fertility. In the past women were always constrained by—and acted against—historically specific laws and ever-changing social norms.

In the eighteenth century, for example, long before abortion became a crime, countless women became pregnant unwillingly and were aware that self-abortion was dangerous. Many of these women turned to medical practitioners for help, even when they knew that these knowledgeable persons might not approve of ending a pregnancy. One doctor described women who came to him pretending to be ill, "coming in the name of others, sometimes bringing their own water, dissembling pains in their heads, sides, obstructions, etc. Thereby, cunningly, as they think, designing to make the physician cause abortion by the medicines he may order for their cure." Assuming this physician was reading his patients correctly, some women in his region clearly hoped (in the context of disapproval but not crime) to combine their own reproductive knowledge with the doctor's medical skill to achieve their goal.[23]

Two hundred fifty years later, in the late twentieth century, a woman contemplating what pregnancy and childbirth meant to her described the reasons she wanted to have babies even though the white-run birth control clinics in her area were passing out pills right and left, trying to get their African American clients "to be a poor version of them, only without our children and our faith in God, and our tasty fried food or anything." The woman explained, "To me having a baby inside me is the only time I'm really alive. I know I can make something, do something, no matter what color my skin is, and what names people call me. When the baby gets born I see him, and he's full of life, or she is; and I think to myself that it doesn't make any difference what happens later, at least now we've got a chance, or the baby does. . . . [The whole family] feel[s] the baby is a good sign, or at least he's *some* sign. If we didn't have that, what would be the difference from death?"[24] Like many poor women in U.S. history (and in the present day), this woman was determined to resist outside pressures and make her own determinations about when and why to have children, or not. Here the woman thought of her reproductive capacity as a psychological as well as a physical lifeline for herself and her family in an otherwise bleak world.

We can see clearly that the eighteenth-century woman perhaps trying to hoodwink her doctor was constructing her own private, personal reproductive agenda. So was the woman I just described. Each woman acted in a particular social and political context, a context where public officials and experts pressed on her life. The circumstances of these women show the limitations of the public-private dichotomy—the way of explaining gendered experience that places women chiefly in the "private sphere" and men in the "public." Reproductive politics clarifies the ways that the "public" is always penetrating "the private," and vice versa.[25]

Once again, slavery provides a clear example. Under the laws of slavery, white men and Black men (some of whom were free) could father a free child or an enslaved child. The English legal principle of *partus sequitur ventrem* provided that the slave or free status of the child followed the status of the mother. White women could give birth only to free children. Only Black women could give birth to enslaved children. In fact, every Black woman who was enslaved and gave birth, gave birth to an enslaved child. Thus, the foundation of the slavery system—the enslaved workforce—was reproduced by Black women and Black women only. No matter what kind of intimate, heterosexual relations an enslaved Black woman had, the rules of slavery governed her fertility, her fate as a mother, and the fate of her child.[26]

In the late twentieth century, many middle-class women felt secure that *Roe v. Wade* and other public policy developments defined their "right of privacy" to make reproductive decisions for themselves. Yet many late twentieth-century public policies have had profound impacts on the "private" reproductive decisions of poor and other resourceless women. For example, the federal government's decision to deny funding for abortions and reproductive counseling services for poor women —the Hyde Amendment—has been described as mandating "forced motherhood" for unwillingly pregnant girls and women who don't have enough money to pay for private services. As a result of public policies, many women give birth against their will or better judgment.[27]

Even in contemporary America, a number of public policies make it harder or impossible for a poor woman to get an abortion or to receive welfare for her child, or even have access to the resources necessary to be a mother. As a result, many poor women have felt pressure to curtail their fertility. Some have used temporary sterilizing agents such as Norplant. Others have turned to permanent sterilization.[28] Is it possible in these cases to imagine women making "private" decisions? Or are their decisions fundamentally shaped by public policies? The state of New Jersey instituted "family cap" policies in the 1990s. These policies limited the amount of welfare money a woman could receive if she gave birth to a new baby while she was receiving public assistance. Studies showed that in the first year, the state recorded fourteen thousand fewer births and 1,429 more abortions than would otherwise have taken place.[29]

In the 1960s, African American writer Toni Cade explained why the newly marketed birth control pill appealed to women. Her description of how women's lives are shaped by the burden of their reproductive capacity thoroughly mixes up private, intimate aspects with the public aspects. Cade points, for example, to racism and sexism in the workplace, laws criminalizing abortion, and the lack of national child care policies, and the behavior of boyfriends. Cade writes, "I think most women have pondered . . . the oppressive nature of pregnancy, the tyranny of the child burden, the stupidity of the male-female divisions, the obscene nature of employment discrimination. And day-care and nurseries being what they are, paid maternity leaves being rare, the whole memory of wham bang thank you ma'am and the Big Getaway a horrible nightmare, poverty so ugly, the family unit being the last word . . . [in perpetuating] the status quo, and abortion fatalities being what they are—of course [we need] the pill."[30]

Reading Cade, it is not hard to recognize that most women, even those endowed with financial and other resources, have made reproductive decisions within the framework of existing public policies. In recent decades middle-class women have typically defined their relation to childbearing as a "choice." But federal, state, court, and corporate decisions about employment policies governing family leave, health insurance, and day care, for example, have all constrained or expanded the individual choices of even these women. Intensely private decisions about reproduction, including decisions about getting pregnant or not, staying pregnant or not, being the mother to the child one gives birth to or not, are always shaped by public laws and policies. This may be a particularly difficult insight to bring into focus, in part because of the way "personal choice" has eclipsed all other ways of thinking about pregnancy and motherhood. Further complicating our appreciation of how the "public" intrudes on the "private" has been the fact that historically, laws and public policies regarding reproduction have been justified by women's physiology—her *natural status* as a reproducer—masking governmental intentions to regulate women's behavior.[31]

REPRODUCTIVE POLITICS: TRACKING CHANGE OVER TIME

At the heart of the history of reproductive politics, though, are two most basic principles that must be cleanly underscored before going forward. The first is that the laws and policies and community attitudes that aim to control women's reproductive experiences—and women's responses to them—have changed over time. The second is that there is no single history of reproductive politics that describes the experience of all—or even most—women in the United States. The story of reproductive politics in this country has always been—and remains—constructed of many plotlines. Race and class have always been key to the ways that women experience their own fertility.

In the United States, reproductive laws and policies and attitudes have changed, and their uses have changed over time. We cannot understand the circumstances of white unwed mothers in late eighteenth-century Maine, for example, by drawing on what we know about single motherhood in the middle of the twentieth century or the beginning of the twenty-first century. To understand solo motherhood at any point and in any place we have to look into questions of population and gender and labor and the distribution of wealth and the nature of various belief systems. We also need to understand how hard women were pressed to obey social norms in that time and place and to understand definitions of nonconformity, virtue, and vice. All of these elements of society and culture are relevant to the life experiences of fertile females. All of these elements shift over time and place in ways that shape quite different lives for fertile and reproducing girls and women.

The unwed white mother, say, the daughter of the village apothecary or a farm-renting couple in eighteenth-century Maine, for example, was not generally shamed by her community, nor was she considered a social or political problem by national leaders. She was not typically ruined or abandoned after premarital sex and childbearing. She might have typically stayed at home with her parents and her baby and eventually gotten married. Laurel Thatcher Ulrich, a historian of this time and place, explains that "sexual activity," even when it led to out-of-wedlock childbearing, "was connected with a comprehensive transition to adulthood," to "good citizenship and economic activity."[32]

The experience of the unmarried white girl or woman who became pregnant in the mid-twentieth century, even in the same state of Maine, was completely different. In this case, the pharmacist's daughter in 1955 or 1965 would typically have represented family failure and shame. The girl would likely have been forced by state law (and in response to her parents' fear of community judgment) to leave school. She might have been whisked out of the community to give birth in secret, under a pseudonym. Maternity-home workers may have pressed her hard to give her child up for adoption. The community did not consider this girl's nonmarital sexuality as a sign of emerging maturity. Instead, the authorities assessed her as pathologically immature. Her out-of-wedlock pregnancy was taken as proof of her deep psychological maladjustments.[33]

By the beginning of the twenty-first century, private and public meanings of unmarried pregnancy, childbearing, and motherhood had changed again, completely. Now, with more than one-third of all babies born to single girls and women, "maladjustment" is no long a viable way to describe this behavior. High schools are no longer allowed to expel female students for pregnancy. White unwed women are no longer coerced to surrender their babies for adoption. Despite the unceasing efforts of many politicians and parents to revive the midcentury stigma of unwed motherhood, more women than ever are becoming mothers without husbands. These mothers are defining their own status in a variety of ways. During the mid-twentieth century, unwed mothers were very likely to be defined by their race and forced into certain outcomes because of their race. This is far less true today.

The historian can locate many of these kinds of dramatic changes in the meanings attached to biological events (sex, pregnancy) over time. The term "fetal viability" is a case in point. Fifty years ago, embryologists and neonatologists were in general agreement that viability—the capacity of the fetus to live outside the womb—was reached after approximately thirty-four weeks of gestation. Scientists and physicians also agreed that "fetal viability" was a technical term, relevant mostly to obstetric emergencies. Over the decades, scientific advances have pushed the date of fetal viability back, so that today, in some cases, a fetus of twenty-seven or twenty-eight weeks' gestation can be rendered viable. New science has fractured old meanings and common usage. Today "fetal viability" is a legal status and an anti-abortion-rights rallying cry. It is a term that often aims to disqualify women and doctors from making decisions.

In contrast, abortion-rights advocates largely use the term "fetal viability" to refer to the fetus as a fetus. Often they use the term in reference to the very small number of abortions performed after "fetal viability" has been reached, almost always in the context of medical disaster and tragedy. These people claim that "fetal viability" is a socially constructed, not a clear, scientifically predictable, status. For instance, they say, a women's access to prenatal care, adequate diet, high-tech obstetrics and neonatal services, and other resources has a decisive impact on when any given fetus achieves viability. This debate shows the value of taking into account older meanings and usages of words that matter in the public discussion of reproductive politics. Taking these meanings into account shows us how basic ideas have changed over time and how none of these concepts have "natural" meanings. They also help us analyze the building blocks of the strategies that constitute reproductive politics.

[handwritten margin notes: Fetal viabil. as technical term; Value of older words; Socially constr. meanings; Terms as building blocks of repro. politics]

Here are two more examples, to drive home the point that language, laws, policies, and attitudes toward women's reproductive behavior continually change, often radically. First, let's stick to the twentieth century and look at relatively recent changes in public and private attitudes toward female contraception. When the grandmothers of many of today's college students were fertile, say in the 1950s, birth control was completely unavailable to almost all unmarried women and to many married women. Not until 1965 was birth control legal in all states for all married persons. In 1972 the Supreme Court legalized contraception for unmarried girls and women.[34]

Throughout the middle decades of the twentieth century, studies have shown, unmarried women who managed to obtain birth control materials were embarrassed to let their male sexual partners know they were equipped for sex. Being "prepared" for sex was generally considered unladylike, partly because to be prepared seemed to reveal an unfeminine willingness—even a slutty desire—to engage in sex. Any young lady associated with birth control could be, and probably was, associated with loose behavior and the "bad reputation" that went with it.[35]

As today's unmarried, sexually active women are well aware, many Americans agree: using birth control is a key sign of taking responsibility for one's life. Teachers and even parents promote birth control as a public health measure, an act, absolutely, of maturity. A great many Americans believe that girls and women who are unmarried and "too poor" to procreate have *the duty* to use birth control. Within a remarkably short period of time, the meanings of unmarried female intercourse and pregnancy prevention have changed dramatically.

The social, political, and personal meanings of abortion have also changed radically over time. Cornelia Dayton, a historian who studies the eighteenth century, for example, has brought attention to the fact that American legal documents from that century do not express "either outrage over the destruction of a fetus or denunciations of those who would arrest 'nature's proper course,'" that is, abortion practitioners.[36] In contrast, at the beginning of the twenty-first century, state legislatures continue to pass laws designed to protect fetuses and limit the professional authority of abortion-providing physicians. A 2003 Texas law, for example, mandated a "reflection period," an interval a woman must wait between an abortion consultation with a physician and the day the procedure is scheduled. During this interval, the abortion-seeking woman is expected to meditate on the images of fetal development

[margin notes: "BC as responsible"; "Poor women DUTY to procreate"]

that the legislature decrees she must look at. In our era, abortion restrictions do not focus on the marital status of the woman or generally on her physical safety as they did in the eighteenth century. They focus almost entirely on questions of fetal development and "fetal personhood," even ignoring risks to women's health. Abortion, like out-of-wedlock pregnancy and birth control, has had different meanings at different historical moments, and has evoked changing legislative, judicial, and personal responses in concert with, and in opposition to, these changing meanings.

Changing meanings > Changing laws.

REPRODUCTIVE POLITICS: NO SINGLE HISTORY

Finally, before moving into the chronology of *Pregnancy and Power*, I want to emphasize again that even after we have established that reproductive politics has a history—that the meanings of these matters change over time—we still need to underscore the most foundational principle shaping this book: that there is no single history of reproductive politics that can be traced from the eighteenth century to the twenty-first century. No one set of events can describe the experiences of all or most women who have lived in the United States. In this multiethnic, multiracial, class-structured society, we need different, sometimes overlapping, often completely distinct histories of reproductive politics to describe the experiences of demographically distinct groups of women.

Different Histories for different groups

Reconstructing these different histories is crucial to the project of showing that sex-and-pregnancy is more than a biological event. It is also a social and political event. When we gather the material that allows us to contrast one group's experience of sex-and-pregnancy with another's, we are compelled to ask questions and develop answers about the mechanisms locking in and sometimes challenging racism and poverty across generations.

Preg = soc + pol event

Capturing how race and class shape reproductive politics means understanding how public policies assign high or low social "value" to different groups of babies. It means understanding how the "value" of different groups of babies structures the experiences of different groups of women differently. These perspectives can underscore how important reproductive capacity—and the politics this biological dimension of life stimulates—is to larger political dynamics in the United States.

If we pay attention to the ways that the politics of race and class have structured distinct reproductive experiences in this country, we can also begin to understand how and why cross-race and cross-class coalitions of women concerned about reproductive health or reproductive rights or adoption, for example, have been so difficult to create and sustain. As always, the mid-nineteenth century provides a stark example. At that time, various white cultural authorities invested white motherhood with "a new glory." This was a status embedding a sentimental mix of love, tenderness, "rigor and bliss," and domestic power —maternal resources in the Victorian "empire of the mother."[37] This was a dominion where little white citizens were sacred and precious.

These same cultural authorities elevated white mothers in part by degrading African American mothers in comparison. Put another way, these white cultural authorities and their followers constructed the African American woman in the white mind as the sexualized, negligent, superfertile "counterimage" that the white Victorian mother was defined against and above.[38] And African American children, sacred in their own families and communities, were enslaved at birth and assigned value, by whites, as chattel. Perpetuating the institution of slavery as an aspect of a "free" society depended upon these distinctions and ensured that African American women could not look across the racial divide for support or a sense of shared identity.

One way to measure the costs of this history is to study the history of reproductive politics. This history tells us about changing contexts in which women of color and white women have sometimes shared little more, reproductively, than a biological capacity. In the early 1970s, for example, sterilization was the most common form of contraception among women over the age of twenty-five in the United States, though Black women and poor women generally were sterilized at twice the rate of white women.[39] Numbers alone do not tell the whole story of race or class differences. Doctors and others were very likely to coerce poor women (but not middle-class women) to undergo sterilization. One survey showed that 33 percent of hospitals involved in the study obtained consent for sterilization while women were in labor.[40]

An obstetrician about to perform a Caesarian section delivery on Jovita Rivera, a Mexican woman in Los Angeles, pressed her—after she had been sedated—to accept sterilization. Rivera reported that her doctor "told her she should have her 'tubes tied' because her children were a burden to the government." Rivera testified as part of a group of women, all of whom had been pressed in the same way to have their tubes tied. None of these women was a recipient of public assistance, but doctors in Los Angeles and elsewhere assumed that women who looked like Jovita Rivera were on welfare and should therefore curtail their fertility permanently.[41]

On the other hand, in the 1970s, after decades of forbidding white women to undergo sterilization, doctors largely stopped interfering when white women asked to be sterilized. After *Roe v. Wade*, sterilization became another liberating "choice" a modern woman might make and pay for. Many white women did not understand why poor women of color saw sterilization as a dangerous medical option and why they called for laws that mandated a thirty-day waiting period before a doctor could carry out a sterilization. The white-feminist-inspired Arkansas Family Planning Act, legislated in 1973, for example, allowed physicians to distribute birth control information and devices to anyone who asked and also legalized voluntary sterilization of anyone over eighteen (and of anyone under eighteen who was married), without waiting.

Because they had different histories and because medical authorities and others assigned different values to their pregnancies, and simply to the fact of their fertility, white middle-class women and poor women of color often had diametrically opposed responses to sterilization. *Pregnancy and Power* will explore racially distinct experiences like these that occurred across the country and across time, creating privileges for some and danger for others.

Clearly, these sorts of experiences have also created enormous difficulties for activists trying to develop a unified movement that stands for reproductive rights for all women. In fact, the history and persistence of reproductive experiences shaped by both race and class in United States have raised difficult questions about full and equal citizenship rights for all women in this country. *Pregnancy and Power* asks whether women can be full citizens in this (or in any) country if they are not permitted—by law, policy, or community and family attitudes—to control their own bodies, including, if they want, to control their fertility. *Pregnancy and Power* will explore the consequences for the meaning of citizenship when some women have greater access than other women to the sorts of resources one needs to control fertility. As part of this exploration, *Pregnancy and Power* will consider relationships over time between economic rights, reproductive rights, and citizenship rights.

Some readers may wonder why so many of the examples in *Pregnancy and Power* illustrate the experiences of "minority" girls and women, sometimes, it may seem, at the expense of examples drawn from the experiences of the majority of American females: white and middle-class. As I explain throughout the book, I believe that the reproductive experiences of different groups of women in the United States have been distinct *and dynamic*.

If the United States ever had been—and stayed—a white-only country, for example, the country's reproductive laws and policies would have undoubtedly been quite different from the history presented here. The presence of racial and class diversity throughout U.S. history has generated and depended on race-based and class-specific reproductive laws and experiences. White women have had the reproductive lives they have, in part, because lawmakers and policy enforcers have historically made certain laws and policies that helped define and qualify certain women as white. Likewise, African American women and other "nonmajority" women have had their reproductive lives structured to various degrees by laws and policies devised to define the nonwhite status of these women and their children.

In short, every time I write about the experiences of white females, I am also illuminating the basis for the experiences of women of color. Every time I write about women of color, I am clarifying the meaning and experience of whiteness.

Often when I speak about reproductive politics in public, a person in the audience may ask me about another apparent problem with my focus: "What about boys and men?" I am sometimes asked. What about their reproductive experiences and their responsibility for the reproductive lives of girls and women?

To be sure, writing only about female experience can be risky or misleading in several ways. This focus can reinforce the old tendency to construct fertility and reproductive politics as a "woman's issue." This focus can simply efface the male role in pregnancies and parenthood. It can also suggest that women are essentially reproducers and that biological reproduction is the special domain of women. A related problem could be reinforcing the idea that reproduction and mothering are necessary conditions of womanhood.

I spell out these possibilities here because I want to explicitly disassociate this book from all of them. I am a historian of women and women's experiences in the United States. I have found that the history of women's reproductive experiences in this country is a large and important enough topic on its own for this—and many other—volumes. I leave for other historians other parts of this history.

Since I am referring here to "other historians," this would be a good place to explain why, throughout this book that draws so much from the work of others, I start so many sentences by referring to the name of a historian or a legal scholar or a political scientist. Throughout the book, a number of sentences start something like this: "Legal scholar Ian Haney Lopez shows how . . ." or "As historian Janet Brodie explains . . ." I decided to name all these scholars in the body of the book rather than simply putting authors' names in the footnotes in the usual way because naming names underscores the fact that knowing about this history—any history—is a collective project that depends on the work of many people. Also, I want to try to evoke in the minds of readers the image of the scholar, deep in the archives, up to her elbows in old newspapers and court records, finding a letter, a piece of testimony, a congressman's dissent. Giving names to the scholars, I thought, might help summon up those very exciting scholarly moments.

My fundamental aim in *Pregnancy and Power* is to draw out a complicated picture of the concept of "reproductive politics," including the meaning of "women's choice," after almost two and a half centuries of reproductive secrets, coercion, resistance, acquiescence, shame, triumph, tragedy, and new life, as women have lived reproductive lives under variously constrained or capacious circumstances.

1

Racializing the Nation

From the Declaration of Independence
to the Emancipation Proclamation, 1776–1865

ON CAMPUS, AT THE MALL, in the supermarket, interracial couples are commonplace in many cities and towns around the country—proof that when people are left more or less alone, millions will form intimate relationships across racial identities. Yet at the beginning of the twenty-first century, we are only one generation away from laws forbidding mixed-race sex, love, marriage, and reproduction. Today, 7 percent of marriages in the United States are interracial. In California the interracial marriage rate is twice that. And nationwide about 15 percent of unmarried relationships are interracial. What's more, these rates are accelerating in all parts of the country.[1]

Historically, though, people in the United States have not been left alone to make their own decisions about intimacy, the kinds of decisions that determine what kinds of babies are born. Religious institutions, family and community traditions, and formal legislation have created and enforced rules about who may be intimate with whom. Historically, racial identity has been a crucial feature of both formal and informal rules about sexual intimacy. In this chapter, we can look back, first, at the founding decades of the United States, from roughly the Declaration of Independence to the Emancipation Proclamation—ninety years—to see what was at issue when the early rules about intimate relations and race were created. What was at issue when colonial and then state legislatures made laws about who could have sex with whom, with what consequences, in a new country?

During the eighteenth century in the American colonies and then in the United States, the men who made and enforced laws governing sexual relations were legislating in an era of complex interracial contact.

Also, this was an era when people had <u>very limited knowledge about how to separate sex and pregnancy</u>. Legislators crafted laws to regulate sexual intimacy for a society in which some people were the property of other people, and in which race and property and population growth all interacted with each other, as reproductive matters.

The early laws show us what all laws show: lawmakers' worries about what ordinary people will do if their behavior is not regulated. The laws show what, in fact, people were actually doing in an unregulated state. The first colonial laws forbidding marriage between white women and African men, for example, suggest that at the time these laws were enacted in the first half of the seventeenth century, white women were forming intimate relations, including marriage, with Africans, even with enslaved African men. If these everyday relations had been rare or non-existent, no laws like these would have been necessary.

Early laws governing sex-and-pregnancy show that founding fathers and the leaders of the next generations believed that regulated reproduction was crucial to building the United States. Famously, the founding fathers and others debated whether the United States should be a nation predominantly of cities, manufacturing, and commerce or a nation of independent farmers producing food in a rural landscape. But the founders did not debate which race was destined to populate and to rule the continent. This goal was a certainty beyond debate. If the United States were to be a "white country," laws and practices would have to make it—and keep it—that way. Laws would ensure that whites alone were citizens and property owners. Laws would ensure that enslaved Africans were—both as labor and as property—the producers but not the owners of wealth. Laws and military victories would ensure that native populations were "removed" from properties that whites could use to consolidate their holdings and their territorial supremacy. All these laws would depend on defining and policing race by regulating reproductive practices, what I call "racializing the nation."

DEGRADING AFRICAN AND NATIVE REPRODUCTION

At the end of the eighteenth century, racial theorists defined race as a quality inhering in the body, a biologically conditioned characteristic, not an environmentally conditioned attribute.[2] They described the color —or the race—of enslaved Africans in the late eighteenth century as a

biological marker of permanent inferiority. Theorists also imposed a biologically based interpretation of inferiority on Indians at this time, an
interpretation that precluded assimilation. As one historian has put it,
"Americans were gradually coming to adopt a color scheme that made
assimilating all but impossible. The old belief that beneath the layer of
bear grease, dirt, or sunburn was a white person yearning to be cleaned
up was slowly being replaced by the notion that Indians were 'red-
skins.'"[3]

Whites used somatic, or body-based, ideas about racial inferiority
to justify the physical domination and exploitation of Africans and Indians whose labor and land they were determined to command.[4] Domination relied at its heart on controlling the reproduction of enslaved
and native women.[5]

White lawmakers and law enforcers believed that controlling reproduction was a strategy for enforcing the distinction between races,
for establishing the "legal meanings of racial difference," for enforcing
the degradation of nonwhite women, and for facilitating white supremacy, generally.[6] Put another way, the reproductive capacity of enslaved and native women was the resource whites relied on to produce
an enslaved labor force, to produce and transmit property and wealth
across generations, to consolidate white control over land in North
America, and to produce a class of human beings who, in their ineligibility for citizenship, underwrote the exclusivity and value of white citizenship.

Reproductive politics—the contest between official authorities and
women themselves to regulate female bodies and their reproductive
capacity—isn't the only way to understand the nation-building strategies of the founding fathers. Nor is a study of reproductive politics the
most complete scholarly route to understanding the meanings or the
experiences of sexuality over time, or to understanding the brutal
process of "subduing" Indians, or to understanding the construction
and maintenance of American slavery, or the interaction between
racism and slavery, or the experience of being enslaved. But none of
these subjects can be adequately explored without paying attention to
the laws, policies, and practices that shaped the reproductive lives of
the population.

To understand the first principles of the new nation, we must look
at the laws and policies and social norms controlling these matters:
Which men could or could not have sex and children with which women?

Which women were coerced to reproduce? Which persons were killed, in part,
so that they could not reproduce? We must consider how these matters
were fundamental to property and citizenship claims and the land and
labor needs of the colonizers and the nation's founders.

The process of constructing a system of chattel slavery took more
than 150 years on the North American continent, from 1619 when the
first Africans were brought to the Virginia Colony, to the second half of
the eighteenth century, when the U.S. Constitution formalized, on a federal level, the status of enslaved persons as property and as "three-
fifths" of a human being. During these long decades of constructing
American slavery, colonial legislators steadily alienated Black men
from many of the rights and privileges that white men enjoyed. This
process continued at the end of the American Revolution, after which a
number of formerly enslaved men were granted freedom in exchange
for their wartime military service. Over time, though, Black men were
denied citizenship rights, including the right to vote, to testify in court,
to sit on juries, to serve in the militia. In many states Blacks were denied
the right to travel freely and to travel without identity papers. Many
laws and practices limited the rights of Black men to own property.
Laws and practices excluding Blacks from public places abounded.
Each of these provisions contributed to creating Africans in America as
a degraded, exploitable pariah class: slaves.

Yet arguably the serial decisions—the formal and informal regulations—to treat Black women as breeders with no formal rights or control over their own bodies, their sexual experiences, and their children
constituted the ultimate degradation of enslaved persons and provided
the foundation of the slavery system. The first of these laws was enacted
in the Virginia Colony in 1662, "An Act Defining the Status of Mulatto
Bastards." The law read: "Whereas some doubts have arrisen whether
children got by an Englishman upon a negro woman should be slave or
Free, Be it therefore enacted and declared by this present grand assembly, that all children borne in this country shall be held bond or free only
according to the condition of the Mother. And that if any christian shall
committ Fornication with a negro man or woman, hee or shee soe offending shall pay double the Fines imposed by the former act."[7]

English common law, the legal model for constructing laws in the
American colonies and later in the United States, dictated that the status of the child, in bondage or free, always followed the condition of the
child's father, not her mother. Thus the Virginia Colony's law was a rad-

ical innovation, adapting an old practice to meet the labor and other needs of an underpopulated land. Under the new system, if the father was enslaved and the mother was enslaved, the child was born enslaved. If the father was a free man and the mother was enslaved, the child would be born enslaved. The older law would have classified the offspring of this union as a free child. Clearly, after 1662 the fertility of the enslaved woman became the basis for the increase of human property. Just as clearly, the new law encouraged white men to seek power, pleasure, and profit by impregnating enslaved women.

In the past, a white man who impregnated a woman not his wife, even an enslaved woman, might have been charged with "bastardy" and expected to take material responsibility for maintenance of the child he sired. Now the legitimacy or illegitimacy of the child was irrelevant. Now, having impregnated an enslaved woman could simply mean that he got ownership of a new person. The 1662 law relieved white masters of punishment for sexually exploiting Black women, replacing penalties with property.[8] The new law also went some distance toward clarifying and hardening racial boundaries. Consider, for example, an enslaved child who could show that while his mother was enslaved, his father was white and free. After 1662 this fact, too, became entirely irrelevant. As legal scholar Adrienne Dale Davis has put it: "Showing that one's father was white was [now] no defense to enslavement."[9]

But what of the children of free white mothers and Black enslaved fathers? These were children born from mothers the courts believed were beneath contempt. According to the law, following their mother's racially elevated though sexually degraded status, these children were free. But they were not "white." Consequently, in communities throughout the North American colonies, these children enlarged the population of free Blacks. Over time, more such children occupied the status—"free"—that lawmakers and others believed should be reserved for "white" people. In response to growing numbers of these children by the end of the seventeenth century, the Virginia legislature passed a law in 1691, "For the prevention of that abominable mixture and spurious issue," resulting from "negroes, mulattoes, and Indians intermarrying with English, or other white women, as by their unlawfull accompanying with one another."[10] This law made intermarriage a crime and mandated that a white person who intermarried must be banished from the dominion.

A more practical, labor-oriented, and profitable solution to the growing number of free Blacks was widely adopted: to hold mixed-race children—typically the offspring of servants—in extended, though impermanent, bondage. Traditionally, children of indentured servants could be held in servitude until the age of twenty-one if a white boy, and the age of eighteen if a white girl. A mixed-race child of a white mother was bound out by law until the age of thirty-one. Historian Kristin Fischer notes that "mixed-race children, though they might be nominally free, effectively spent most of their productive and reproductive years as servants."[11] In addition, mixed-race children were marked indelibly as illegitimate, unable to inherit property or names from their fathers.[12]

These early Virginia laws set the pattern for colonial and then state legislatures for nearly two hundred years: using sexual regulations—who had the right to have sex and reproduce with whom—to reinforce and police racial boundaries. These laws also played a major role in allowing whites to construct and dominate the labor system. These laws sexualized race and racialized sex.[13] The North Carolina legislature, for example, passed laws in 1715, 1723, and 1741 criminalizing interracial sex and marriage. If the woman giving birth were indentured, she would have her term extended the usual two years, plus two more years for having "a Bastard child by a Negro, Mulatto or Indyan."[14] In Louisiana, an 1807 law, modified in 1827, 1830, and 1831, prohibited a free Black man from buying and freeing his enslaved wife until she was thirty years old, that is, through her childbearing years. The law also provided that the children of this union, born before the wife was manumitted (freed), would be born slaves and remain enslaved for at least thirty years. Shortly before the Civil War, Louisiana outlawed all manumission, so even these opportunities for freedom were dead.

Again and again state legislatures made laws allowing slave owners and their families to use the reproductive capacity of enslaved women for their own enrichment. One state's law allowed the formally acknowledged illegitimate child of a deceased owner and his "concubine" to be freed at the owner's death only if the value of the child did not exceed the portion of the estate's value that such a child was entitled to. If the child were worth a substantial sum on the slave market, or if the master's estate were paltry, the master's illegitimate slave child would have to remain enslaved.[15] The law was written to protect the property interests of the dead slave owner's white family in this way.

The experience of giving birth to a child who was the property of one's owner was a devastatingly complex event for enslaved parents. In many cases, the birth was the outcome of coerced sex, forced on an enslaved woman by her owner, a man who might or might not acknowledge a child born of that rape. From the mother's point of view, the interracial enslaved child she gave birth to could represent the essential mark of sexual and reproductive powerlessness, and could be a symbol of the terrorism on which slavery depended: "the immense power whites held over the most intimate sphere of black life."[16] For the enslaved mother who had no laws protecting her body, her reproductive capacity, and her sexual safety, rape was truly a "weapon of terror" that reinforced "white domination over their human property."[17]

The child embodied the enslaved mother's sexual degradation and also her degradation as human property. The child defined her as chattel who reproduced a commodity, not a person, at the will of the owner. The owners' freedom to rape enslaved women depended on the traditional definition of sexual violation as a crime against a man's legal rights over an economic dependent: his property. When a slave owner raped his own possession, no man's property interests were hurt. As historian Kathleen Brown writes, "The only man with legal claims to a female slave's labor and reproductive capacity was her master. Rape did not jeopardize his investment"—and may well, in fact, have increased it.[18]

According to Brenda Stevenson, a historian of the enslaved family, for some raped women, the potential interracial child might be a symbol of the shame enslaved women experienced as a result of having been the degraded victims of their owners. They "were afraid of the consequences for themselves, their families, and the children they might have conceived. They tried to conceal the sexual assault from their husbands."[19] In this way, the interracial child conceived out of the violence of slavery could be a dreadful threat to the entire Black family. And yet, in addition to being a symbol of degradation, that same enslaved child could represent for his or her mother "the continuity of a people," the extension, the enrichment, and the potential of the community of Black people, and its renewal: a new life.[20]

From the owner's perspective, the new interracial child enlarged his slaveholdings but at the same time represented a threat to racial status—a "monstrous amalgam." No matter that the slave owner was more often than not the father of this "monster." Elite whites were horrified that by sometimes appearing "white," though not legally "white," the interracial child represented racial corruption. Such children, breaching the borders of "white," symbolized abominable "infractions against the color line" and became the occasion for new laws —ever more finely calibrated definitions of whiteness—ensuring the continuing degradation of interracial children.[21] The sexual behavior of owners created new opportunities for elite whites to tighten the noose of slavery.

Thinking about the complexities of giving birth to and mothering an interracial child within the slavery system helps clarify how sex and reproduction were central to social practices of racial degradation and racial privilege. It is important here to spell out the aspects of sex and reproduction that became vehicles of racialized degradation and racialized privilege during the slavery regime. Naming even the most basic aspects lays bare the essential dynamics of a slave society.

To begin with, as we've seen, often the enslaved woman did not have the right to choose her sexual partner. With no reliable contraception, many enslaved women, therefore, did not have the right to choose their procreating partner. In American slave society, then, making such deeply intimate partnering decisions was a racial privilege.

Because I use the term "racial privilege" repeatedly in this chapter, I want to be clear about what I mean by this expression. I am using "racial privilege" in this discussion as a way of describing a status or an opportunity that the law and other instruments of power reserved for whites and generally denied women of color, on the basis of race. I am not suggesting that all white women were able freely, for example, to choose their sexual partners in a male-dominant society. But I do mean to indicate that white women were very much more likely than women of color to be able to exercise preference or claim personal dignity in this and other related matters discussed in this chapter. I also mean to indicate that denying African Americans these opportunities or privileges was key to racial degradation and enslavement.

Regarding the matter of choosing partners, historical sociologist Wilma Dunaway shows us that on many plantations, especially on the smaller ones in the mountainous areas of the South, owners picked mates for enslaved men and women. Also in this geographical area, through sales, forced labor migrations, and wills, and by sending enslaved men to work in locations distant from their families, owners broke up approximately two of five marriages. Owners justified these "business decisions" by claiming "slaves did not construct permanent marriages, did not establish strong emotional ties to their children, [and] did not value extended kin networks."[22]

We've also seen that slaveholders appropriated power over the reproductive capacity of their enslaved property, effacing women's decision-making power over procreation, pressing enslaved women to reproduce for the owners' economic gain. At one point, Thomas Jefferson proposed a fixed market value for African American babies of $22.50. Here we can grasp that giving birth to a child, not a commodity, was a racial privilege in a slave society. Commenting on the intentions of slave owners in the Upper South, Dunaway notes: "While not orchestrating barnyard breeding methods, mountain plantations did indeed structure an exploitative reproductive system aimed at generating surplus slaves whose labor could be sold or hired."[23]

If the slave child was a commodity, then the womb of the enslaved woman was a manufactory, a site of value only if it churned out product. A nineteenth-century plantation mistress noted that the bondswomen on her husband's plantation had "a most distinct and perfect knowledge of their value to the owners as property." According to the mistress, one of the women told her, "Missus, tho' we no able to work, we make little niggers for Massa." This particular mistress, a person who had no children, was aware that her value as a white woman was not ultimately or definitively determined by her fecundity. This, too, could be a white privilege: to have value as a female person beyond and ultimately regardless of one's reproductive performance.[24]

An enslaved man, Charles Ball, told about a woman rendered worthless by her failure to reproduce: "When I joined the coffle . . . , there was in it a Negro woman named Critty, who has belonged to one Hugh Benford. She was married, in the way that slaves are, but as she had no children, she was compelled to take a second husband. Still she did not have an offspring. This displeased her master, who sold her to Finney. Her anguish was intense, and within about four days from the time I saw her first, she died of grief. It happened in the night, whilst we were encamped in the woods."[25]

Owners of small numbers of enslaved persons often made their slave property "marry abroad," to an available enslaved person on a different plantation, so that valuable reproduction could proceed. One nineteenth-century observer noted, "The small fry (and 99 out of every 100 are small fry) class of owners can't think" of prohibiting abroad marriages. "Old Amy without a husband," he continued, "would scarcely have been the 'goose who laid the golden egg' had she been denied a husband from home, seeing her master had none at home 'for her."[26]

Even given the value of enslaved women as "golden geese," the reproductive experiences of many of them, particularly those on small plantations, show how reproductive health was a racial privilege under slavery. Of course not all white women lived out their pregnancies in health or with access to decent food, shelter, and medical attention in this era. Still, most enslaved women were forced by their slave status into reproductive danger. Dunaway shows how these women were endangered: "On average, a pregnant slave was removed from field work only about twenty days throughout her entire pregnancy." She worked until a week before delivery, in some places working to fill cotton baskets weighing seventy-five to one hundred pounds. "In contrast, Southern doctors recommended that affluent pregnant women limit their physical exertion to activities no more strenuous than those conducted 'in carriage' and elite women took regular afternoon naps."[27]

Owners calculated how to increase their capital in slaves while also increasing slave labor. This naturally led to contradictory practices, many of which harmed slave women. For example, owners routinely enforced practices that would enhance fertility, such as pressing enslaved girls and women into early sexual relations and pressuring them to wean their babies early. The same owners would likely force pregnant enslaved women to work in the fields almost up to their due dates. In this way owners were taking the chance that laborers would "miscarry right there in the fields," an event that occurred on many of these plantations, especially since profit-maximizing owners refused to call in physicians to supervise the birthings of enslaved women.[28]

Historian Richard Follett has found that on Louisiana sugar plantations terrible work conditions and other factors created reproductive havoc. He wrote, "Overwork induced miscarriage and stillbirths shortened birth intervals, high levels of infant mortality ensured that women would resume early menses, inadequate postnatal care further limited the delay between births, while relatively poor nutritional content and quantity of the slave mother's milk probably triggered early weaning and shorter birth intervals."[29]

One formerly enslaved woman, Josephine Bacchus, looked back, remembering: "I ain't never been safe in de family way." She recalled experiencing constant hunger and rape, and being pressed back into the fields soon after childbirth. Not surprisingly, all of her babies except one died at birth.[30] Under this regime, mothers died too. Edward De Bieuw, an enslaved man in Lafourche Parish, Louisiana recalled, "My ma died 'bout three hours after I was born. . . . Pa always said they made my ma work too hard. . . . He said ma was hoein'. She told the driver she was sick; he told her to just hoe-right-on. Soon, I was born, and my ma die[d] a few minutes after dey brung her to the house."[31]

Women were also forced to perform the reproductive labor of wet-nursing, that is, nursing a baby born to another woman. Ellen Betts, an enslaved woman, reported, "I don't do nothing all my days, but nuss, nuss, nuss, nuss. I nuss so many chillen it done went and stunted my growth and dat's why I ain't nothin' but bones to dis day."[32]

The system also stunted enslaved babies, many of whom, especially on the sugar plantations, were born tiny. Follett tells us that this was, in part, the result of enslaved women working sixty to seventy hours a week "while standing or stooping over cane shoot in ninety-degree temperatures." These women had an insufficient blood supply to their placentas; they often suffered from hypertension, which causes slowed fetal growth.[33]

Slavery established the right to choose a sexual and procreating partner as the privilege of whites. It also established the right to marry and raise one's children with one's marital partner as a similar privilege. The slave code forbade enslaved persons from contracting marriage and disregarded the meanings of partnering practices among enslaved persons. Codes referred to slave matrimony as "the association which takes place among slaves, and is called marriage, [but is] . . . properly designated by the word contubernium, a relation which has no sanctity, and to which no civil rights are attached."[34] A by-product of disallowing slave marriage was the denial of "legitimacy" status to all enslaved children, rendering "legitimacy" the privilege of whites.

In addition, by denying enslaved people the right to marry, owners protected themselves and the church against the need to reconsider the meaning of marriage and of sin. This was especially relevant if an owner sold a man but wanted that man's "wife" to continue increasing his slaveholdings by having more children. If the owner had allowed marriage, how could he—and the church—define the woman's relationship to the man he paired her with after selling her husband? Also, by denying enslaved people the right to both "religious ceremony and public recording," owners justified their claim that "blacks didn't construct families that were moral and cultural equivalents of whites'."[35]

Making a claim for personal dignity, one enslaved man wrote, "I was married to Lucilla Smith, the slave of Mrs. Moore. We called it and considered it a true marriage."[36] But others looked back, remembering that enslaved women had no right to decide for themselves who and when to marry. A formerly enslaved woman, Katie Blackwell Johnson, described how slave masters had the final say. The slave women she knew had "no choice in the matter as to whom they would marry."[37] Charles Gandy, an ex-slave, recorded, "Marsa used to sometimes pick our wives fo' us. If he didn't have on his place enough women for the men, he would wait on de side of de road till a big wagon loaded with slaves come by. Den Marsa would stop de ole nigger-trader and buy you a woman. Wasn't no use tryin' to pick one cause Marsa wasn't gonna pay but so much for her. All he wanted was a young healthy one who looked like she could have children, whether she was pretty or ugly as sin."[38] Whether an enslaved person lived in a sustained, loving relationship or an imposed arrangement, the slave owner's economic and labor calculations could end a family arrangement as easily as they could construct them, so making family itself a white privilege.[39]

Especially in the slave-exporting states, where enslaved persons were the most valuable commodity small farmers "produced," the right to family was particularly violated. These owners sold children much more often than owners in the Lower South and regularly structured labor arrangements for men that sent them away from home. One man from Appalachian Virginia remembered, "White folks in my part of the country didn't think anything of breaking up a family and selling the children in one section of the South and the parents in some other section."[40]

For the purposes of this book, "reproductive politics" refers to struggles over who decides whether, when, and which women can reproduce legitimately *and* also to struggles over which women have the right to be mothers of the children they bear. Under the slavery system, the right to be the mother of one's child was, on top of everything else, a racial privilege—that is, a privilege reserved for white women. Legal scholar Dorothy Roberts has written, "Black women bore children who belonged to the slave owner from the moment of their conception."[41] Under these circumstances, any definition of "mothering" was deeply compromised.

Booker T. Washington described how his mother, as an enslaved woman, had few rights to make decisions. Even her right to decide how and when to be motherly was severely constrained: "My mother, of course, had little time in which to give attention to the training of her children during the day. She snatched a few moments for our care in the early morning before her work began, and at night after the day's work was done."[42] Others described what kinds of control were exerted over nursing mothers. In one case, mothers who left the fields to nurse their children were threatened with the whip. Going further, the owner tried to establish a rigid three-times-a-day schedule for infant feeding. Apparently the enslaved women on this plantation were able to band together and eventually force the owner to allow them to "tolerate" the schedule they devised for their children.[43]

Owners had ways of dealing with older children, attempting to "socialize" them to obey the master, not the parents. Owners pressed enslaved children to grant the master all due authority, as he prepared them for a lifetime as slave labor.[44]

Most tragically, unlike a white mother, an enslaved mother did not have the privilege to protect her children from sale or, in many cases, to maintain a relationship with her children. On plantations large and small, family breakup was a distinct possibility. One former slave described an auction at which his enslaved mother's children were sold off, one by one, while the mother looked on "in an agony of grief." Next, the mother herself was on the block: "My mother was then separated from me, and put up in her turn. She was bought by a man named Isaac R. . . . and then I was offered to the assembled purchasers. My mother half distracted with the parting forever from all her children, pushed through the crowd while the bidding for me was going on, to the spot where R. was standing. She fell at his feet, and clung to his knees, entreating him in tones that a mother only could command to buy her Baby as well as herself, and spare to her one of her little ones at least. Will it, can it be believed that this man, thus appealed to, was capable not merely of turning a deaf ear to her supplication, but of disengaging himself from her with such violent blows and kicks as to reduce her to the necessity of creeping out of his reach and mingling the groan of bodily suffering with the sob of a broken heart."[45]

A slavery-era newspaper commentary on the slave trade in Washington, D.C., underscores once again the degree to which the rights to be a mother of one's child and to maintain one's family were racially determined—as well as a crucial part of the definition of race in the United States in that period. Describing the slave market, the commentator wrote, "Here, you may behold fathers and mothers leaving behind them the dearest objects of affection, and moving slowly along in the mute agony of despair; there, the young mother sobbing over the infant whose innocent smile seems but to increase her misery. . . . Such is but a faint picture of the American slave trade."[46]

Recent research has shown that between 1820 and 1860, as the cotton kingdom boomed, one-tenth of all Upper South slaves were relocated to the Lower South each decade. Nearly one out of three children living in the Upper South in 1820 were gone by 1860. Thus a very high percentage of slave families were broken in this era by owners' strategies for maximizing profits. Wilma Dunaway asks: "How could the horror and grief not have been a shaping force in the family lives of mountain slave women, a majority of whom suffered losses of spouses, children, parents, or siblings?"[47]

When possible, enslaved women nevertheless did what they could, within their circumstances, to assert ownership over their own bodies and their reproductive capacities.[48] This meant trying to protect themselves "totally beyond the control of the master," sometimes by resisting rape, by choosing one's own sexual or life partner, by attempting self-abortion or seeking the services of knowledgeable enslaved people on the plantation, or by other means.[49] In studies of slavery and resistance, a Georgia physician is much quoted because what he had to say in 1849 was so revealing both about white fears of Black reproductive autonomy and about the constant need of enslaved women to manage their fertility. He said that "slave women had far more abortions and miscarriages than did his white patients, either because of the excessive work slaves were compelled to perform or, 'as the planters believe,' because slaves were possessed of a secret by which they destroy the fetus at an early stage of gestation."[50]

Historian Stephanie Shaw has defined efforts of enslaved women to exert reproductive control as expressions of maternal responsibility: "[E]ven when slave women had abortions, refused to conceive or committed infanticide in order to protect children from a life time of slavery, they often did so in the interests of mothering. And even when they made such decisions without considering the child's future, they made mothering decisions—decisions not to mother." This is a bold interpretation, in part because anti-abortion-rights forces in the United States today have effectively pressed many people in this country to imagine the act of terminating a pregnancy as an irresponsible and selfish act. Here we need to consider the relationship between reproductive autonomy and maternal judgment.[51]

Women's acts of resistance—these efforts to exert control over their reproductive capacity—were, in any case, related to efforts that animated the entire abolitionist and Black freedom movement: demands for the "freedom to make meaning by taking chosen rather than dictated paths."[52] Secret acts in the interests of enslaved women's desire to be human and free expressed an understanding that sexual autonomy and reproductive autonomy are fundamental to human freedom —and that no person's productive or reproductive labor should be owned.[53]

Writing about these matters, legal scholar Peggy Cooper-Davis explains, "The promise of emancipation and Reconstruction was more than freedom from ownership by a master. It was freedom to live as morally responsible agents, able to mark the social fabric. This greater freedom is nurtured in intimate communities, where families are freely formed, and wanted children absorb and reshape the mosaic of values that constitute an American culture." As enslaved women trying to own their reproductive bodies realized, freedom meant "the exercise of moral and intellectual capacities—of choice."[54]

At the same time that the laws, policies, and practices of the slavery system racialized the nation, the United States was also racialized by cultural and military violence waged against Native Americans. The age of the cotton boom and slavery expansion and rampant marketing in the bodies of enslaved persons overlapped the age of Indian "removal." As early as 1802, President Thomas Jefferson had supported the idea of transporting Indians from their tribal lands east of the Mississippi River to western destinations. In 1830, President Andrew Jackson signed the Indian Removal Act that empowered the military to carry out massive movement of Native Americans westward, "beyond the chartered boundaries of states."[55] Tribal disputes, court cases, an important treaty, and political opposition delayed government action. But in the winter of 1838–1839, the U.S. military rounded up approximately fourteen thousand Cherokee and forced them to walk one thousand miles to the Oklahoma Territory. For between one-quarter and one-third of these people, this was a death march.

The Cherokee and thousands of other Native Americans whose lives were harmed or ended by federal policies and military campaigns had lived for as long as a thousand years on ancestral North American lands. Like all peoples, the lives of Native Americans had been shaped by elaborate ritual practices associated with sexual intercourse, pregnancy, and childbirth. These practices, unimpeded for centuries, were important to definitions of life, maturity, manhood, womanhood, and other foundational concepts of culture.

Historian Theda Perdue has given us insight into the rituals and meanings of reproductive matters that characterized Cherokee culture. She describes the ways that female fertility was understood as both a blessing and a curse. Cherokee treated menstruation, the first and continual reminder of reproductive potential, as a sign of female power and as an occasion for separating the bleeding woman from the community. This woman wasn't "unclean" so much as "possessed [of] great power," and therefore dangerous. After all, signs of her fertility were also signs of her capacity to bring a new person into life and thereby change the shape of the community.

Perdue defines the restrictions and rituals constructed around procreation as marking the "community's apprehensions, as well as [marking] any personal anxiety women might have about childbirth." The rituals, she finds, "allayed fear" and helped the community "control the direction of change." Perdue explains that "through sexual abstinence [and a group of other practices] women attempted to control the danger and minimize its negative effects." Also, women could "gain a spiritual power" through undergoing the trials of menstruation, pregnancy, and childbirth. Not incidentally, all of these events involved women's blood, a substance that "dangerously unleashed the spiritual power of life." Blood that flowed from fertility-related events marked women as most specifically female, just as the blood of men that flowed as a result of hunting or warfare marked them as most specifically male.[56]

Cherokee rituals and rules acknowledging the blessing and the curse of fertility were extremely specific. For example, Perdue writes, "The Cherokee did not eat food prepared by a pregnant woman or walk on a path she had traveled. If she waded in a river upstream from fish traps, she spoiled the catch, and if she looked on a person suffering from snakebite, the victim died." Pregnant women had to avoid certain foods to preserve the health of the fetus or the newborn or protect it from harm during birthing. Some rules reflected the kinds of medical diffi-

culties that threatened parturient women and confounded their atten-
dants in this premedicalized era: "Because squirrels climb trees the
Cherokees believed that the consumption of squirrel meat by an expec-
tant mother caused the baby to go up instead of down during labor."

Prescriptions for an expeditious birthing experience were detailed
and copious. They involved instructions about the proper setting for
giving birth, for who may and may not attend the birth, for what to
drink and what to avoid drinking, for what words to recite during labor,
and how the mother's body would be situated—never lying down,
only standing, kneeling, or sitting. A baby was to be plunged into the
river upon birth, a ritual that was to be repeated every day for two
years. A parturient woman had to stay separate from her family for
seven days following the birth.[57]

Perdue shows how the prestige or status of women declined
sharply as whites penetrated Cherokee land and culture and worked
hard to "civilize" and Christianize these people. In the late eighteenth
and early nineteenth centuries, women's power as reproducers and
their power as members of the Cherokee polity were reciprocally diminished. To a significant degree, government officials and Christian
missionaries defined their task as interrupting old meanings associated
with communal property, clan-based power, and female reproduction.
In the 1820s, for example, as part of the program of bringing "civilization" to Indians, missionaries and their Cherokee allies restricted and
then outlawed polygamy, a practice Perdue and others associate with
strong female bonds. In 1825, matrilineality, a foundational source of female power, was seriously compromised when the Cherokee council allowed "the children of Cherokee men and white women, living in the
Cherokee nation as man and wife," to become citizens of the Cherokee
nation.

Fundamentally, whites who concerned themselves with Indian culture and nation measured the value of Indian women against a standard that governed early Victorian-American, white women's lives: enforced dependency and gentility. Ironically, "policy makers, agents, and
missionaries" found Indian women "degraded" because they were not
politically powerless and economically dependent like proper white
women. Therefore, a first task in civilizing Indians was to raise the status of their women "to its proper rank and influence" by restricting female authority. A minister in 1822 expressed his belief that Indian
women who "nurse and nourish every one that cometh into the world"

were in a special position to do God's work, exercising "authority over the mind in its most pliant state." This was the most important task Cherokee women could perform. Their social roles should be constructed accordingly.[58]

Perdue shows how missionaries further stunted the authority of Cherokee women when they acknowledged women's special position but then placed themselves between mothers and their children: missionary creed allowed that the most effective way to Christianize families was by making a spiritual impact on the youth. Foreshadowing the practices of the boarding school system later in the century, missionaries positioned themselves as "surrogate parents" presiding over a "new Christian family" in place of "the extended matrilineal kin network."[59]

During this period of cultural contact and change in the first decades of the nineteenth century, matrilineal family structures were under stress and decomposing, but the Christian, patriarchal, nuclear family had not yet taken hold.[60] Perdue describes this period as a collection of disastrous impacts: "War and disease decimated the Cherokee population, and Cherokees bought peace with land cessions, trade sucked them into a world economic system over which they had no control and 'civilization' promised a loss of culture, sovereignty, and land."[61] At this time, a variety of whites assessed the "civilizing" project a failure—in part because of the partial persistence of matrilineality and its manifestations in Cherokee society. Women still held on to some economic power, some personal autonomy, and remnants of political and familial authority. Also at this time, the U.S. government and its allies determined to "remove" the Cherokees westward and claim Cherokee lands as their own.

Historical evidence shows that Cherokee women resisted land agreements with the U.S. government, that is, treaties providing for the trade of ancestral land in the East for tracts a thousand miles away. Women argued from a position of power derived from reproductive and maternal capacity. They spoke forcefully about how their "duties as mothers" gave them the right to speak to "Chiefs and warriors in council." They insisted, "The land was given to us by the Great Spirit above as our common right to raise our children upon, and to make support for our rising generations." The women declared, "We have understood some of our children wish to go over the Mississippi, but this act of our children would be like destroying your mothers. Your mothers and sisters ask and beg of you not to part with any more of our lands."[62]

Historians have preserved records of the terrible wrenching of a people from their land and of the "Trail of Tears," the ghastly forced march of Cherokee to the Oklahoma Territory.[63] Here is one account of what happened when the U.S. military arrived to "remove" the Cherokee: "Men working in the fields were arrested and driven to stockades. Women were dragged from their homes by soldiers whose language they could not understand. Children were often separated from their parents and driven into the stockades with the sky for a blanket and the earth for a pillow." Violations of Cherokee life- and death-related rituals began at once: "One family was forced to leave the body of a child who had just died," and the distraught mother "collapsed of heart failure." Another mother "could only carry her dying child in her arms a few miles." Eventually she had to "consign her much loved babe to the cold ground." Accounts of life along the trail have been described as "a litany of the burial of children, some born in an 'untimely' way."

One can imagine that along the trail, all rituals and rules governing birth—what women ate, who saw them, who attended birth, and the many other traditional prescriptions—were distressingly suspended. But birth went on. A variety of sources report that nearly seventy newborn babies were among the Cherokee who arrived in Oklahoma Territory. Perhaps it is surprising that so many infants were born and survived. After all, a missionary reported that "troops frequently forced women in labor to continue [marching] until they collapsed and delivered 'in the midst of the company of soldiers.'"[64]

Cherokee women now living in the West as well as other native women faced huge demographic challenges—as well as diminished status—in the second half of the nineteenth century. For example, historian Albert L. Hurtado shows that "in every age cohort in every country" in California in the late 1850s, there were "substantially fewer women than men." The gold rush, in particular, created special horrors for native women. Hurtado explains that they "had to run a sexual gauntlet while their kinfolk and friends helpless watched their sense of community, chastity, and morality being assaulted by white men who dreamed of a new community of racial purity, sexual continence, and Christian ethics—a community that they would found with white women." Hurtado finds gendered danger in California and beyond: All Indians were at risk in this period, "but women's chances for survival were measurably worse than men's. Brutal assaults, deadly diseases, and general privation killed women and left their community's repro-ductive potential in doubt."[65]

Far from regretting this gendered endangerment, many prominent white Americans approved. Charles Francis Adams Jr., a descendant of presidents and himself an important industrialist in the late nineteenth century, judged U.S. Indian policy as harsh but efficacious because it "saved the Anglo-Saxon stock from being a nation of half-breeds." Prominent missionaries such as Rufus Anderson, secretary of the American Board of Foreign Missions from 1832 until 1866 and author of *The Hawaiian Islands, Their Progress and Condition under Missionary Labors* (1864), approved of the reduction of the native population of that island by 90 percent. He found the obliteration of natives only "natural," similar to "the amputation of diseased members of the body."[66]

Many years later, historian Rebecca Tsosie reflected on the ways that government policies of removal and obliteration and gender standardization were reflected in the novels that white people wrote about Indians in the nineteenth century. She found that in these white-authored stories, the native woman appears "originally" as gentle and beautiful, nurturing "sheep, corn, and babies." Later she is alienated from her reproductive capacity and from nurturance. She becomes "a promiscuous, manipulative, materialistic creature," beyond redemption.[67] A figment of the white imagination, this transition is a contemporary expression of official military and cultural aims.

The United States became a racialized country in the late eighteenth century and beyond not simply under the mechanisms directly enforcing and perpetuating racial slavery, Indian removal, and white supremacy. The nation was fully racialized when laws and practices explicitly linked the degradation of Blacks and Indians to the elevation of whites. White privilege depended on this process. The special status of whites was built out of the rules, laws, and norms governing white sex-and-pregnancy every bit as much as the slave system and Indian degradation depended on reproductive control of nonwhite people. The social privileges and protections of white people depended on laws, policies, and attitudes continually affirming and policing racial boundaries. Often the most direct way to police these boundaries was by prescribing and monitoring the sexual and reproductive behavior of white women.

CEMENTING WHITE SUPREMACY

For the rest of this chapter, I will look at how definitions and enforcement of white women's sex-and-pregnancy-related behavior contributed to the process of racializing the nation. To reiterate, I am using this term, "racializing," to refer to the process carried out by elites whereby the nation's inhabitants were divided into racial groups. Each group was subject to special laws and rules depending on race, with the overall goal of maintaining white supremacy.

[margin note: Racializ. def'n]

We can start the consideration of white women's reproductive experiences in the early decades of the United States by exploring changes in the meanings of white motherhood in the late eighteenth century. We can ask what those changes had to do with definitions of race and the nation. Second, we can look at the idea of chastity and its role in underwriting new ideas about white motherhood, as well as its dynamic role in defining the racial identity of females. Finally, we can take a look at the simultaneous rise in the United States in the first half of the nineteenth century of a vibrant abolitionist movement and a vibrant claim for fertility control.

In 1787, a Cherokee woman, Katteuha, wrote to Benjamin Franklin proposing a wise course for their respective nations: peace. She built her letter on a metaphor, the life-giving, revered, nation-shaping Mother of All, a woman so wise that even powerful white men such as Franklin "ought to mind" what she says. Katteuha assumed that Benjamin Franklin and his people would "have a beloved woman amongst [them] who will help put her Children right if they do wrong." Katteuha assumed that the white man would credit her trope: motherhood as a source of wisdom and state power.[68]

In truth, the Cherokee woman's metaphor described a mother who was grander and more potent than even the most endowed white mothers in the United States at the end of the eighteenth century. Even many of the most privileged lived in a society where married mothers could not own property, work for pay, divorce and claim custody of their children, or look for legal protection if they'd been sexually violated. Even for privileged women, motherhood could be "the last straw in enforcing women's subordination to men."[69] But throughout white culture, as the slave system hardened and spread, white motherhood increasingly appeared as Katteuha described it: an ennobled status. White mothers

[margin note: White Motherhood = ennobled]

increasingly appeared in prescriptive literature as dependent but dignified, innocent and pious but knowing, domestic but able to shape the affairs of the nation through their child-rearing responsibilities, deeply emotional but judicious. Above all, white mothers were paragons of white purity. Even the process of becoming pregnant—fertilization— was imagined at the end of the eighteenth century as a "miniaturized version of monogamous marriage," the citadel of white women's purity: "the animalcule/husband managed to get through the single opening of the egg/wife, which then closed and 'did not allow another worm to enter.'"[70]

Even (or especially) in an era when every woman faced the prospect of death in childbirth, educated white women increasingly described the stages of pregnancy as marking their own "progress toward spiritual perfectibility."[71] In the era when the fecund enslaved woman was commonly regarded as a profitable "brood mare," a fecund white woman was encouraged to imagine that each time she gave birth she was elevated to a "higher place in the scale of being." According to prescription, with each child she had firmer claim to white women's "sacred and singular occupation."[72]

A number of historians have written about the "rise of the moral mother" or "republican motherhood" at the end of the eighteenth century and into the nineteenth century.[73] Popular literature at that time prescribed the "moral mother" as provider of nurturing guidance to future citizens of the republic. Writers defined motherhood as the noblest status of women. But this literature never referred to race. Clearly, though, the prescription described an exclusionary, racialized ideal. Both the moral mother's children—future citizens—and the republic they would serve were imagined as white.

This venerated white mother, the wife in a patriarchal household, emerged in the late eighteenth century as a cultural icon for a number of reasons. First of all, by this time, infant mortality had declined, so fewer births were needed to produce a desired number of living children. Also parents understood that they had to stop subdividing their landholdings into ever-tinier plots, if their offspring were to inherit farms big enough to survive on. For these reasons, women began to try to limit their fertility. And as women had fewer children, each one seemed more precious. White motherhood became an upgraded status as infant care was now defined as complicated and demanding expertise.

Now white women living in patriarchal households were less likely than earlier to be busy producing cloth or other goods for the market. They were more likely to "devote" themselves to domestic tasks and child rearing. At the same time, in part because of increasing urbaniza-tion, more people could read the ever-growing number of published pamphlets and books, including those that instructed literate white mothers in the glories and duties of their familial and national roles.

The intense religiosity of married white women in the early decades of the new nation meant that many of these women went to church regularly. There they heard evangelical white preachers speak to largely female congregations about their special maternal powers and duties. And, again, in a nation, part of which was engaged in under-writing an aggressively expanding slavery system and the genocide of native people, racial distinctions were crucial. No distinction was more crucial than the one accorded to the white married mother who was supposed to engage in sexual relations in order to give birth to white citizens.

The process of racializing the nation was complicated. We can get some sense of how complicated by looking at the situation facing poor white women who engaged in sex and reproductive activities when they were unprotected by male relatives. Like Black women, these women were excluded from the category of white nation-building mother, despite their racial identity. Unprotected impoverished white women continued to earn punishment for sex-and-pregnancy-related behaviors even though white women who were married to, or the daughters of, property-owning men no longer faced punishments by the end of the eighteenth century. Like those of Black women, the wombs of these poor white women in the growing cities of the free-labor North produced the future laboring class. Their children would become workers generating wealth for white property and business owners.

One sex-and-pregnancy-related behavior that poor white women continued to suffer punishment for was infanticide. No one knows how many women—enslaved or free, white or Black, married or unmarried, poor or not, killed their newborn babies in the eighteenth century—or why. Historians believe that some women in all these groups commit-ted infanticide. Lawmakers and those who enforced the law tended to interpret an unmarried woman or perhaps a very poor one with a dead newborn as a likely murderer.

Kristin Fischer has described infanticide as the outcome of illegitimate pregnancy for many servant women. Fischer has invited the modern reader to imagine the details: "Pregnant servant women had to carry on with the usual chores of domestic service and reveal no special hardship or else risk the dangers of absconding during late pregnancy for a secret childbirth. Few if any servants had private bedrooms; they had to give birth quickly, quietly in a private place outdoors in the privy. The mother had to cut the umbilical cord, kill the baby before its cries could give them away, hide its body without being seen, and dispose of the soiled sheets or clothes and the afterbirth. The trauma, fear, and guilt involved in such actions must have been enormous." The historian goes on to underscore the servant woman's likely motive: "That some women elected this difficult route testifies to the terrible burden and shame that could accompany illegitimate pregnancy."[74]

In addition, the white servant girl, unprotected by any male, along with African and sometimes Indian women who committed this crime, was much more likely to be prosecuted in the second half of the eighteenth century than "daughters of middling or elite householders." The prosecuted girls had no dowry and no parents nearby to protect them. They were "particularly vulnerable to abandonment by their lovers." They were especially likely to be prosecuted for having killed their infants in a desperate effort to protect themselves, in a society where no laws and no persons protected vulnerable females.[75]

Unprotected poor white women in the bondage of servitude blurred the difference between white women or mothers and Black. Their unfree status and their unchaste actions blurred the distinction between slaves and free women, between the dignity and indignity of sex-and-pregnancy. So they, along with racially marginalized women accused of infanticide, were pulled into the criminal court.[76]

Once indentured servitude began to decline as a labor arrangement in the second half of the eighteenth century, white servant women were usually defined as "free." Juries were now less likely to convict these women in cases of infanticide and more likely to look at them with "sentimental pity." Having been redefined as white, they could also be defined as loving mothers and as tragically victimized women.[77]

Like the official treatment of infanticide, the official treatment of fornication—the crime of sex outside of marriage—was complicated and ever-changing. Early in the history of the American colonies, both men and women were publicly shamed and punished for fornication, but by the middle of the eighteenth century, fornication had become a "female crime."[78] As historian Cornelia Dayton describes it, "By 1740, the Puritan system of prosecuting and punishing men alongside women for fornication had collapsed. Lawyers, judges, and sexually active young white men had brought off a coup: [white] men would be exempted from confessing to philandering while women, still presented for the crime and convicted by both their confessions and their pregnancies, would continue to appear in public as repentant sinners until the end of the century."[79]

But now only some women were likely to face prosecution: only "marginal women—poor domestics, women in interracial relationships, women who repeatedly bore children without marrying" were prosecuted for committing fornication. These were white women whose behavior blurred the distinctions between slaves and free women.[80] The vulnerable fornicating female was the woman who refused or failed to be properly "white," who was not sexually restrained and enfolded within the patriarchal family.[81]

When authorities stopped bringing charges against fornicating wives and daughters of "middling sorts," that is, females attached to men owning at least some property, then only family members or the church could punish these women. Sexual misbehavior could be treated as a private matter. One could say that sexual privacy, even when unconventional sexual activities were involved, became a privilege of race and class.

Without prosecution or a trial, the male fornicator was less likely to be named in public—a highly desirable situation for the male. In fact, a woman, if she herself were respectable and protected by family, could simply threaten to name her sexual partner if the court leaned toward prosecuting her. That might well convince the magistrate to desist.[82] On the other hand, if the girl had been raped or abandoned, if her parents were dead or destitute, her experience in court and in the community could be "difficult or bitter."[83] If she were a Black fornicator, she might still be whipped. Having one's sexually misbehaving body mortified in public became a mark and a definition of race and racial degradation.[84]

The prescriptive and cautionary literature of the eighteenth century brought the stories of sexually errant young white women into public view. The stories demonstrated that when an unprotected white girl threw off sexual restraint and revealed her carnal nature, she was regarded like a slave. Her story was tragic because she had so much to lose in an era in which chaste white girls who became chaste white wives and mothers had a role in shaping the destiny of the nation. The famous 1807 story of Polly Middleton's "fall from grace" began with the girl, motherless, uncared for by her father and his new wife, banished to the kitchen. "There among the slaves [Polly and her sisters] lived and labored, coarse, ignorant, and neglected." There she was vulnerable to a young man's predations. There she lost all.[85]

Polly Middleton's tragic story firmly instructed the early nineteenth-century reader: the cult of white young womanhood and white motherhood utterly depended on family protection and chastity. Chastity, above all, distinguished white females from slave women who were, in the white mind, completely alienated from sexual purity. According to many abolitionists, this distinction was key to maintaining the system. The great abolitionist Sarah Grimké explained to white women that the racialized privilege of chastity was grounds for antislavery work. She wrote in 1838, "The virtue of female slaves is wholly at the mercy of irresponsible tyrants, and women are bought and sold in our slave markets to gratify the brutal lust of those who bear the name of Christians. In our slave States, if . . . a woman desires to preserve her virtue unsullied, she is either bribed or whipped into compliance, or if she dares resist her seducer, her life by the laws of some of the slave States may be . . . sacrificed to the fury of disappointed passion. . . . In Christian America, the slave has no refuge from unbridled cruelty and lust." Grimké begged every white woman to see that her own claim to moral purity and chastity was "contaminated" if she looked "at these scenes of shocking licentiousness and cruelty, and fold[ed] her hands in apathy and [said], 'I have nothing to do with slavery.'"[86]

Indeed, looking back, religious and cultural prescriptions that defined the proper sex-and-pregnancy behavior of white women seemed to guarantee one thing above all: the rules promised white females that if they behaved as instructed, they would not be *slaves*. Evangelical Protestants in the post-Revolutionary era taught that women who could suppress their innate sexual impulses would be like "angels," raised from slavery, "elevated . . . above the weakness of animal nature."[87] Chaste white women, close to God, were relieved of the dangerous lustiness of the body. And being relieved, they were free to become moral mothers, intellectual persons, the human equals of men.

In a society where white men were all-powerful, prescriptive chastity became a way of curtailing unlimited male power over white women, including the power of sexual domination.[88] At the same time, the chastity of white women enforced white men's property interests in their wives. Only a chaste wife could ensure that her husband really was the father of his heir. Also, as one historian has put it, "[A] cuckolded husband unable to control his wife's sexual behavior forfeited respect as head of the household."[89] According to prescriptive literature, white chastity was key to the orderly transmission of property, to the orderly functioning of the family, generally—and thus to the order and dignity of the nation shaped by white patriarchal families, reproducing white citizens.

In 1799, Hannah More, an Englishwoman concerned about improving the education of women, wrote about the role of culture and society in categorically creating and distinguishing between free women and enslaved women. She noted that in countries where interest in the "mere person," the "mere external charms," *the sexual bodies of women,* was "carried to the highest excess," women were "slaves."[90] In white America in this era, white female chastity could stand for the self-ownership of free white women as a republican claim and an emblem of national virtue.

It may have been that everywhere a young white woman turned in the post-Revolutionary and slavery era, she encountered cultural messages about white chastity. This requirement of proper white womanhood was probably so ever-present as to be acknowledged only when absent and only to mark a negative distinction. By definition, slave women were not chaste. Nor were Indian women, long described by European men as sexually free and possessing secret contraceptive knowledge that allowed sex with no consequences. (Englishmen imagined native women as capable of going through childbirth without pain, another emblem of unwomanly unchasteness.)[91] As we've seen, poor white women could be chaste or unchaste. As servants they were likely to be "unchaste," their class status opening them to sexual exploitation and marking them as sexually degraded, like slaves.

The record exists of a servant girl's plight in the early eighteenth century, showing how white unfree labor was incompatible with chastity, dignity, and self-ownership. A young servant woman, Anne Adams, reported to the county magistrates that her master, "Mr. William Swann, . . . had made her pregnant. The judges cross-examined Adams and then proclaimed Swann guilty of having had 'Divers times Bodily and Carnal Knowledge of the said Anne During her being

Pedisnt at ye Said Swann's house.' Swann had to pay his servant two shillings per week until the child reached eight years of age; at that time the child would be apprenticed to learn a trade. Although Swann was responsible for her pregnancy, Adams had to serve him two extra years, during which time she remained vulnerable to continued sexual involvement with him."[92]

Surely many young women and their mothers remembered these kinds of events that underscored the profound value of chastity—and the association of chastity and freedom. Chastity was especially valued and valuable in a society so deeply committed to seeing the world as composed of binary opposites: chaste and unchaste, white and Black, male and female, dependent and independent, slave and free.

Ultimately, in practical terms, however, prescriptive literature and racial ideologies were not enough to maintain the chastity of white womanhood in America. Ultimately powerful religious, medical, and legal authorities came to believe that white chastity depended on enforcing the strictest relationship between sex and reproduction. Authorities determined that such a relationship had to be vitalized and enforced by law: through the criminalization of abortion and the criminalization of contraception.

The womb became public territory in the first half of the nineteenth century in order to bring the force of public laws into the most intimate aspects of women's lives.[93] We can get a sense that this kind of enforcement was new by looking back for earlier examples. A legal scholar finds that before 1745 there are no records in record-rich New England of a court bringing charges against anyone for performing an abortion.[94] The same historian finds that in the eighteenth century abortion was defined as a problem because of its association with the promiscuity (the separation of sex and reproduction) of unmarried females.[95] But generally, until the 1820s, abortion, following English common law, was not a crime, especially not a crime before the woman herself reported that she had felt the fetus "quicken"—that is, show life—in the womb. A woman seeking an abortion would typically do so only after she had described this quickening sensation to the midwife or physician. A woman might also report to the abortion-performing midwife that she was seeking to "restore" an absent menstrual period.

In the eighteenth century and after, the person performing the abortion was likely to be a midwife, the traditional female professional charged with overseeing women's reproductive functions and events.

The law was rarely invoked to manage or punish either the abortion-seeking woman or the abortion-providing midwife. In fact, early nineteenth-century law tended to validate abortion as a women-centered practice. For example, in 1812, the Massachusetts Supreme Court decided that abortion before quickening was legal. The Massachusetts court allowed early abortions even though nine years earlier the British Parliament had overruled the English common law (the model for lawmakers in the United States), criminalizing abortion before quickening.

Beginning with Connecticut in 1821 and continuing across the nineteenth century, one by one, state legislatures criminalized abortion, although for decades afterward, the quickening doctrine prevailed in many states. Generally abortion was folded into omnibus anticrime bills but rarely prosecuted in cities and towns across the nation.[96] And yet, in the middle decades of the nineteenth century, a woman-centered practice that countless numbers had depended on across history had become a crime in the United States for the first time.

Historians trying to understand why abortion was criminalized in this era have noted that in these years the incidence of abortion was probably increasing sharply and that advertisements for abortionists in city newspapers made abortion a much more visible practice than before. It is also possible that abortion-seeking women in the early to middle decades of the nineteenth century were more likely to be urban, married women, not "promiscuous" single women trying to mask their sexual impropriety.[97]

Historians have also paid attention to what doctors and others wrote at the time about the importance of criminalizing abortion. Many physicians expressed concern about the mortal dangers women faced at the hands of unskilled practitioners. The subtext here expressed, in part, physicians' concerns about regularizing and professionalizing the standards of medicine and the standing of physicians in the community, as against older, traditional folk practitioners such as midwives. But whether one listened to the evangelical Protestant authorities of the period proclaiming sacred motherhood, or listened to newly minted physicians concerned about safety, or listened to social commentators speaking as champions of white children as future citizens of the republic—all the voices in favor of marshaling the law to stop abortion invoked abortion as a crime against chastity. All these voices implicitly or explicitly defined abortion as a crime against the chastity of white women.

The organized effort to outlaw contraceptive devices in the United States overlapped with the campaign against abortion. But by the time the federal Comstock Law (1873) promised to crack down on contraceptive purveyors, most state legislatures had had their laws against abortion on the books for some years. Studies have shown that women in the second half of the eighteenth century were likely to rely on breast-feeding to limit their fertility, a strategy that proved itself "a feeble method."[98] Looking for a better method, women tried oral, herbal preparations and douching. When their sexual partners agreed, they tried periodic abstinence. Whatever effort a white woman made, however, was made inside of a culture that disapproved of white females engaging in sex without the possibility of impregnation, an "unthinkable" practice that would surely "turn the world into a universal brothel."

According to historian Helen Lefkowitz Horowitz, "At the outset of the debate over contraception in America, opponents voiced what remained a primary theme for at least fifty years: if given the means for not suffering the consequences of sexual intercourse in pregnancy, women would be more easily seduced by men and would become promiscuous." Robert Dale Owen, a sexual reformer of the time, spoke often and favorably about fertility control. For one thing, he believed that devices to limit fertility would have the beneficial side effect of wiping out "the resort to masturbation in a single generation."[99] But in the end, Owen and other advocates held back full endorsement because they believed that when white wives and daughters gained contraceptive information, nothing would stop them from becoming prostitutes.[100] Like abortion, contraceptives raised the intolerable specter of white female licentiousness. After all, the most defining attribute of white womanhood in this slaveholding country was nothing less than white chastity.

CONTROLLING FERTILITY IN THE ABOLITIONIST ERA

Across the first half of the nineteenth century, white chastity was championed in the form of increasingly moralistic and legalistic campaigns. But all the while, information about how to limit fertility or how to find an abortionist was available to the young men and women living in cities, away from their families, reading the newspapers, perusing the advertising columns, having sex.[101] Historians have found rising abortion rates at this time on the frontier as well as in cities and towns, suggesting that information spread quickly and widely.[102] We know that women were finding and using information about fertility limitation because we can see that the birth rate was declining fairly rapidly at this time. On average, women born between 1710 and 1759, for example, had 8.37 pregnancies. Those born between 1760 and 1799 had 8.33 pregnancies. And the first generation exposed to the explosion of urban newspapers and other complexities of urban life—those born between 1800 and 1839—had 5.81 pregnancies.[103]

No matter how unthinkable this pursuit may have been in the past, by the end of the 1830s, ordinary white women were assumed to be reading the books and pamphlets published in the United States about fertility limitation.[104] The first of these, Robert Dale Owen's *Moral Physiology; or a Brief and Plain Treatise on the Population Question*, a sixty-nine-page booklet published in the 1830s and sold for thirty-nine cents, provided information and advice. We know that women were doing activist work together in the 1830s and 1840s, as union-builders, strikers, urban laborers, and abolitionists. Political scientist Rosalyn Petchesky has made a connection between the existence of these kinds of women's information networks and expansive reproductive practices: "Where there are strong and cohesive women's communities, either through shared neighborhood cultures or shared work, and where women have access to local 'wise women' or midwives or active communication networks, abortion practices flourish."[105] It's not surprising that lecturers and others began to talk about sex and reproduction in public, as issues about women's status in society. These issues were discussed in terms of women's power and powerlessness.

Public discussions about white chastity had, in the past, emphasized the relationship between sex and pregnancy as the key to white women's identity and their protected status. Now, in the abolitionist era, those concerned with white women's sexual and reproductive capacities grappled with the idea that separating these capacities might be key to white women's full personhood.

To be sure, this idea of separating sex and pregnancy—the possibility that the wives and daughters of ordinary white men might routinely adopt the "devices of the brothel"—was radical. Many people spoke out against the "political and social revolutionaries" who advocated separation, worrying that "the power to curtail pregnancy and thus to separate sexual intercourse from reproduction threatened to alter relations between men and women, to diminish the power of husbands over their wives, and of parents over their children, especially over their daughters."[106] To these people, birth control stood for unchaste and unfaithful women before and during marriage and the impossibility of knowing whether one's child was legitimate or illegitimate—a condition of society that would, intolerably, make white children the same as slave children.

Yet in the abolitionist era, the arguments in favor of fertility control were increasingly made out of the same ingredients as the arguments against slavery—and drew on antislavery language and imagery. To begin with, a wide range of advocates of the "anti-contraceptive art" used ideas and terms mandating the body as the site of self-ownership, not the vehicle of enslavement. Historian Linda Gordon has shown how for women, "normal 'sex' in the nineteenth century meant a form of intercourse dictated primarily by male desires . . . and involving the risks of venereal disease, unwanted conception, and dangerous and painful parturition or abortion."[107] Here is male-imposed sex as multiple acts of enslaving the woman's body. For sex reformers like Robert Dale Owen, reproductive control could save unmarried women from the syndrome of seduction and shame. Reproductive control could liberate all women from the role of "sufferer" in a sexual system that, like the slave system, allowed the dominating man to go "free" and blameless.[108] A New York abortionist advertised her service as a "sanctuary" to which women enslaved by the "uncharitableness of general society" could flee—and there find a kind of liberation.[109]

Sometimes uncontrolled reproductive capacity itself was the cruel master, capable of enslaving and impoverishing both man and woman: "In how many instances does the hard-working father, and more especially the mother, of a poor family, remain slaves throughout their lives, tugging at the oar of incessant labour, toiling to live, and living only to die; when, if their offspring had been limited to two or three only, they might have enjoyed comfort and comparative affluence!"[110] Owen and others associated mechanisms of reproductive control with human liberation—self-determination, redistribution of wealth, and the end of cruel forms of oppression.

Also in the abolitionist era, the need to manage fertility was often associated with the need to control unbridled male lust. Abortion and birth control were sometimes described as ways for women to protect themselves against male lust that rendered both the sexually domineering man and his victimized wife less than human—enslaved by sex.[111]

Like antislavery advocates in the 1840s and 1850s, the new sex educators, including advocates of reproductive control, spoke across the country to deeply concerned urban white crowds. Lecturers were addressing subjects that for the first time admitted public debate and multiple perspectives. Mass audiences were drawn in because they believed new information could reshape the ways they thought about old subjects. Frederick Hollick, an author of books and tracts about reproductive matters, spoke twenty-six times in Philadelphia in a five-year period, plus in Baltimore and Washington, St. Louis, Cincinnati, Louisville, Pittsburgh, and Hartford, throughout Massachusetts, and on a steamship bound for New Orleans, at the request of the passengers. Hollick, in the style of mid-nineteenth-century lecturers, offered scientific demonstrations in the form of wax and papier-mâché manikins so that his audiences could understand the basic biological principles of human reproduction. The lecturer offered white Americans across the country a startling dose of learning in the cause of human liberation. (A newspaper of the time reported, "[M]any have fainted away at first view of Hollick's manikins.")[112]

Specifically, Frederick Hollick, in his book *The Marriage Guide* (1850), laid out a new theory of female sexuality and reproductive biology, one that proposed "the female body as governed by its own laws." This claim demanded the ennoblement of woman, even as it rendered her body a mere collection of biological functions that operated independent of her volition. The ovum, Hollick taught, was released on a regular schedule, whether or not intercourse occurred. A woman could become pregnant whether or not she experienced "sexual feelings" during intercourse. In identifying and describing these inexorable, normal processes, Hollick redefined female reproduction. He said, in essence, women do not ovulate or become pregnant simply in reaction to male penetration and ejaculation. The reproductive event occurred as the result of dynamic reproductive capability—occurring at the right time.

As it happened, Hollick identified a woman's fertile period incorrectly. But the concept was correct, and it pushed forward the notion of human liberation through reproductive control. If women possessed the information to gauge the days during their cycle when pregnancy was least likely, they could exercise the rational choice to have intercourse at those times. They could achieve freedom from endless rounds of pregnancy and childbearing. According to some nineteenth-century "freethinkers," if women had this kind of information and if sex and reproduction could be uncoupled, then both men and women would be freed to realize their human potential more fully.[113]

Surely thousands of women attempted to practice reproductive control in the abolitionist era whether or not they saw one of Hollick's manikins, heard a freethinker's lecture, or saw an abortionist's advertisement in an urban newspaper. And surely many women did not—either because they lacked information or because they did not approve of such activities. In the increasingly urban, immigrant, and class-riven society of the United States at the middle of the nineteenth century, responses to public discussions about fertility control were extremely various and complicated.

Historians have written many books and articles about the attitudes of midcentury women's rights activists, the generation of "First Wave" feminists who met at Seneca Falls in 1848 and proclaimed women's equality as humans with men. Many of these women were philosophically close to and actively involved in abolitionism. They based their theory of gender rights on the antislavery theories of racial equality and human rights. At the same time, many of these women opposed the division of sex and pregnancy. They interpreted the separation that reproductive control could facilitate as a danger for women, not a liberatory development. Many reasoned that fertility-control mechanisms, including the male condom, perfected in 1844 with the discovery of vulcanized rubber, could make it easier for men to have sex outside of marriage. By separating sex from pregnancy, these devices could also diminish white women's claim to the cultural status of moral mothers.[114] A woman who used a device would dangerously compromise her claim to male protection.

Many midcentury women's rights advocates hated the idea of abortion. One defined the practice as "an outrage on my body and soul, and on my unconscious babe. . . . My womanhood," she wrote, "rose up in withering condemnation." Elizabeth Cady Stanton called abortion "the degradation of women."[115] Stanton and others argued that "voluntary motherhood" was women's salvation—that education, the right to vote, and the right to say no to one's husband's sexual demands were the necessary ingredients of sexual and personal dignity for women.

First Wave feminists and their ideas about "voluntary motherhood" have played a very big role in the story that historians of white women have told about mid-nineteenth-century attitudes about sex-and-pregnancy. Yet we also know that thousands of women were attending lectures in these years, lectures dealing, in part, with fertility control. And rates of abortion were escalating rapidly, especially, according to historian James Mohr, the rate for married women.[116] Mohr estimates that in the period 1800–1830, perhaps one out of every twenty-five to thirty pregnancies was aborted. Between 1850 and 1860, he estimates, the ratio may have been one out of every five or six pregnancies. At midcentury, more than two hundred full-time abortionists reportedly worked in New York City.[117]

According to the *Boston Medical and Surgical Journal* of 1864, "the veil which preserves the decencies of society" had been removed.[118] Now physicians all over the country began to speak out, write, and organize against fertility control, especially against abortion, as a threat to women's lives and to their traditional roles. As James Mohr put it, "over and over" in these years "physicians warned that the growing self-indulgence" of women who used fertility control to separate sex and pregnancy, represented a blow "at the very foundation of society."[119] Doctors, many of whom had long associated women's rights claims with the rise of abortion (despite the antiabortion attitudes of the movement's leaders), were part of a powerful, conservative force putting enormous resources in the abolitionist era and beyond into preserving and restoring the traditional, distinct roles of white women and African Americans, while enhancing their own professional position.[120]

The physicians' campaign against abortion and, as we will see, the moralists' campaign against fertility control of all kinds in the late nineteenth century were extremely effective. Together the campaigns yielded laws giving the state the right to deny women the opportunity to control their fertility. These laws, both the ones against abortion and the ones forbidding sale of birth control information and devices, were enforced inconsistently, and sometimes not at all, in the nineteenth century. But the existence of these laws constituted an expression of official state policy. And these laws ensured that the shadowy practices that huge numbers of women used in the United States in the interests of what might be called women's emancipation remained shadowy, furtive, often shameful, and more unsafe than they would have been in daylight.

The existence of these laws also represented a state policy mandating the continuation of an indivisible relationship between sex and pregnancy: the basis of white chastity. In sum, in the emancipation era, white male authorities organized strenuously to force their vision of *the race* onto the bodies of white women. In effect, doctors and legislators ensured that no matter the outcome of the Civil War, the future of slavery, or the demographic viability of the Indian, laws over women's bodies would make sure that white women would remain chaste and thus remain white.

2

Sex in the City

From Secrecy to Anonymity to Privacy, 1870s to 1920s

AFTER THE CIVIL WAR, in the 1870s, if Martha D., seventeen years old and unmarried, living with her parents on the outskirts of the Hudson River town of Rhinebeck, New York, became pregnant, who cared? Whose business was Martha D.'s out-of-wedlock pregnancy and impending motherhood?

Looking back, historians have shown us—whether Martha D. was white or African American or Native American—her sexual experience and her pregnancy were family matters. These events probably became community matters, too. Most likely, Martha D. would have tried to keep the fact of her sexual relations secret. Having been discovered, though, Martha's situation was not what we would consider today a personal matter, a matter of individual "choice," or a private problem. Nor did Martha's situation call for a response from public officials or from people in charge of institutions. Martha's family and various people in her community very likely took care of what needed taking care of. That might mean making sure that Martha and her sexual partner married. Or it might mean ensuring that Martha was tending her baby safely and well, with the help of her mother and sisters.[1]

But decade by decade after the Civil War, thousands of daughters like Martha D. moved away from their communities, away from the protection of families. Many of these young women, mostly white in the last decades of the nineteenth century, migrated alone to cities. They left home because of economic hardship and because they had heard that a girl could get a decent job and find a room in New York or Boston, St. Louis or Omaha. Daughters left home before sons, often because their labor was less valuable to their farming families. Many women left rural areas because widowhood or divorce set them "adrift." For some, when their sexual secrets became community matters, they left in shame or defiance.[2]

A young woman who arrived in the city in 1870 would have discovered that most jobs she could get involved domestic labor, that is, being a maid living in another family's household. Many girls found work in the needle trades. Neither job paid enough to live on decently.[3] Still, there were jobs. And by the end of the 1880s, there was even an increasing demand for female labor as manufacturing and clerical jobs opened for females.[4]

Every city in the United States experienced this new phenomenon: girls in the city, alone, at work, living in boarding houses, walking in the streets, now vulnerable, now a bit savvy, absorbing street culture, anonymous. If we were able to see what they saw as they negotiated the city streets, going from work to rooming house, glancing at the newspapers, we'd see, for one thing, an astonishing public display of matters that these new city dwellers had traditionally been trained up to consider *secret*.[5] Historian Andrea Tone tells us about an observer of city life in 1872 who claimed that "hardly a newspaper [exists] that does not contain . . . open and printed advertisements [for contraceptive devices or methods] or a drugstore whose shelves are not crowded with [these items] publicly and unblushingly displayed."[6] Everywhere one looked, apparently, contraceptive information, ads, and materials were visible: "[A]lmanacs, joke books, even cookbooks contained advertisements for contraceptives or abortion-inducing agents—inserted by author, publisher, book-seller, or druggist."[7]

This intense commercialization of contraception and abortion after the Civil War reflected a striking cultural development: many women were eager now to separate sex and reproduction. They were eager to buy products that promised to help them do this. In the city, they could make those purchases anonymously. There were others, also new to the city, who were concerned about urban challenges to female propriety and worried about how to sustain traditional female roles. These people believed that contraception and abortion, especially in the service of female pleasure, were gross symptoms of "society dissolving into chaos."

To these people, the *traditionalists*, the city was a sink where politics and business were infected with corruption. The traditionalists defined a mission for themselves: to clean up the city. When the traditionalists walked the city streets, they saw women living alone, abortionists beckoning, filthy, disease-ridden tenements, manufactories bedeviled by labor strife, social relations fueled by racial hatred and sometimes racial violence. Foreigners choked the landscape.[8] The economy was horrifyingly unreliable, as likely to bust as to boom.

The traditionalists, often white men and women who, themselves, had migrated from small towns to the city, disliked the idea of young women living freely in an urban "zone of tolerance."[9] The traditionalists looked at these young women and saw innocent, small-town girls who weren't innocent anymore. Now they were participating in trade union activities, claiming identities as workers, apparently rejecting parental supervision. Most upsetting of all to the traditionalists was the sight of young women challenging sexual conventions, breaching codes of sexual conduct that had, the traditionalists claimed, prevailed forever.[10]

What had been women's secrets in a New England village or in an Ohio farming town had turned into commercial transactions in the city, depersonalized and *anonymous*—a mark of fearsome female independence.[11] Historian Robert Wiebe describes how the traditionalists consoled themselves in this urbanizing context by reading "a flood of fiction [that] sighed over the lost virtues of another day." These made-up stories may have tenderly reminded former village dwellers of a more virtuous past. But the stories also reinforced readers' frustration. They invoked a decent world where moral standards were honored and families were secure. The stories clarified the truth, that this decent world was "either rapidly passing or had already disappeared."[12]

Historians have told this story—the urbanization of America—in many ways. One of the core pieces is always about how the federal government haltingly stepped in to control aspects of life that had been secret business in the past. These were aspects of life—"gambling, drinking, lotteries, narcotics, child labor, reproductive control"—that a weak nineteenth-century federal government could never really hope to master. The government could, though, exert its power to publicize and sometimes punish people who engaged in these secret behaviors.[13]

This chapter is concerned with the last item on that list, the state's efforts to criminalize and punish reproductive control, against women's growing determination to manage their own fertility no matter what the government, the church, their parents, or their husbands believed was proper. Chapter 2 records the slow but steady mainstream acceptance of fertility control between the 1870s and 1930.

Chapter 2 has five sections. The first section looks at the final decades of the nineteenth century just before and after the U.S. Congress passed the Comstock Law (1873) in an effort to define contraceptive materials and information as obscene and immoral and ban their dissemination. This section will show how urban law enforcement officials, pushed by a variety of worried religious and cultural authorities, sometimes prosecuted violators of federal and local laws against contraception and abortion. The second section, "Practicing Privacy," deals with the period from 1900 to the end of the 1920s and considers from a number of angles both the dangers of anonymity and the benefits of sexual and reproductive privacy. Throughout this chapter, this question, "Who had access to reproductive privacy and who did not?" is important. The third section, "The Public Body," describes how laws, policies, and ideologies aimed to influence what kind of babies were born in the early twentieth century. Next, "Caught between Public and Private" describes the reproductive experiences of ordinary women in this era, and last, "Strange Allies in the Public Square" shows the emergence of a cultural thaw. By the end of the 1920s, the Comstock Law was still the law of the land. But officials in many domains and millions of heterosexually active women opposed the law in public—or paid no attention to it at all.

FROM SECRECY TO ANONYMITY TO COMSTOCK LAWS

Historian James Mohr has explained why a small-town young woman in the mid-nineteenth century, looking to control her fertility, might get on the train to the closest city. As Mohr wrote, "[A] trip to the city offered anonymity."[14]

Urban reformers aimed to pay close attention to this girl getting off the train in the center of the city, and to other girls coming in from the outlying districts. Many of these reformers were evangelical Christians concerned with making sure religion did not fall away from the lives of new urbanites. Many reformers were concerned with encouraging worldly, urban sinners to remake themselves in the image of Christ. They focused on young women and the dangers that could compromise femininity and sexual purity—key conditions, as we've seen, of white privilege. These dangers included rooming houses that lacked both privacy and supervision. They included lurking male lodgers, leering and groping employers, workplaces that mixed men and women together, and low wages that pressed some young women to steal or to prostitute themselves.[15]

According to urban reformers, most dangerous was the basic fact that young white women in the city were far away from their own mothers and from family supervision. Who would train them up for their natural roles? Who would protect their virtue? Who would lead them to ruin? Most disconcerting was the fact that the traditional lines defining "good girls" and "bad girls" were breaking up.

In 1873, the same year that Congress enacted the Comstock Law, Myra Bradwell sued the state of Illinois because officials there refused, on the basis of her sex, to grant Bradwell a license to practice law. When the case was ultimately settled in favor of the state, one of the judges wrote, explaining why Bradwell should not be allowed to become a lawyer, "The paramount destiny and mission of women are to fulfill the noble and benign offices of wife and mother. This is the law of the Creator." The Supreme Court justice was expressing a belief that many white Americans defined as a bedrock fact of white civilization—and only white civilization—in the mid-nineteenth century. By the 1870s, this "fact" called for judicial reinforcement.[16]

When the Supreme Court justified curbing the work of white women and when evangelicals crafted reforms to protect white womanly virtue, both centers of authority were responding to real changes in society and changes in the behavior of young white women. First of all, marriage rates declined in the late nineteenth century. Four years before the Comstock Law was enacted, a prominent demographic study suggested that because 250,000 more women than men lived in states along the eastern seaboard, many women would never find a man to marry. In 1883, an expert testifying before Congress provided this information: one-third of all women over twenty-one were not married; therefore, clearly, young women should not assume that marriage would inevitably constitute their "career."[17] The great African American social scientist W. E. B. Du Bois found a related problem in the Black neighborhoods he studied in Philadelphia: "a large excess of young women in a city where young men cannot afford to marry."[18] These data were terrible news in a society where a white woman—and thus all "real" womanhood—was so closely and officially associated with being a proper wife and mother.

Sometimes when reformers looked for evidence of females adrift—unmarried and sinful—they did turn up proof of prostitution and

Blaming Victim *

unwed motherhood. In response to these findings, they did not mount campaigns to raise wages for single women or to change male behavior, arguably the best ways to protect traditional womanhood.[19] Instead they tried to convince single young women in cities to stop misbehaving, especially regarding sex and reproduction.

Historian Joanne Meyerowitz found a series of fifty-seven letters sent into a Chicago newspaper in 1873, all written by people concerned about housing for urban women vulnerable to poverty and prostitution. Many of the writers believed these degradations could be surmounted if young women would return to domestic service. Even if these "women adrift" were far from their own homes, at least as maids they would be under the protection of a man at the head of some household.[20]

Many late nineteenth-century reformers worried most about the illicit sexual lives and illegitimate maternity of white working-class girls. They worried that these females would probably not have the capacity to be adequate mothers. Having lost their chastity, they had lost their womanly identity. Historian Sherri Broder's important study of the lives of such women in Philadelphia at the end of the nineteenth century shows how middle-class women prescribed only one remedy for poor, unwed girls who had babies. Only by keeping and learning to mother her infant would this kind of girl redeem her womanhood and her value as a human being. Reformers cast both those who abandoned their babies (generally because of extreme poverty and desperation) and the unwed mothers whose babies died as unwomanly, unredeemed failures.

By focusing on the bad behavior of poor women, reformers directed attention away from the horrible rates of infant mortality.[21] Many single mothers who worked away from home for pitiful wages had no money to pay for medical care for sick babies. A poor woman who worked long hours was vulnerable to the charge of neglect. Her children might be taken away. Broder shows how child-rescue strategies at that time clarified a new, contingent relationship between poor white women and their children. If a poor mother fulfilled her parental duties properly, that is, in ways approved by self-appointed charity and reform authorities, she could be a mother to her child. If she did not meet standards —if she was not married or could not afford to stay home all day—she had no biological or custody right to keep her child. Experts used this rule of thumb: women were suspect, mothers were sacred. But achiev-

Not so different

ing socially sanctioned motherhood could be hard or impossible for women without economic resources.[22]

Bereft young women who became pregnant and gave birth were troublesome enough. But worse, according to traditionalists, were white women who committed what one clergyman called in 1868 "this horrid home crime," obtaining abortions at such a rate as to end a "full one-third of the natural population of our land." The speaker considered abortion a worse crime than intemperance or even slavery, and believed with many of his peers that its cause was the weakness of women: "fashion, inexorable, tyrannical, with its whirl of amusements and frivolous enjoyments" and "a low life of pleasure and ease."[23] A Michigan doctor, however, spoke for many in 1874 when he pointed to a larger problem than selfish women: "The annual destruction of fetuses [has become so] truly appalling [among native-born, white American women that] the Puritanic blood of '76 will be sparingly represented in the approaching centenary." In other words, abortion was dangerous because it thinned the population of Anglo-Saxon white people. Abortion risked the racial future of the United States.[24]

It is true that some Americans were upset because so many women obtained abortions. But other evidence suggests that abortion was a less-than-burning issue in the United States in these years, even for American Catholics. James Mohr tells us, when Pope Pius IX renewed "medieval censures" of the Catholic Church against abortion in 1869, this news was not reported in U.S. diocean newspapers. (The bishop of Baltimore did take note. He issued a statement that year that read, "The murder of an infant before its birth is, in the sight of God and His Church, as great a crime as would be the killing of a child after birth. . . . No mother is allowed, under any circumstances, to permit the death of her unborn infant, not even for the sake of preserving her own life.")[25]

It is important to note, though, that at the time the minister and the doctor each decried the prevalence of abortion and the horridness of women for pursuing this solution, abortion had just recently been criminalized in most states. For more than two hundred years since English settlement on the North American continent, abortion had not been a crime, but now it was. Before and after the law changed, many women made an old argument justifying their abortions—that regardless of the law, before quickening, there was no baby. Abortion was not killing. It was simply a way to make their own reproductive bodies "regular."[26]

Abortion as making the body regular

The commercial explosion of contraceptive sales, a phenomenon that overlapped in time with the successful efforts of state legislatures to outlaw abortion in the 1830s forward, was in full flower after the Civil War.[27] Women of all economic means bought contraceptive materials wherever they were available. Middle-class women, now practicing privacy as a key mark of middle-class status, began contraceptive douching in their private WCs (water closets, or toilet rooms) newly outfitted with doors and locks. Despite the enormous expenditure of money and hope, many of the new contraceptive preparations and devices for women were unreliable or downright ineffective. They did not prevent pregnancies, or self-blame, or maybe another abortion.[28]

In short, the anonymity of the city gave women, married and unmarried, unprecedented need for and access to contraception and abortion. The secrecy of the small town had always depended on the discreet pharmacist, a willing network of female friends and relatives, or family members scared not to assist a girl in trouble. In the city, girls and women could melt into a crowd of strangers. A young woman could scurry into and out of an apothecary shop where no one knew her. She could visit an abortionist she'd never seen before and would never see again. Dangers of many kinds went with anonymity, but so did a new independence.

Doctors, ministers, and others who saw or imagined evidence of this new freedom spoke out against the impertinent sexual liberties of white working-class girls. They condemned "the aborting matron" who stood as an emblem for "all that was problematic in the social order." For several decades by now, doctors and others had spoken out against the women's rights movement, popular health reform movements, and odious free love movements as among the causes of high abortion rates.[29]

Yet many doctors, treating their work as a private business, continued to perform abortions at the end of the nineteenth century. Many doctors provided this criminal service despite the opposition of the new American Medical Association. After all, the AMA began life concerned with making sure that the public saw physicians as disciplined, ethical professionals. Nevertheless, historian Leslie Reagan shows how an abortion exposé in the *Chicago Times* in the 1880s "made it obvious that physicians were an important source of abortions and that abortion was part of regular medicine," despite its criminal status. The exposé named forty-eight doctors "who when approached, agreed to help."[30]

When physicians wouldn't help, women's work and neighborhood networks in the city might well provide the information a woman was looking for. A popular self-help book published in 1886 called *The Mother's Guide and Daughter's Friend* advised its readers, "Many women, being refused by honest physicians to relieve them of what they consider a burden, learn from other women what to take or what to do to produce abortion upon themselves."[31]

This crazy quilt of post–Civil War urban elements—thousands of young women separated from family authority and protection, libertarian and reform organizations espousing varieties of personal freedom, growing immigrant communities and other demographic trends away from a "pure-white" population, commercialization of contraception and abortion services, the rich array of accessible medical personnel, including midwives and physicians—altogether stimulated a determined group of moral reformers to act against sexual license in the interests of reproductive restraint. The goal was to save America.

The man who figured out how to sell this proposition and to translate his idea for a solution into congressional action was Anthony Comstock. Here was a young man in New York desperately determined to cleanse obscenity from the streets of the city, from the streets of all cities.[32] Comstock worked with a YMCA-sponsored group, the Society for the Suppression of Vice, mixing traditional Christianity-based language and moralism with a new concept of state control over sexual and family matters. In 1873 he convinced Congress to pass a law placing the U.S. Post Office in charge of finding and censoring all "obscene" information passing through the mail.[33] No one was certain how abortion and contraception came to be included in the final bill that Congress enacted. Apparently, there was hardly any discussion or debate in Congress regarding this matter, and afterward, no politician dared speak against the new Comstock Law, "for fear of appearing 'lewd,' 'lascivious,' or 'filthy' himself."[34]

The postal system created by Congress was meant from the beginning to support the growth of commerce and to ensure a free flow of ideas and information. In these ways, until the Comstock Law, the U.S. mail was a proud symbol of democracy: accessible, dependable, and above all, as Comstock himself put it, "It goes everywhere and is secret."[35] In 1873, Comstock would convince the Congress that this secrecy made the postal system dangerous. Comstock and his army of moral reformers had made the mail into a symbol of urban debauchery, especially a symbol of female sexual and reproductive misbehavior.

The Comstock Law provides a fascinating perspective on the challenges facing proponents of democracy in the nineteenth century. At the time of the law's enactment, the United States had recently rededicated itself to freedom in the form of the post–Civil War amendments to the Constitution. But to Comstock and others, the specter of contracepting and aborting women—like the specter of a woman in a voting booth—was threatening to the social fabric. To protect the social fabric, the governing class of men reinforced the restricted and gendered meaning of freedom.

Comstock oversaw the construction of an apparatus that used modern state power, including federal courts and municipal police, to strike at a sign of modern life: female sexual independence. He made sure that public resources would be dedicated to policing female behavior and the purveyors of "obscenity." The punishment for violators was not trivial. The law provided that a person convicted of sending obscene material, including information about preventing pregnancy, through the mail "shall for each offense, be fined not less than one hundred dollars nor more than five thousand dollars, or imprisoned at hard labor not less than one year nor more than ten years, or both, in the discretion of the judge."[36]

Comstock himself used the mail to entrap those who would disobey. Historian Constance Chen found this letter that Comstock wrote and sent to six doctors in 1873. Posing as a young woman in trouble, the evangelical reformer wrote to the doctors this way:

> Dear Sir,
>
> I am an employee of the Treasury and I have got myself into trouble. I was seduced about four months ago and I am now about 3 months gone in the family way. The person who has seduced me has run away and I do not know what will become of me if I do not get relief. . . . I . . . have to keep a widowed mother and a crippled sister, so that I send you all, in fact more than I can spare, hoping that you will send me something that will relieve me. . . . Now, dear Doctor, send it right away and send it by mail. . . . For God's sake do not disappoint a poor ruined and forsaken girl whose only relief will be suicide if you fail me.[37]

All six doctors accepted the twenty dollars that Comstock had tucked into each envelope. All wrote back to the "girl in trouble," sending herbal preparations to help her abort her "pregnancy." All six doctors were arrested and imprisoned.

Anthony Comstock and the antiabortion physicians who worked successfully with state legislatures to outlaw abortion were powerful men. But power alone did not lead to their success. These men would not have achieved their objectives if they had not been speaking about matters that deeply concerned the governing class of men in late nineteenth-century America. Men concerned about the possibility that women might manage their fertility spoke about two threatened, overlapping spheres: the health of the nation and the meaning of womanhood. Typically, a woman who practiced fertility control was condemned because her behavior was said to hurt her ability to meet her marital obligation. Both abortion and contraception were tagged as "disastrous to a women's mental, moral, and physical well-being." But quickly, the argument slid into the public realm. A white woman did not owe children to her husband so much as she owed them to the state. *Children to State* Passing laws against abortion and contraception was crucial to protecting "the public's interest in procreation." The "public," a concept used to incorporate the new, white, urban middle class and their families still living in rural communities, had a profound stake in the reproduction of the social order. Making laws to regulate intercourse and its outcomes was important for ensuring the demographic advantage and the political power of the "right" social class and racial group.

Legal scholar Reva Siegel shows that the medical profession was disturbed by the "aborting matron" at the end of the nineteenth century. But doctors, she argues, were even more appalled by white middle-class women attempting to enhance their status in the domains of marriage and motherhood. They argued that a woman who wanted to manage, limit, or curtail her fertility revealed an unattractive and dangerous *Egotism* egotism. The medical profession, writes Siegel, interpreted fertility-controlling behavior, especially abortion, as self-indulgent, on the one *FPlan* hand, and as "a rebellious, incipiently political act," on the other. Doctors associated fertility-controlling women with women's rights activists.[38]

As I noted in chapter 1, this association was not one that most well-known feminists such as Elizabeth Cady Stanton or Susan B. Anthony would have accepted. These women and their allies publicly opposed contraception and abortion. They believed these methods of fertility control, which separated sex from reproduction, were not in women's best interests. These methods would protect unfaithful husbands from the risk of disease and from "bastard" babies. Many women's rights activists feared that the separation of sex and pregnancy would emphasize the connection between womanly sex and pleasure. They worried that this emphasis would undermine the only dependable basis of a white woman's claim to family and social respect—her physical purity and her moral authority.[39]

Women's rights advocates continued through the nineteenth century to take positions against contraception and abortion and in favor of "voluntary motherhood"—the absolute right of a woman to say no to her husband's request, or demand, for sex. Yet Reva Siegel finds that even the most prominent among the feminists was compelled to explain why, under the gender regulations that governed society, a woman might turn to these methods.[40] In "Marriage and Maternity," an 1869 editorial in their publication, Revolution, Stanton and Anthony wrote, "I know men who call themselves Christians who would insist that they are gentlemen, who never insult any woman—but their wives. . . . They never think that even in wedlock there may be the very vilest prostitution; and if Christian women are prostitutes to their husbands, what can we expect but the natural sequence," abortion?[41]

Another prominent women's rights advocate, Matilda Joselyn Gage, spoke about women's sexual and reproductive needs in the most encompassing terms, without ever naming sex or fertility: "Woman must first of all," she wrote, "be held as having a right to herself." Gage spoke into a culture in 1878 in which a woman could hardly take this right. A woman could make demands, but ultimately she had to rely on her husband's benevolence, if he was a benevolent man. The granting of women's rights, including a woman's right to "herself," was still a male prerogative, unless a woman could employ contraception secretly.[42] (Ironically, many purveyors of contraception appealed to potential female clients by emphasizing that women could use their products secretly. In the 1860s, a prominent promoter of a female contraceptive device wrote, "The husband would hardly be likely to know that it was being used unless told by the wife."[43] This advocate understood that secrecy could be powerful when associated with contraception.)

In an era lacking the concept of "marital rape," women did not have formal or informal power to control whether and when to have sex with their husbands. So, clearly, "voluntary motherhood" could not meet most women's need for reproductive control in this era. How could women as second-class citizens set schedules and conditions for intercourse in a world that was legally male-dominant? Angela Haywood, a "free love" advocate, defined sex for women under the Comstock Law as rape and forced childbearing: "Since Comstockism makes male will, passion, and power absolute to impose conception, I stand with women to resent it. The man who would legislate to choke a women's vagina with semen, who would force a woman to retain his seed, bear children when her own reason and conscience oppose it, would waylay her, seize her by the throat and rape her person."[44] Offering a remedy to sex as rape, Haywood suggested that every man "should have solemn meeting with, and look serious at his own penis until he is able to be lord and master of it rather than it should longer rule, lord and master of him and of the victims he deflowers."[45]

Lacking sexual partners who had these solemn meetings, many women taught each other the methods that seemed most effective. Many women obtained what contraceptive materials and abortion services they could, ignoring state and federal laws. In 1874, an Illinois doctor estimated that where he lived in a rural section of the state, one out of every ten pregnancies ended in abortion. This man, Dr. Smith, told an interesting story about the variety of ways that women got information and services. "I know three married women, respectable ones, who are notorious for giving instructions to their younger sisters as to the *modus operandi* for 'coming around.' After the failure of tansy, savin, ergot, cotton root, lifting, rough trotting horses, etc., a knitting needle is the stand by. One old doctor near here was so obliging as to furnish a wire with a handle, to one of his patients, which did the work for her, after which she passed it to one of her neighbors, who succeeded in destroying the foetus and nearly so herself."[46]

The historical evidence we have today shows that women all over the country in the 1870s and 1880s and 1890s were seeking to end pregnancies they could not manage. A doctor-pharmacist in the Syracuse-Troy area of upstate New York (population ten thousand) estimated that more than nine thousand "female pills"—sold as aids to bring on menstruation and/or to end a pregnancy—were purchased annually in that region.[47] An article in a New York City newspaper announced that the city was home to two hundred full-time abortionists performing thousands of abortions a year and making pregnancy termination as safe as childbirth.

Physicians, clearly aware of all these abortions, worked harder to criminalize the procedure. After they succeeded state by state, many doctors continued to describe abortion practitioners as perverted lowlifes. They described the growing number of practitioners as a proliferation of "inhuman wretches" in "almost every neighborhood." Many physicians taunted the nonphysician abortionist, characterizing the criminal practitioners in terms like this: an "old woman of one sex or another, who is known for her ability and willingness for a pecuniary consideration" to perform abortions.

Still, hundreds of thousands of women sought abortion practitioners.[48] By the end of the nineteenth century, abortion rates may have been even higher than before the Comstock Law. In 1898, the Michigan Board of Health found that approximately one-third of pregnancies in that state were aborted. By far the most likely customers, according to the board, were "respectable married women."[49]

Neither the state of Michigan nor the state of New York nor the federal government had an effective strategy—or an adequate law enforcement bureaucracy—to stop women from buying contraceptives or seeking criminal abortion providers. The Comstock Law did enable postal agents to seize huge quantities of contraception-related items. Historian Janet Brodie provides this extraordinary list of Comstock's yield in 1880, giving us some idea of the industriousness of his agents but also a glimpse of what was surely only a tiny fraction of the total amount of materials in circulation that year:

Seized and Destroyed
24,225 lbs of books and sheet stock
14,420 stereotype plates
165 different obscene books
64,094 rubber articles for immoral use
4,185 boxes of pills and powders for abortion
3,421 letters and packages ready for mailing
70,280 opened letters
6,000 names of dealers in obscene materials

901,125 names and addresses of people to whom "smut dealers" sent
goods[50]

We know for sure that many of those six thousand "dealers in obscene
materials" suffered multiple arrests in these years. The profits one could
make from selling even totally ineffective contraceptive information
and devices trumped the fear of arrest, even given the harsh punishments promised by the Comstock Law. Men and women tempted by
the likelihood of huge profits knew that many purveyors of fertility
control had gone to jail. They also knew that many had resumed their
lucrative businesses the day after they got out of jail.

Andrea Tone, historian of the business of contraception, found an
example of this syndrome. When Henry Hymes, a seller of diaphragms,
was arrested, he told police that "500 Brooklyn ladies" were his clients.
Because these women believed that Mr. Hymes had what they needed,
they were unlikely to forget the gentleman during his short stay in jail.[51]
In the end, the demand for female contraceptive information and materials was simply too insistent and too massive in the age of the burgeoning marketplace-of-everything to yield to state or local control.
Urban and rural women alike may have had to draw on secrecy and
anonymity to purchase Frederick Hollick's incredibly entitled *The Marriage Guide, or Natural History of Generation: A Private Instructor for Married Persons and Those about to Marry Both Male and Female; in Every Thing
Concerning the Physiology and Relations of the Sexual System, and the Production or Prevention of Offspring, including All New Discoveries Never Before Given in the English Language.* But whatever thousands of women
had to do to educate and protect themselves, they did. Two hundred
editions of this book were published between 1877 and 1883, years
when its distribution was completely illegal.[52]

For women who had little or no money to spend in the urban marketplace of contraception and abortion, and who had little personal
capital of any kind to protect themselves sexually and reproductively,
"voluntary motherhood" was an especially impotent or irrelevant
strategy.[53] Poor young women employed in factories toward the end of
the nineteenth century were targets of multiple studies, many of which
focused on their moral (sexual) behavior as much as on their output as
workers. Labor historian Alice Kessler-Harris found, for example, that
a study of working girls in Cincinnati revealed that the "moral tone"

among them "was low." In Richmond, Virginia, "immorality is much more noticeable than elsewhere," due to white women working in mixed-race environments in tobacco products factories. In Philadelphia the "moral tendencies" were of a "distinctly high order." It is important to remember that many young women in these sorts of workplaces were nearly destitute, barely able to feed, clothe, and house themselves.[54]

Many of these young women labored in cities experiencing falling marriage rates, but not necessarily falling rates of sexual intercourse. For many poor young women in these settings, heterosexual flirting, intimacy, and sexuality may have been just about the only available form of diversion from the grim workday life.[55] In the 1890s, when the cost of a diaphragm equaled a week's wages for a female domestic servant (and when the purchase of this item was patently illegal), such diversions naturally led to pregnancies, the birth of babies, no husbands, and no money.

Urban reformers created rescue homes at the end of the century to house small numbers of these desperate women and mounted campaigns to stamp out infanticide, the occasional act of the most profoundly resourceless mothers. Reformers also tried to end another desperate practice of destitute mothers—leaving babies anonymously on doorsteps, a "pervasive" problem in the 1880s and 1890s.[56] For a woman whose baby was "illegitimate," abandonment may have seemed the only option, especially if the matron at the rescue home informed her that the home did not take infants born to unmarried women, or did not take the baby if the mother would not also agree to come into the institution and obey all rules. This second condition was impossible for women with other children or responsibilities that they had to meet.

Most resourceless women tried to keep their babies, some by putting them in the care of "baby farms," boarding facilities that sprang up in cities to meet the need of working but destitute mothers. Sherri Broder describes how these arrangements were dangerous for babies. Many "farms" provided careless tending and poor nutrition, leading to terrible rates of infant mortality, particularly for African American babies, more of whose mothers had to work for wages immediately after giving birth. Society placed very low value on either African American or white babies born to poor, unmarried mothers. Dr. Charlotte Abbey of the Women's Directory of Philadelphia in 1898 discovered that "Fifty

Baby Farms

dollars is the usual amount paid by an unfortunate mother to the proprietor of a lying-in hospital for the disposal of her child."[57]

Sherri Broder explains that when investigators and newspaper reporters and ordinary people got upset about baby farms in the cities, they set the blame on resourceless women themselves: "fallen women, mercenary caretakers, and non-maternal, possibly murderous destitute mothers," cautionary icons for all women of the era. Women everywhere were being warned not to do what these poor women did: work outside the home, have sex outside of marriage, try to separate sex and its maternal consequences, and reject "maternal self-sacrifice in the face of conflicting needs of mothers and children." The judgments of poor women were very harsh, indeed.[58]

By the end of the nineteenth century, social and economic inequality in American cities created an increasingly stratified range of reproductive experiences. Historian Janet Brodie suggests that state laws against abortion and by extension the Comstock Law may have had little impact on the lives of middle-class married women. "Most," she writes, "had abortions and babies in the privacy of their own homes."[59] Poor women did not have relationships with private doctors, nor did their homes provide private spaces. These women were likely to encounter sexual and reproductive dilemmas anonymously, but with little access to privacy. *Anonymous ≠ Private*

PRACTICING PRIVACY

In the early decades of the twentieth century, before the Great Depression, from approximately 1900 to 1929, new social theories and practices tied *privacy*—that is, the ability to pursue some aspects of life substantially free from state or community interference—tightly to middle-class status. As the urban middle class became a larger segment of the population, a number of supports helped members of this class build *Priv. + Middle Class.* lives that depended on and stood for privacy. Architects and city planners designed for the middle class pursuit of privacy. Doctors, lawyers, and bankers provided confidential, privately purchased services to the middle-class and their upper-class models.

In a related development, American mental health professionals adapted Freudian theories about sexuality to the diagnosis and treatment of American women. Now they defined normal white females as capable of some sexual passion and some sexual pleasure.[60] These psychiatrists and psychologists and social workers drew on Freudian definitions of sex as an "irrepressible drive" that must not be suppressed. What's more, they located the stimulus for sexual activity and sexual pleasure in the *mind* of the middle-class female, the most deeply private venue of all. Mental health theorists and law enforcement agents used racist distinctions to draw a thick line between white, middle-class women and others. In professional journals, at charity agencies, in the courts, and elsewhere, experts described the sexuality of poor women and women of color as hot, rapacious, and dangerous, a public menace, and an appropriate target of restraints.[61]

In the eighteenth and nineteenth centuries, the sexual and reproductive degradation of women had been associated with (and facilitated by) race. Now relatively resourceless girls and women of all races, whose sexual and reproductive lives were not governed and protected by privacy, were targets of degradation. Indeed, access to privacy permitted some measure of female sexual and reproductive dignity, even —or especially—in the age of the Comstock Laws. When public policies and municipal policemen defined a woman's body and her sexual and reproductive behavior as public matters, such a woman was denied both protection and value.

As middle-class females depended on a cadre of professionals to help them achieve privacy or to leave them alone, working-class and poor women routinely lacked these possibilities. In the age of Freud, for example, female, heterosexual, monogamous, marital (and even some premarital) sexual passion—and its consequences—was normalized, as long as it occurred in private. But a working-class woman might be dragged into court to account in public for the illegal abortion she'd had, forced by male officials into "humiliating interrogation about sexual matters."[62] If she had the resources to end her pregnancy within "the bounds of discreet secrecy," male officials might well keep their distance. But a woman forced by lack of resources to pursue pregnancy control beyond these bounds might be risking everything.[63]

Birth control advocate Margaret Sanger, the public health nurse who became the driving force behind legalizing and disseminating "family planning" in the United States, understood the wages of living a reproductive life beyond the bounds of privacy. In the years before World War I, drawing on socialist politics and tactics, Sanger constructed a direct appeal to working-class women, the ones most lacking reproductive privacy. She spoke in public and wrote and distributed literature arguing the close relationship between sexual and reproductive and economic oppression. She encouraged women to break the law by using birth control and by coming to her birth control clinics. She urged women to demonstrate in the streets to demand legal access to information and materials that would control their fertility. Sanger knew what women wanted. When her first birth control clinic opened in New York in October 1916, women showed up in droves, Catholics, Jews, and Protestants.[64]

Interestingly, many of the working-class women who came to the clinics tried to protect their privacy when they applied in person for reproductive advice. When a clinic doctor tried to follow up on patients for a study of the effectiveness of the clinic's work and methods, she was unable to locate many of the women. The doctor noted, "Some who came to the clinic undoubtedly gave false addresses."[65]

When Mary Ware Dennett, the founder of the first activist organization devoted to ending the reign of the Comstock Laws and to legalizing contraception, imagined the road to success for her causes, she envisioned birth controllers meeting "in private homes, churches, labor unions, clubs, anywhere." She saw birth controllers distributing literature "all over town," giving up privacy, going public.[66] Yet deep into these decades of the twentieth century, those who shaped mainstream thinking and practices about these matters counseled dignity and privacy. One influential physician described how if privacy were relinquished, the issue could "go to the radicals" and might "receive harm by being pushed in [an] undignified or improper manner."[67]

Many private doctors, members of the same "fraternity" that had overseen the criminalization of abortion in the nineteenth century, continued to protect the reproductive privacy of their middle-class patients. A Louisville, Kentucky, physician, for example, described his commitment in 1904: "If I was called in, I would not give testimony compromising a young lady, and I would not put it on the record, no matter what the facts were, and I would not 'give away' a girl, but would attempt to protect her."[68] A few years later, a Chicago doctor who had officially studied the criminal abortion situation in that city announced that he was convinced that neither the public nor doctors wanted the laws against abortion enforced.[69] In 1923 an observer spoke out on behalf of physicians and against a charge that was sometimes levied against those who performed abortions: "If every physician who

75–90% murders [handwritten margin note]

even once in his career—under the stress of tragic circumstances, in order to save the life and reputation of a young girl and the happiness of her parents—performed an abortion is a murderer, then 75 percent, nay probably 90 percent of the medical profession are murderers."[70]

Private doctors also flaunted the law by providing contraceptive advice. As one prominent doctor put it in the 1920s, no laws can stop this practice because "physicians generally deprecate laws which prevent them, in the honorable discharge of their duties, from giving [service] to patients urgently in need of it."[71] Middle-class women who went to Margaret Sanger's new birth control clinics in New York City in these decades might be quietly referred to private doctors who fit diaphragms for women "presenting no health indications whatsoever." They might even be referred to the doctors who performed abortions in secret.[72] Clearly, women with access to private doctors and the information they dispensed were safer, reproductively. One study in the 1920s compiled striking data showing that the more information a woman had about contraception, the less likely she was to have an abortion.[73]

The same commitment to privacy that justified quiet medical decisions in favor of the needs of middle-class women could also create difficulties for individual women or members of middle-class women's organizations. How, in a culture of middle-class privacy, could a proper middle-class woman speak out in favor of women's need and women's right to manage their fertility? Historian Ellen Chesler described this situation in 1916 when Margaret Sanger faced trial for publishing radical and "obscene" material about birth control. At an event to honor Sanger, "anthropologist Elsie Clew Parsons stood up and asked fifty married women to sign a manifesto demanding that information about birth control be made public and admitting that they used it themselves." While some of the women called upon did not want to associate themselves publicly with Sanger's radical politics, Chesler points out that most "[shrank] from public identification with birth control."

Women's organizations responded similarly. Members of the new League of Women Voters decided in 1924 to study the issue of sterilization for "the unfit." But the organization would not touch the subject of birth control. The National Women's Party studiously avoided the subjects of voting rights for Black women—and birth control. Both feminist organizations responded defensively to the charge that women's suffrage was a threat to family life and, as historian Wendy Kline has pointed out, avoided any issues that "smacked of promiscuity."[74]

Birth control scholar Carole McCann explains that in some ways, by the 1920s these matters had not changed since the days of Stanton and Anthony: "Birth control threatened to undermine the ideology of feminine chastity that grounded political authority of those organizations." Even more pointedly, the subject of birth control could simply poison the wellspring of white woman's political agency: her maternal capacity.[75] Generally, the most ardently public feminists of these decades, committed to fighting for first-class citizenship for women, defined reproductive matters as individual, private business, not a fit subject for women to speak about publicly.[76] Privacy could be a source of political weakness, as well as a source of personal power.

In another development, jurors and judges did not generally convict birth control entrepreneurs in the early twentieth century. Instead, they nullified the Comstock Law in the courtroom and tacitly accepted the populace's need for contraception.[77] Jurors and judges quite often affirmed contraception and even abortion (as long as there was no death involved) as private decisions. Beginning in the 1920s, another group of professionals and volunteers advocating legal contraception —doctors, lawyers, activists, intellectuals, policy experts—also began to associate fertility control with the needs of modern women. This group crafted a concept of privacy that defined female fertility as a private matter and also defined women's right to use birth control as a right based in personal privacy.[78]

THE PUBLIC BODY

While the concept of reproductive privacy and "the right to privacy" were gestating, however, we've seen that most poor and working-class women did not have access to privacy. They often lacked even the varieties of privacy that depended on the kindness or ideological bent of individual doctors. In fact, their sexual and reproductive misfortunes were used in public to warn all women about the dangers of breaking the rules, and also as a form of instruction about the differences between classes in the United States.

Having your naked body imagined and discussed in a newspaper exposé or in a courtroom while you were alive, for example, was something that marked a female as low-class. This type of female did not deserve the protections that middle-class women deserved. A well-known professor of gynecology in the 1920s categorized female sexuality by class, associating middle-class women in families with "self-control, high ideals, and a pure Christian faith." The other, the low sort, the woman using birth control to separate sex and reproduction, he likened to the "road-house," a public drinking establishment catering to lowlifes, inviting patrons "down into the corruption pit."[79]

Abortion trial transcripts from this era show how poor and working-class women became hideously vulnerable and publicly exposed in the courtroom. They show how hard some women tried to craft a claim to privacy out of virtually nothing. When Julia McElroy's sister Eunice died from an abortion in the 1920s, Julia was forced in public to answer questions about her sister's sex life and her monthly periods. At the trial of the person who performed the abortion, Julia was threatened with jail if she refused to answer all the questions put to her in open court. Julia said later, "I knew everything but I could not answer [all the questions] on account of all the men around. . . . Because there was so many men around I hated to talk about my poor sister more than I had to."[80]

Women lacking families with resources to protect either their lives or their privacy were sometimes forced to give "dying declarations," that is, to provide police and prosecutors with the name and address of the abortionist whose poor skills brought them to the brink of death. They were also pressed to give the name of the man "responsible." This information was likely to end up in the newspaper, the venue where the death notice confirmed which women's sexualized and violated bodies were public business. Leslie Reagan describes how if a woman refused to use her last breath to provide the name of an abortionist or lover, police told the doctor in charge to walk out of the hospital room, leaving the woman to die unattended. In a truly sad gesture invoking a personal commitment to privacy and loyalty, many women refused to comply with the demand for names, saying, "She [the abortionist] was the only one who would help me, and I won't tell on her."[81]

Not surprisingly, there is little evidence that these kinds of spectacles were mounted when African American or other women of color were involved. These spectacles almost always involved white, working-class women, those who could not buy privacy or protection but whose race made them objects of public interest and concern. Law enforcers pushed the sexualized bodies of this group into the public sphere, reinforcing the ways that danger and privilege played out across gender *and* race *and* class.

Leslie Reagan shows how, at every stage of obtaining an abortion in the criminal era, a poor woman's actions were likely to bring her body into public view. A woman with resources, on the other hand, was likely to be able to keep her abortion a private matter, even if disaster ensued. The poor woman was more likely to self-abort, to delay calling a doctor if she was damaged or ill afterward, and to end up coming to "official attention" because the self-abortion and the delay could lead to medical crises. The woman with money, even if she were shamed, typically went to a private doctor or reputable practitioner of some sort, was never expected to participate in the ritual of the dying declaration, and would have relatives who put a fake name on her death certificate and who would pay off whomever needed to be paid off in order to keep the woman's name private.[82]

In the late nineteenth century and beyond, some Native American women who got pregnant, stayed pregnant, and never entered the abortion arena were nevertheless in danger because of a different opportunity their reproductive capacity provided public officials to remake "American culture." These women were pushed into the public sphere through the federal government's project to take their children away from the reservation and place them in boarding schools. A late nineteenth-century commissioner of Indian affairs explained the project this way: "The Indian youth should be instructed in their rights, privileges, and duties as American citizens; should be taught to love the American flag; should be imbued with a genuine patriotism and made to feel that the United States, and not some paltry reservation is their home."

The commissioner strongly recommended that Indian youth should be placed with or near "white families," where they would be "brought into intimate relationship with the highest type of American rural life." This way, native children would develop proper "enthusiasm for home," by which the commissioner did not mean the reservations where their own mothers and fathers lived. The removal of children from their parents and their placement in boarding schools is an episode that illustrates how some women—and only some—have faced officially sanctioned obstacles to exercising the right to be mothers of the children they bear.

Implicitly and explicitly, the commissioner's report and the boarding school system in general aimed to denigrate the parenting capacities of native mothers and fathers. At the same time, the boarding school project aimed to use the "raw material"—the children born to native women—to strengthen American homogeneity and American nationalism. The commissioner observed, "Whatever steps are necessary should be taken to place these children under proper educational influences." He added ominously, "If, under any circumstances, compulsory education is justifiable, it certainly is in this case."[83]

By the time Commissioner Thomas J. Morgan submitted his report on Indian education to the secretary for the interior, the U.S. government had been pursuing military campaigns against Indians for more than half a century. The U.S. military had changed millions of acres of tribal lands into white-held private property. The military had killed thousands of Indians and consigned thousands more to reservations. But still, prominent white Americans continued to picture the Indian as a primal threat to American life. In July 1876, the august American writer William Dean Howells published an essay in the *Atlantic Monthly* that commemorated the country's one-hundredth birthday. Howells wrote: "The red man, as he appears in effigy and in photograph . . . is a hideous demon, whose malign traits can hardly inspire any emotion softer than abhorrence."[84] Recognizing that military victories were not enough to dissipate the power of the "demon," the federal government, together with late nineteenth-century reformers like Howells who wanted to civilize Indians, determined to create educational institutions to achieve the most thorough results.

In many ways, both the representatives of government and the reformers assessed Native American women as lacking some biologically based capacity for proper motherhood that white women possessed. A government agent to the Shoshone tribe in the 1880s observed that despite his efforts, Indians were not making good progress toward becoming "civilized." He identified the problem this way: "It's not in their mothers' milk."[85]

Reformers such as members of the Women's National Indian Association, a group of white women "devoted to the cause of Indian uplift and assimilation," also identified this deficit. In response, they focused efforts on remaking Indian girls through education. They believed that as future mothers, young females had to be transformed. This process would be most effectively undertaken at boarding schools, "seedbed[s] of republican virtues" and "democratic freedoms."[86] The schools were designed to suppress "tribal languages and cultural practices." Students were taught English and Christianity. The girls were taught white people's domestic arts; they were imbued with the cryptoreligious meanings of "a ritual calendar intended to further patriotic citizenship." The girls were made fit to become American mothers.[87]

Not surprisingly, many Native American mothers and fathers were horrified to be officially defined as inadequate and inappropriate parents for their own children. Many resisted as hard as they could when federal Indian agents came for the children. In 1882, a Crow agent described parents as "bitterly opposed to sending their children to [boarding] school." He said they "invent[ed] all kinds of excuses to get the children out or keep from sending them." Often when parents resisted, agents withheld food rations or called in agency police. In 1886, an agent to the Mescalero Apache vividly described what parents were up against: "Everything in the way of persuasion and argument having failed, it became necessary to visit the camps unexpectedly with a detachment of police, and seize such children as were proper and take them away to school willing or unwilling. Some hurried their children off to the mountains or hid them away in camp, and the police had to chase and capture them like so many wild rabbits. This unusual proceeding created quite an outcry. The men were sullen and muttering, the women loud in their lamentations, and the children almost out of their wits with fright."[88]

Just over sixty years after this agent wrote his report, the United Nations Convention on the Prevention and Punishment of the Crime of Genocide defined genocide as including the act of "[f]orcibly transferring children of the [target] group to another group."[89] Historian David Wallace Adams affirms the profound sense of obliteration that parents felt on the reservations when their children were removed from their care and from the community. He records evidence that the acts of removal "severed the most fundamental of human ties: the parent-child bond."

A Navaho parent, for example, described the particular rupture of family bonds that so many Native Americans experienced: "It has been with us like a tree dropping its leaves. They fall one by one to the ground until finally the wind sweeps them all away and they are gone forever. . . . The parents of those children who were taken away are crying for them. I had a boy [taken] to Grand Junction. The tears come to our eyes whenever we think of [our lost children]. I do not know whether my boy is alive or not."[90] In 1893, in a major concession, the federal government agreed to a rule that stopped Indian agents from removing children from the reservation to boarding schools without parental consent.[91]

In the meantime, at the boarding schools, teachers were charged specifically with obliterating Indian culture. They gave their students new names and in many ways tried to convince them that the school, not the tribe or the family, was the locus of authority. One Sioux girl called Nellie Robinson at the boarding school wrote to the head of the school in 1881:

> Dear Sir Captain Pratt:
> I write this letter with much sorrow to tell you that I have spoken one Indian word . . . and I felt so sorry that I could not eat my supper, and I could not forget that Indian word, and while I was sitting at the table the tears rolled down my cheeks. I tried very hard to speak only English.
> Nellie Robinson[92]

All these years later, we cannot judge the authenticity of Nellie Robinson's regret. We do not know if she wrote this letter freely or if writing it was part of her punishment for uttering an English word. We cannot tell whether Nellie's heart was full of humility or full of resistance. But we do know that many young people caught in these institutions of assimilation did object to what was being done to them, and why.

One Indian woman in the Pacific Northwest described how at her school in the 1920s, forty-six children ran away one year, seventy the next. Generally, when runaway children were caught and returned, the punishments were harsh: "Two of our girls ran away . . . but they got caught. They tied their legs up, tied their hands behind their backs, put them in the middle of the hallway so that if they fell, fell asleep or something, the matron would hear them and she'd get out there and whip them and make them stand up again." What would the parents of these girls have thought of this punishment?

Late in the 1920s, a government report on the boarding school system found that institutions were characterized by "poor diet, overcrowding, below-standard medical service, excessive labor by the students and substandard teaching."[93] Nonetheless, the system persisted for several more decades. Thousands of children of Indian women, like the children of enslaved African American women and hundreds of children of poor, white, urban women in the nineteenth century, were snagged by laws and policies and by public and private projects that assigned the children of vulnerable women roles as commodities, laborers, and cultural agents.[94] The women who gave birth to these children were reduced to engines of reproduction. They were publicly and sometimes permanently denied the dignity of motherhood.

Unfortunately, there were even further ways that poor women's fertile bodies became public in this era. The famous Supreme Court case *Muller v. Oregon* (1908) shows how the reproductive capacity of working women became the basis for justifying prevailing labor practices. In this case, the majority opinion expressed the position that the reproducing body of the working woman was "an object of public interest." Her maternal strength and the quality of the baby she produced were the concerns of the nation. Her reproductive capacity obligated employers to restrict her work to certain jobs and to a certain number of hours of work. Her employment choices and her earnings could be legally restricted, "for the benefit of all." As Alice Kessler-Harris has written, this decision "wrote into legal precedent a conception of citizenship rooted in motherhood and family life that could and did override women's rights as individuals under the law."[95] Certainly this Supreme Court decision limited the relationship between reproduction and privacy for working-class women.

The sexual and reproductive bodies of poor and working-class women were also made into public business in the early twentieth century through explosive interest in the "science" of eugenics. In these decades, politicians, philanthropists, intellectuals, and others avidly studied ways to promote *human racial improvement through selective breeding*. In 1927, deep into the eugenics craze, Paul Popenoe and Roswell Johnson, leading proponents of eugenics, claimed that based on IQ test results (the test itself was a new craze at the time), as many as ten million Americans were "undesirables," unfit for reproduction.[96] The eugenicists counseled reproductive strategies that would ensure higher rates of reproduction among the fit and lower rates among the unfit. Most white elites were wedded to what they saw as the natural truth of eugenics. They believed that only by applying the principles of this science to the reproductive behavior of Americans, especially women, would this country avoid "race suicide," that is, the decline of

Anglo-Saxon numerical superiority and power. Even Margaret Sanger, the great proponent and popularizer of contraception as a woman's basic need, joined with eugenicists to move her cause forward when they championed birth control even for healthy women.

Historian Linda Gordon makes the excellent point that the eugenicists' desire "to reproduce the entire American population in the image of those who dominated it politically and economically" represented, essentially, "a defense again the growth of democracy." Eugenicists wanted to curb the demographically and politically complex America that would result from a population reproducing without the interference and guidance of eugenicists. Gordon adds that "race suicide," understood properly, was "a way to reject the implications of democracy without rejecting democracy."[97]

In the early years of the twentieth century, public images of "the unfit" included all nonwhite persons, mixed-race persons, many immigrants whose "race" was indeterminate, as well as many poor and working-class whites who produced "too many children." The "unfit" also included the blind, the deaf, the insane, the feebleminded, and criminals. Women whose reproductive capacity could yield babies associated with any of these categories were targets of eugenical experts, especially in this period of heightened racism and nativism (or bias against those with origins outside of the United States).

Eugenicists in the American South were particularly concerned about miscegenation, that is, sexual liaisons that produced mixed-race children "who slipped back and forth across the color line and defied social control." White Southerners spoke out their fears about blurring the meaning of "white." They also worried publicly about increasing the number of the eugenically "tainted, shiftless, ignorant, worthless class of anti-social whites" in the South, added to and mixing with inferior African Americans.[98] In the Southwest, Americanists or nativists targeted Mexican-born women whom they defined as sexually primitive and reproductively wanton. Historian George Sanchez shows how eugenicists and others at this time believed that, first, Mexican children had to be trained to be dependable and obedient workers. Only the "trained" Mexican girls would grow up to limit their reproduction and weaken the impact of the "greaser invasion."[99]

Eugenicists worked closely with members of the U.S. Congress in the early 1920s to craft an immigration policy that would mix the "right sort" of adults into the population. They wanted an immigration policy that would guarantee that the "right sort" of first-generation American babies would be born. A small, elite group, the Committee on Selective Immigration of the Eugenics Committee of the United States of America, laid out its rationale this way: "Immigrants from northern Europe furnish us the best material for American citizenship and for the future upbuilding of the American race." Regretting the huge number of "inferiors" who had poured into the country in recent years, the committee's report added, "Had mental tests been in operation [years ago] . . . over six million aliens now living in this country, free to vote, and to become the Fathers and Mothers of future Americans, would never have been admitted." On May 26, 1924, President Calvin Coolidge signed the Immigration Act of 1924, often called the National Origins Act because it limited the inflow of any group—Poles, Russians, Italians—to 2 percent of its representation in the 1890 census. For example, the Italian quota was cut from forty-two thousand a year to four thousand. This law, enforced until 1952, aimed to radically reduce non-Nordic immigrants. It was designed to curtail the reproduction of "lower" immigrants.[100]

Legal scholar Ian Haney Lopez shows how immigration laws, naturalization laws, antimiscegenation laws, and segregation laws—all cornerstones of public policy in the early decades of the twentieth century—shaped the population. These laws made rules about who could live in the United States, who could become a citizen, who could live where, who could be "white," who could love whom. Lopez also shows how these laws structured the reproductive lives of people living in America, "alter[ing] the physical appearance of this country's people." Further, the laws created definitions of "race" that were based, to an astonishing degree, on appearance. They "established material conditions of belonging and exclusion" that we call "race."[101] A twenty-five-year veteran of the U.S. Navy, for example, was denied citizenship in 1909 because though his father was white, his mother was one-half Chinese and one-half Japanese. The judge, denying the application, explained, "A person, one-half white and one-half of some other race, belongs to neither of those races, but is literally a half-breed."[102]

Eugenics policy was embraced by politicians and policymakers, and also by doctors, speaking to each other and to their patients about proper ways to think about reproduction. Dr. William Cooper, a close associate of Margaret Sanger's in the 1920s, provides us with a classic mainstream prescription for eugenically inspired reproduction. His perspective, offered to fellow doctors, suggests a blueprint for public policies limiting the reproductive lives of many women in the United States, at a time when any given politician, doctor, or religious leader might well have accepted the Comstock Laws but secretly practiced birth control himself. Dr. Cooper explained, "The better endowed biologically [should] maintain a higher birth rate than those who are less fortunate. Those who have a vicious inheritance or are socially incompetent," he went on, "such as dependents, delinquents, incorrigible criminals and the like, should be discouraged from breeding indiscriminately."[103]

In these first decades of the century, often called the Progressive Era, a robust raft of organizations and public policies aimed to achieve the eugenicists' dream. The American Eugenic Society (AES), founded in 1923 to educate the public in eugenic thought and action, sponsored all kinds of events and programs, including "Better Baby and Fitter Families" contests at state fairs. This organization and others helped solidify and spread a climate that approved of certain women's reproductive output, but not that of others. The new IQ test became a tool for determining which child could become a good citizen, a good soldier, a good worker, a legitimate reproducer, and which child should not have been born to begin with. Many social planners in the United States were explicitly racist and in fact produced models for the racialist policy initiatives that were nascent in Germany in these years.[104]

In the United States there was probably never a majority supporting eugenics or eugenics-based reproductive laws, such as sterilization of the unfit. In fact, after state legislatures began to pass eugenic sterilization laws—Indiana was the first in 1907—few eugenically motivated sterilizations were actually carried out. In time, a number of the laws were overturned. But many well-positioned scientists did believe that eugenics was a science. They wrote, published, and taught from eugenics textbooks flooding into high school and college classrooms. They focused on marriage and reproductive selectivity as key to a strong nation. They excoriated "those who adhere to the obviously false doctrine that men are born equal and therefore it really doesn't matter who marries whom."[105]

Over time the eugenicists had the funding, the influence, and the access, as well as the "science," to trump the doubts of the majority. Between 1907 and the mid-1920s, twenty-three states enacted legislation providing for eugenical sterilization. By 1940, nearly forty thousand persons had been sterilized under these laws.[106]

In 1927 one young resourceless woman, Carrie Buck, became a national symbol of the eugenics campaign against unfit reproduction and of the nation's interest in racial betterment. Eugenicists presented her in the courtroom as a symbol of the nation's commitment to bring the undesirable reproductive behavior of women who did not meet middle-class standards of fitness into public focus and under public control.

Carrie Buck was the daughter of one of the "least respected citizens" of Charlottesville, Virginia, a woman who had apparently been a prostitute and who told the city authorities that she had syphilis. In 1920 Carrie's mother was labeled "feebleminded." Acting without any restraints, the local authorities assigned this woman to Ward 5 of the state's Colony for Epileptics and Feebleminded for the rest of her life. Carrie was sent to live with the family of a Charlottesville peace officer, where she stayed until she was seventeen. Up to that point, Carrie had been a decent student, and apparently a good and trustworthy housekeeper. In 1923, Carrie told the family she lived with that she had been raped and was pregnant. The peace officer immediately began the process of having Carrie declared feebleminded in preparation for sending her to the same institution that housed her mother.

It was not unusual for authorities in this era to label women who had been publicly associated with sex as "promiscuous," and then to classify them as "morons" or "feebleminded" persons. But by the 1920s, the expense of institutionalizing all these labeled women was becoming too much for the state. Many eugenically minded experts counseled a cheaper solution: sterilization. Also, experts believed that sterilization made women "more amenable to discipline and less restless," further reducing the public costs of dealing with such persons in society.[107]

Carrie Buck gave birth in the colony to a daughter, Vivian, and the historical record shows that local social workers were manipulated into defining the baby as another "subnormal female." Soon thereafter, the institution's review board ruled Carrie "feebleminded, and by the laws of heredity . . . the probable parent of socially inadequate offspring." The board determined that Carrie should "be sexually sterilized . . . and that her welfare and that of society will be promoted by her sterilization."[108]

Ultimately, in May 1927, the U.S. Supreme Court upheld this treatment of Carrie Buck—including the right of the state to carry out eugenical sterilization. Justice Oliver Wendell Holmes issued one of the Court's most famous opinions ever when he wrote for the majority that Carrie's sterilization would promote society's welfare. Here is Holmes's deathless pronouncement on the public nature of reproduction for some women and the public's responsibility to regulate the reproduction of those women as a public health measure: "It is better for all the world, if instead of waiting to execute degenerate off-spring for crime, or to let them starve for their imbecility, society can prevent those who are manifestly unfit from continuing their kind. The principle that sustains compulsory vaccination is broad enough to cover cutting the Fallopian tubes. Three generations of imbeciles is enough."[109]

The Supreme Court's 1927 decision affirmed the government's right to interfere with—even terminate—the reproductive capacity of "socially inadequate persons." *Buck v. Bell* expressed the government's acceptance of a eugenic reproductive politics and policy. Also, this case remains an important moment in U.S. history because it expresses the state's willingness to pursue policies based on the premise that individuals are qualitatively different from each other and that the differences may call for reproductive freedoms or constraints, to be determined by the state.

In the era of *Buck v. Bell*, legislatures were enacting measures to "eliminate defective germ plasma" by regulating the reproduction of females like Carrie Buck. At the same time, Progressive Era civic groups were building organizations and institutions across the poor neighborhoods of the nation and mounting programs dedicated to protecting and reforming young girls in danger of sexual and reproductive misbehavior. These included girls' clubs, protective leagues, sex education campaigns, delinquency prevention programs, maternity homes, and new programs within the criminal justice system specially designed to reform promiscuous girls.[110] The reformers who designed and implemented these efforts were sometimes interested in providing safe havens, even a measure of privacy, for young women whose families could not provide such a luxury. Surely many young women received supports of many kinds. Ironically, though, the construction of these programs and institutions, and the public conversations they stimulated, brought the bodies and behaviors of working-class and poor young women under more public scrutiny than ever.

CAUGHT BETWEEN PUBLIC AND PRIVATE

Many young working-class women were clear, on their own, about the relationship between fertility and privacy, and about the ways that privacy was related to dignity and health. W. E. B. Du Bois wrote in the interests of these women when he explained in 1922 what "the future woman" needed: "a life work and economic independence." He identified "knowledge," probably information about birth control, as crucial, and added, "She must have the right of motherhood at her own discretion."[111] During this period, African American communities organized themselves to look after young women who lacked the knowledge and thus lacked the ability to avoid unwed motherhood. According to a Harlem social worker in the 1920s, members of this community would do what they could to avoid institutional solutions. "Secrecy is maintained if possible," she wrote, when unwed pregnancy caused "shame and grief." According to the social worker, the suffering of slavery had conditioned the community to offer compassion and service to its own.[112]

There is plenty of evidence that legions of African American women and others ignored the Comstock Laws, informed themselves about contraception, and obtained birth control products. For one thing, the average number of children born to white women declined from 4.4 to 2.1 between 1880 and 1940. The decline for African American women was even more dramatic: from 7.5 to 3.0 during the same period.[113]

In addition, organizations within African American communities worked on the problem of making birth control directly accessible to their young women. For example, the Harlem Community Forum invited Margaret Sanger to give a lecture in 1923.[114] Entrepreneurs ran ads in community newspapers about how to prevent conception and how to obtain birth control materials.[115] Many community leaders supported a two-pronged advocacy of birth control in this era. First, they argued, in those African American families where the women used contraception, the family had a better chance of improving its economic and social status. Second, they stressed what African American women themselves, and other poor women, fully understood: if they could limit their fertility by using contraception, proponents of eugenic sterilization would be more likely to leave them alone.[116]

Legal scholar Dorothy Roberts notes, though, that many Harlem residents, potential patients of the Harlem birth control clinic founded jointly by Margaret Sanger and the National Urban League in the 1920s, stayed away from that facility. They feared that "the clinic was really intended to promote race suicide [not] racial betterment. . . . Others feared white doctors [at the clinic] would subject them to medical experiments."[117]

The fact was, however, that with the Comstock Law on the books, and private doctors out of the question for most women, millions were unable to manage their fertility. For women living in burgeoning Mexican communities across the Midwest in the 1920s, in Kansas, Iowa, Nebraska, Indiana, Michigan, Minnesota, Missouri, Wisconsin, and Ohio, the "nerve-racking hardships of sub-standard and overcrowded housing, the lack of running water [and] the discomforts of outdoor bathrooms"—and the lack of money to pay doctors—made reproductive hygiene and the practice of contraception, which required running water, extremely difficult or impossible, even when they had information about how to limit their pregnancies.

A Davenport, Iowa, resident of the Cook's Point section in the 1920s, for example, remembers that the area "was a barrio that had no modern facilities. We had outhouses, kerosene lamps, wood-burning . . . kitchen ranges . . . and no running water. There were four taps located at several points in the neighborhood where people went for their water for washing clothes, baths, cooking, and drinking. The streets were all dirt with no lights nor sidewalks."

Women who did not live in cities—the 1920 U.S. census was the first to show a majority of the population living in urban places—were especially desperate. One woman living on a farm in Kansas looked to the government's office of information and special programs for child welfare, the Children's Bureau, for help. She wrote about the "hard row" that was her life and about how she was losing her health from "hard work and Bearing babies." Mrs. E. S. had a very pointed question for the government about birth control: "Now what I Want to know is Why can't We poor people be given Birth Control as well as Dr's. & the Rich people that could provide [for] and Dr. their families." Mrs. E. S. did not hesitate to instruct the government: "We need help to prevent any more babies. . . . I think it unfair Drs. And Rich seek Birth Control & the poor can't seek nothing, only poverty and more babies." Showing her appreciation of the value of privacy, Mrs. E. S. closed her letter,

"Please don't publish this letter with my name signed to it thou[gh] I'm sure it would be enjoyed by the Poor class of people."[118] Other women wrote to the Children's Bureau about wanting to keep their husbands' love but needing to curb their fertility. They were, they wrote, ill, exhausted, old before their time.[119] A Louisiana woman wrote to the Children's Bureau: "I have children so fast it is wrecking my life."[120]

Because desperate letter writers and countless others did not receive answers to their birth control questions from this—or any—government agency, they used whatever they could to stop from having babies. Self-induced abortion was widespread, especially among poor women, African Americans, and unmarried pregnant women living in rural areas.[121] Poor working women, pregnant and unmarried, could rarely make enough money to support themselves, much less afford a baby. Many must have realized that if they went forward with the pregnancy and gave birth but lacked the resources to care for the child, they might be targets of child welfare officials, charged with neglect. Leslie Reagan reports that many of these women used the implements they had at home, including knitting needles and crochet hooks, hairpins, scissors, or a bone stay from a corset.[122]

Sometime in the 1920s officials of various sorts recognized the dangers that reproductive capacity created for these women. Now a judge might acquit a mother who stole to feed her children. A judge might speak out in court about the woman's need for birth control.[123] Municipal elites might support new or reviving organizations dedicated to overturning the Comstock Law. But these efforts touched the lives of a limited number of women. Many city women, themselves living ever more complicated lives as workers and consumers, were determined to find contraception as they pursued what historian Ruth Alexander has called "a romantic and erotic identity." This new identity incorporated emerging urban technologies and spaces—the telephone, the dance hall, cars, and nightclubs—as young women reached for "the autonomy they desired."

Many young African American women coming up to northern cities as part of the Great Migration escaped the sexual terrorism of predatory white men in the South. And they traded the strict church-focused lives of their families for the sophistication and freedom of the city.[124] Under these urbanizing, eroticizing conditions, young women seeking pleasure and autonomy and safety found that contraception was a basic need—and one worth side-stepping the law to procure.

STRANGE ALLIES IN THE PUBLIC SQUARE

Young women from all social and economic classes, married and un-married, were now stepping aside of the law. They needed ways to control their fertility even though enemies of both premarital sex and contraception still commanded a great deal of public space. And middle-class rules of conduct still demanded the sexual double standard. But partly because of the needs and determination of urban women, the third decade of the twentieth century was a time of explosive, increasingly public debate about the roles of conception and contraception in modern life, especially the role of female-centered birth control.

An unexpected stimulus for this explosion was the government's own contraceptive program mounted during World War I to protect American soldiers who might contract diseases from prostitutes working near military bases in Europe and at home. Sex education programs for soldiers stressed the fact that "all loose women are dirty" and warned soldiers with pamphlets sporting titles such as "Live Straight If You Would Shoot Straight." The military praised soldiers who stayed away from prostitutes as having "honored and protected the sisters, wives, and future mothers of the race we are fighting for." But soon, faced with an epidemic of venereal disease among soldiers, military authorities realized the limits of the abstinence campaign. Now the military stressed the inevitability of male sexual activity and the fact that soldiers simply had to be supplied with condoms in the interests of public health. The contraceptive role of condoms may not have been a topic of public conversation during this campaign, but by 1918, the government itself had begun to promote a strategy for separating sex and reproduction.[125]

The strategy—decriminalizing condoms—incorporated a new and modern orientation to sex and its consequences. The new way was part medical and scientific and reflected the state's new responsibility for social welfare. It also reflected the cultural recognition that sexual intercourse, at least for white males (at least those serving their country), was a private act.

At the end of the war, in the context of urbanizing trends in the 1920s, with more women at work, with traditional gender constraints weakening, prostitution itself began to fall away. Now ordinary women entering into consensual, nonpaying sexual relations needed to have the same information and access to protection that many prostitutes and their clients had.[126] Historian Constance Chen has found a striking expression of the way that attitudes about birth control where changing —and changing rapidly—in the 1920s. She quotes Senator Albert B. Cummins of Iowa: "When I introduced the bill [to remove the contraceptive clause from the Comstock Law], I was denounced in my home city. Prominent clubwomen protested against the bill. I was criticized for having introduced it and I was asked not to introduce it again." Cummins went on, "To-day women's organizations are holding public meetings in its behalf, are passing resolutions in favor of it and are telegraphing Congress to pass it. . . . I have seen this change occur in these few years."[127]

Senator Cummins and his colleagues were surely aware of robust centers of opposition in the 1920s: those who insisted that birth control was against "the will of God and the laws of nature"; and those who feared that contraception would make prostitutes out of all women; and maternalists who championed public policies that promoted "better," not fewer, children and more virtuous mothers. Enemies of birth control also included followers of Black nationalist Marcus Garvey, who called birth control genocidal and urged African American women to have more babies.[128] A prominent center of opposition to birth control was composed of doctors, politicians, and others attempting to shore up traditional gender roles. A "famous neurologist" spoke for this group: "Any woman who does not desire offspring is abnormal."[129]

When Mary Ware Dennett testified before Congress about legalizing contraception, Senator Knute Nelson of Minnesota yelled at her "about fifty times," "at the top of his lungs," "You ought to be ashamed, an intelligent American woman like you, to want everybody to be like the . . . women who are too stuck up to have children, or just raise a few dudes."

Dennett observed that congressmen "are remarkably like men outside of Congress."[130] She meant that they privately supported birth control, had wives who used it, and used condoms themselves. A few, she said, had become convinced and even helpful to her cause. Those congressmen, like Senator Cummins, may have joined the anti-Comstock, pro-contraception forces for any one of a number of reasons in the 1920s. To begin with, many public figures and others began to speak out in favor of contraception at this time as a way of stamping out abortion, which was widely seen as dangerous, damaging, alarmingly common, and immoral. A well-connected doctor in the 1920s estimated that one-third of all pregnancies in the United States were still terminated by abortion, an extraordinary percentage apparently sustained across the criminal era. This doctor believed that the practice of abortion was "on the increase." Reports indicated that women from every walk of life sought abortions, and only a tiny percentage of them was ever stopped by law enforcement. (Like "dying declarations" in the illegal era, nearly all abortion prosecutions involved abortions provided to white women, a fact that suggests again how law enforcement defined which women's bodies required policing and which women's bodies existed *beneath the law* in this regard.)[131]

Many supporters of contraception became devoted to birth control in this era because they believed it created national strength, public health, and a better race. A number of contraception advocates identified themselves as Progressives, a political orientation that identified economically "rational," efficient, scientific solutions to social problems. Progressives aimed for solutions that, through good management, would restabilize a society reeling its way through the impact of decades of urbanization, industrialization, and immigration. Margaret Sanger coined the term "birth control" in 1914 in part to appeal to the Progressive sensibility. She wanted the public to understand that using birth control was consistent with Progressive goals.[132] Without birth control, society would be "inefficient." "The right sort" would not have enough babies, and the rest of the population would have too many.[133] A number of traditionalists who had wanted to send working-class girls, new to the city, back to their patriarchal households in the late nineteenth century now imagined birth control as the only realistic solution.[134]

Many physicians took the position that medically prescribed birth control would protect the health of their patients and, at the same time, reinforce the structures of privacy that properly guarded the lives of middle-class patients. Dr. James Cooper wrote to his colleagues in the 1920s explaining that facilities for dispensing contraceptive advice would serve only "such women as may be sent . . . by reputable physicians." Cooper assured wary colleagues that women "who are not entitled to treatment do not get past the attendant's desk." Those women who were properly referred and whose mental or physical condition would be "aggravated by further childbearing" would receive contraceptive advice and materials. But no others.[135]

Very few advocates justified their support for birth control as a woman's right. Margaret Sanger most famously did, even if her feminism was increasingly eclipsed by her efforts to win support from non-feminist proponents such as doctors, politicians, eugenic scientists, or foundation executives. "No woman," said Sanger, "can call herself free who does not own her own body."[136] Sadly, over the decade of the 1920s, birth control became a more bitterly contested subject than ever —a eugenic prescription, on the one hand, and a matter of private decision making, on the other. Elite doctors tended to efface the needs of most women as they privately tended to the reproductive dignity of their middle-class patients.[137]

Private doctors, justifying prescriptions for birth control devices on whatever grounds they endorsed individually, began to counsel their patients to use contraception on a daily basis. One doctor told his patients "to make the insertion of the pessary [a diaphragm-like device] a part of her evening toilet if desired so as to be always prepared." He added, "It takes only a few seconds. Some women find it distasteful to place anything in the vagina, but when the insertion of the pessary is made a part of the daily routine of undressing it soon becomes a matter of habit and the psychic aversion to the practice disappears." Here we can see the doctor's sensitivity to and condescending approval of a middle-class woman's genteel squeamishness about her own body.[138] We can see the doctor encouraging his private patient to separate sex and reproduction.

Some doctors even sterilized their private, middle-class patients upon request. Wendy Kline has found letters women wrote to a prominent advocate of sterilization, praising the results of their operations precisely because of their increased sexual pleasure afterward. One woman wrote, "Now that conception is impossible . . . I have no worry and can enter into relations with my husband with a freedom and zest I never enjoyed before. I believe sexual impulse is stronger since the operation—probably due to the fact that my physical condition is improved in every way."[139]

Public acceptance of birth control continued to grow in many arenas. By 1931, official bodies of Unitarians, Reform Jews, Universalists, and the Committee on Marriage and the Home, created by the Federal Council of the Churches of Christ in America, representing more than twenty million Protestants "from Presbyterian elites to Baptist fundamentalists," endorsed birth control.[140] High-profile organizations such as the Voluntary Parenthood League, the National Birth Control League, and the American Birth Control League vigorously competed with each other to set and control the political agenda for legalizing contraception.

In the early years of the twentieth century, Leta Hollingworth, a psychologist and longtime faculty member at Columbia University's Teachers College, published a brilliantly modern and pointed essay in the *American Journal of Sociology* entitled "Social Devices for Impelling Women to Bear and Raise Children." Hollingworth revealed a pervasive absurdity in American society: "There could be no better proof of the insufficiency of maternal instinct," she wrote, "than the drastic laws which we have against birth control, abortion, infanticide, and infant desertion." Maternal instinct, Hollingworth argued, was so weak that it had to be constructed and enforced by laws ensuring population growth. It had to be reinforced by "opinion, illusion, education, art, and bugaboos." Hollingworth believed that it was only a matter of time until American women became "fully conscious" of the "devices" that controlled their fertility and mandated their maternity. When women realized how their fertility and maternity were being manipulated, she predicted, these devices would become "useless." Presumably, at that point, American women would make decisions about fertility and maternity on their own, privately, out of personal desire to be mothers—or not.[141]

When religious organizations found birth control acceptable, and when respectable women formed and led pro–birth control organizations and testified before Congress about the most intimate needs of fertile females, and when doctors began to hand out advice to their patients about fitting contraception into their "evening toilet," clearly birth control was moving into the mainstream of acceptable behavior. When Mary Ware Dennett prepared a leaflet as part of her anti-Comstock campaign, she started it off with these words: "Attention! Every man and woman in this town!" Dennett understood that the road to privacy had to be laid through the public square.[142]

By the late 1920s, this crucial feature of life—fertility control—that women had always had to treat as a guilty secret was further on the way toward becoming a matter of privacy for more women than Hollingworth might have acknowledged, though not for all.

3

No Extras

Curbing Fertility during the Great Depression

BY 1933 one-quarter of American workers were out of a job, and the average family's income had fallen 40 percent since 1929. As usual, men who couldn't earn a living stayed away from matrimony. But during the Great Depression, there was an especially large number of these men. The census showed that a quarter of a million fewer couples married in 1932 than had married in 1929.[1] Naturally, many of those unemployed workers and unmarried couples had sex anyway. In the context of the Great Depression, these developments meant two things for many women: unintended pregnancies, and a lot of determination to curb fertility until economic times improved.

By the 1930s, most women—the married and quite a few of the unmarried—had heard about contraception. They knew that something—some object, some substance, some method—was out there. And they wanted it for themselves. They also wanted to be able to get what they needed legally.

Activist women, following Mary Ware Dennett, Margaret Sanger, or other advocates of birth control in cities and towns around the country, pressed the government unrelentingly to get rid of the Comstock Laws and to legalize contraception. To a certain extent, activists tried to make their case by marshaling the voices of women from across the socioeconomic spectrum. For example, Margaret Sanger herself testified before Congress, but she also tried to convince the Milbank Memorial Fund, a philanthropy concerned with population issues in the 1930s, to "finance a campaign to have poor women seeking contraceptive advice write to their Congressmen." Sanger, always reaching out, also appealed to middle-class women to add their clout to the political campaign for birth control. The text of one such appeal is a classic expression of the troubled and divided subject of women's relationship to birth control in the 1930s and beyond.

Sanger wrote in part, "Do you, a woman, realize that true emancipation and acknowledgment of an equal status for women can never be realized until motherhood is by choice and not by chance? This is the first time in the world's history that an organized drive at race betterment, through conscious, intelligent, forward looking parenthood, is being launched and women must lead the way since women are the Mothers of the race."[2]

Sanger's appeal is classic because it divides the purpose of contraception into two: emancipation for women, and race betterment for society. Sanger did not apparently stop to consider whether these goals can coexist or if the second goal must, by definition, be gained only at the cost of giving up the first. Arguably, when society depends on women's reproductive capacity to produce "quality" offspring and exhorts women to reproduce "quality" babies, then experts, not women themselves, will decide with whom, when, and under what circumstances intercourse and pregnancy should occur. These are not favorable circumstances for women who want to achieve emancipation.

Sanger laid out the two goals, side by side, the twin, core purposes of birth control. She argued that these goals constituted the rational basis of public policy. Speaking directly in this appeal to middle-class women, Sanger offered a rational justification for their private actions, especially in the midst of the national crisis of the 1930s Depression.

The impact of the Great Depression was so dramatic partly because not only the poor got poorer. Millions of middle class people suffered its effects as well. Whenever possible, though, women who had become used to private doctors in previous decades, and who had come to embrace the relationship between privacy and middle-class status, continued their trips to the doctor's office, the only place where birth control was really available. (The growing number of public clinics served a very small number of women.)[3]

Women with various kinds of resources who didn't make it to private doctors for contraception, or who didn't use the methods successfully, might have converted the resources they possessed into backup solutions: seeking out information, advice, and one of the thousands of competent, if criminal, abortion practitioners who worked in cities and towns across the country. But even these relatively lucky women had to manage their bodies in the context of shame, fear, and often secrecy. They often had to seek out strangers for help. Sometimes they paid practitioners who only pretended to know what they were doing. There is no question at all that frequently women entered the criminal arena to manage their own bodies. And sometimes, in some places, even women with resources ended up doing the single most dangerous thing of all: self-abortion.

We need only look at the experiences of the *other* girls and women in the Great Depression—the ones who did not have access to the various kinds of resources that could be converted into reproductive privacy and personal protection—to see how much trouble their fertility bought to them in a time of economic want. Here we can see the costs of lacking privacy and the costs of living inside of a "public body."

For one thing, social critics and struggling neighbors sometimes looked at poor women who reproduced in the 1930s and called their children "relief babies." Historian Laura Briggs explains ambivalence in the 1930s about "excessively" fertile poor women and about activist government this way: "'Relief babies' entered the lexicon of headline writers [during the Depression] as an unnecessary and unwelcome drain on the public coffers, a commentary on the immorality of the poor, and a critique of the New Deal programs."[4]

In this context of economic insecurity and reproductive shame and danger, many women believed that no matter what the law said, or what the church said, or what the government said was legal or illegal, birth control and abortion were basic and daily needs. Women willing to defy the laws governing their fertility understood that when a basic need is against the law and also associated with shame and vulnerability, degradation is always a strong possibility. Managing fertility during the Great Depression was often an act of great determination.

In this chapter I will review some of the ways that the courts and the Catholic Church responded to the fertility-related dilemmas of women during this era of economic hardship. I will also look at how federal and local governments tried to boost the white population of the United States during the Great Depression. Moving in closer, to look at the lives of real women, I will show that in this difficult time, many tried a variety of strategies, including ones that broke the law, to manage their fertility. Finally, I will suggest that reproductive *consumerism* (the burgeoning Depression-era marketplace of contraceptives, for example) and the strong strand of cultural *individualism* (represented by the rise of psychoanalysis and other developments that focused on "self") reinforced the belief in *reproductive privacy* during the 1930s.

THE COURTS, THE CATHOLIC CHURCH, AND POPULATION RESTRICTIONS

With the Comstock Laws still in force during the Depression, many women were denied reproductive privacy by law, and many had no alternate access to the kinds of illegal reproductive privacy that money could buy. During the Great Depression, then, reproductive capacity was a source of danger for millions of women lacking privacy, money, and the means to manage their fertility. Margaret Sanger spoke regularly in this era about the power of the law to cause reproductive misery, especially for the poor. In a series of historic decisions in the 1930s, though, the law began to thaw.

Throughout the twenties, Mary Ware Dennett had "chipped away" at the Comstock Law. Most famously, she struck back through the courts when her sex education pamphlet for young people, "The Sex Side of Life," was labeled obscene and banned from the mails. Ultimately, Dennett prevailed when an appeals court judge ruled in 1930 that "an accurate exposition of the relevant facts of the sex side of life in decent language and in manifestly serious and disinterested spirit cannot ordinarily be regarded as obscene."[5] This decision redefined *information* itself. After this case, sexual information was no longer a privatized commodity. This was a considerable breakthrough.

In the same year as the "Sex Side of Life" decision, another legal case, *Youngs Rubber Corporation v. C. I. Lee & Co., Inc.,* also broke ground. In this case, the U.S. Court of Appeals for the Second Circuit determined that "transporting" contraception under certain conditions, for certain purposes was legitimate. Specifically, devices could be legally distributed under a doctor's prescription for the purpose of protecting against disease or for preventing a pregnancy in places "where that is permitted by law." Here is an example of a judicial decision that had an immediate and enormous impact on the lives of ordinary people. The *Youngs* case arguably laid the cornerstone for anyone and everyone's right to make a personal claim for contraception, if desired. In practical terms, the marketplace of contraceptive materials underwent "vast expansion" after *Youngs.* Anyone and everyone could claim the need to protect him- or herself against venereal disease and to promote his or her own personal hygiene.[6]

The third momentous birth control–related decision during the Depression forever changed the status of contraception. In the descriptively entitled *United States v. One Package of Japanese Pessaries* (1936), the U.S. Court of Appeals ruled that there was nothing obscene about a doctor's prescription for contraception, even in the absence of a medical justification. Judge Augustus Hand made a historical case for his ruling, arguing that if Congress had "understood the facts" about the purposes and social value of contraception in 1873 when it considered the Comstock Law, this legislation would never have been enacted. The *One Package* decision did have its limitations. Coming after more than half a decade of brutal economic hardship, it removed all federal bans on birth control but did not address the question of state bans. And even after the "Sex Side of Life" case, women with private doctors and well-filled pocketbooks still had a substantial advantage. They were able to purchase reproductive privacy much more readily than other women.[7]

No longer responsible for policing contraceptive practices, the federal government pursued a Depression course that was still sexist and timid. This was the case both before and after the now-prestigious American Medical Association gingerly endorsed birth control in 1937 as a "proper sexual practice." On the one hand, following up "quietly" on its World War I provisions for sexual and reproductive protection for soldiers, the army and navy slipped condoms onto their list of "approved prophylactics" in the 1930s.[8] On the other hand, in the same years, Margaret Sanger could drum up no support from the Roosevelt administration for her Depression-era campaign to recognize birth control as "an instrument to diminish human misery and reduce the staggering economic burden" created by the economic calamity. (At one point, Sanger, appealing fruitlessly to Congress to pass legislation supporting women's reproductive needs, referred to birth control as a "Mother's Bill of Rights.") Ironically, one branch of the government could facilitate male pleasure while other centers of government turned away from women's basic need, fearful of being associated with the taint of sex and also afraid of crossing another powerful institution: the Catholic Church.

Soon after the onset of the Depression, the Catholic Church emphasized its official position against contraception. In 1930, Pope Pius XI issued "Casti Conubii" (Of Chaste Marriage), a ringing pronouncement
directing Catholics to honor the civil rights of wives and mothers, and
at the same time condemning the "false liberty and unnatural equality"
of modern women who, the pope mandated, should be subject to the
authority of their husbands. The pope unequivocally condemned any
interference with fertility, including interference for eugenic purposes.

But Catholic authorities found a way to respond to the needs of
parishioners who wanted to limit the size of their families. In 1929 American doctors had confirmed the span of days within a woman's menstrual
cycle that constituted the "sterile period." Using this information, authorities counseled, Catholics could obey the pope while still limiting fertility. Couples could use the "rhythm method." That is, they could time
intercourse to coincide with the woman's sterile period. Catholic
churches distributed calendars women could use to keep track of their
cycles. Thousands, won over both to the rhythm method and to the
pope's stance against artificial fertility control, wrote to their congressmen warning them not to jump on the birth control bandwagon. The
Catholic Church tagged birth control "a national menace," and suddenly,
politicians and government officials, recognizing the size and importance of their Catholic constituency, pulled back sharply. Now, according
to one pundit, politicians saw birth control as "political dynamite."

Historian Ellen Chesler argues powerfully that in the 1930s, the
Catholic Church marshaled its forces and sounded every alarm. "Not
just prudish politicians, but the . . . political sophistication and power of
American Catholics stopped birth control reform in the 1930s." Even
the president's wife, Eleanor Roosevelt, a supporter of women's causes
and a forward-thinking reform-minded political force, refused to mention birth control publicly at all throughout the 1930s.[9]

The Catholic Church would not need to mobilize quite so forcefully
around reproductive issues again until the birth control pill was put on
the market in 1960 (and then again in 1973 and beyond, after the U.S.
Supreme Court decriminalized abortion). In the meantime, millions of
heterosexual Catholic couples adopted the rhythm method of contraception while other Catholics secretly used condoms, diaphragms,
coitus interruptus (withdrawal before ejaculation), illegal abortion, and
other means of limiting their fertility, just like other Americans.

In a sense, the counterforce to the Catholic Church during the Depression was the eugenics movement. Opposed vigorously by the church, eugenics was supported by many Americans concerned about widespread poverty and what this poverty could mean for the future of the country. Eugenicists claimed that if poverty persisted, and poor women continued to reproduce while middle-class women made more prudent reproductive decisions, then the quality of the population would be degraded to the point where democracy could not flourish. Some eugenicists supported the continued use of immigration laws to protect the "quality" of *American* babies and the jobs of *American* workers. This became an effective argument in the 1930s against Mexican workers, Chinese immigrants, and African Americans.

Since the passage of the immigration laws of the 1920s, the entry of southern and eastern Europeans had been severely restricted, and the entry of Asians had been restricted since the Chinese Exclusion Act of 1882. This law especially controlled the admission of the wives of laboring men, while allowing more lenient access to the United States for the wives of Chinese merchants, men who had come to this country earlier and alone. In 1880 females constituted 3.6 percent of the Chinese population in the United States, in 1920, 12.6 percent, and in 1940, still only 30 percent. Clearly this dramatic underrepresentation of women had a huge impact on reproductive possibilities and opportunities for family formation among Chinese in the United States. Not until 1940 did the number of Chinese born in this country exceed the number of Chinese living in the United States who had been born in China.[10]

Scholars have identified many reasons why so few Chinese women came to the United States in these decades. Explanations usually begin with restrictive immigration laws but also include labor and economic conditions and family responsibilities in China that pressed women to remain in their home country; the cost of passage; and the dangerous conditions Chinese women faced in the United States as many were forced into prostitution and other degrading work. U.S. authorities typically treated Chinese women as if they were lowlifes.

Historian Sucheta Mazumdar cautions against assuming "*a priori* that [Chinese women] wanted to join their husbands in forming a nuclear household and were prevented from doing so only by U.S. racism and restrictions." Mazumdar tells us that immigration scholars have focused on the family unit as the normative model of immigration. But she shows that very often Chinese women did not emigrate with their husbands even to destinations without immigration restrictions.[11]

Mazumdar explains that Chinese women lived at home within "an economic system . . . built around male migration and female domestic labor." She adds that Chinese women may have rejected living in the United States because it was an "alien world." She suggests that "the secluded worlds of [U.S.] Chinatowns" may have repelled many Chinese women who preferred to stay in China as well as many who returned home after a few years in the United States.

Yet the fact remains that U.S. immigration policy, favoring Chinese merchant-class women over poor women, shaped the demographics of Chinatowns around the country.[12] In 1930, a California congresswoman spoke out against the "deplorable situation" in which the laws of the United States deprived many laboring Chinese people "of one of the fundamental rights of the human race, namely the right to enjoy family life." Making matters worse, antimiscegenation laws in California forbid Chinese men from marrying "white" women, leaving many of these men unable to enjoy legal, marital companionship or children. In the end, immigration laws and race prejudice, in combination with other factors, had a long-term impact on the reproductive, family, and community lives of Chinese in the United States before, during, and after the Great Depression, as well as immigrants from other Asian countries.

The Depression also stimulated a set of immigration policies that shaped the lives and reproductive experiences of hundreds of thousands of relatively recent immigrants: men and women born in Mexico and their U.S.-born children. This population became a chief "scapegoat of the depression" as powerful American nativists accused "cheap" Mexican laborers—"the most unassimilable of aliens"—of taking the jobs of "real Americans" and also of filling up the relief rolls. Mexicans, recruited by U.S. employers for work on the railroads, in the crop fields of Michigan, California, and Texas, in southwestern coal mines, in the steel mills of East Chicago and in Gary, Indiana, from the 1890s to the late 1920s, were now the targets of "repatriation" campaigns. In Los Angeles, Detroit, Gary, San Antonio, and many other cities and towns, municipal authorities organized "forced exodus" programs, pushing Mexicans out of the United States, back to Mexico.

The federal government, along with state, county, and city governments and other centers of power, participated in this project in a variety of ways—some inadvertent, some explicit. Federal legislation such as the Agricultural Adjustment Act of 1933 displaced thousands of Mexican tenant farmers and agricultural laborers whose landlords quickly evicted them from their homes. The Works Project Administration excluded "alien" employment on federal work-relief projects, often the best hope for unskilled workers. Many state relief programs also excluded Mexicans, and cities and counties often insisted on "local labor" and long-standing citizenship for all workers on publicly funded jobs. These were conditions most Mexicans could not meet. A study of anti-Mexican campaigns in Gary, Indiana, showed that coalitions of businessmen, social workers, out-and-out nativists joined together to mount campaigns to "send Mexicans back to Mexico."[13]

In the early years of the Depression, many local governments carried out deportation raids in cities and towns where Mexicans lived. A Southern California official sent a telegram to the United States secretary of labor, William N. Doak, describing his hopes for the raids in his area, including his expectation that simply news of the raids would have a big impact: "This apparent activity will have tendency to scare many thousand alien deportables out of this district which is the result desired."[14] The Southern California official and many others pursued tactics guaranteed "to establish an environment hostile enough to alarm aliens." Along with carrying out raids and deportations, officials alarmed Mexicans by illegally imprisoning many immigrants, deporting U.S.-born children, confiscating property, withholding wages, and separating families.[15]

Typically, officials justified anti-Mexican activity using facts and fantasy, often focusing on the costs of Mexican fertility. A spokesman for the California Federation of Labor, for example, used this explanation: "In Los Angeles, where the Mexican population is estimated at 150,000 [out of a total municipal population of about 1.5 million], the outdoor relief states that 27.44 percent of its cases are Mexican. . . . Twenty-five percent of the budget of the General Hospital is used for Mexicans, who comprise 43 percent of its cases. The city maternity service reports 62 1/2 percent of its cases Mexicans, using 73 percent of its budget." And the president of the Immigration Study Commission of Sacramento, California, argued, "[A] normal Mexican family produces about 32 children and 1,024 grandchildren as opposed to three children and only nine grandchildren in the typical American family." The commissioner wrote, "We are therefore daily adding newcomers to the 3,000,000 Mexicans now here breeding against us."[16]

These policies and pronouncements had harsh impacts on Mexicans and their American-born children. Historian Camille Guerin-Gonzalez calculates that just before the "repatriation" era, about 650,000 Mexican immigrants lived in the United States, about one-third of them in California. By 1940, she finds a population of about 325,000.[17] Another historian estimates that between 50,000 and 75,000 Mexicans left the Los Angeles area in 1931 alone. Accounts from that time report that the roads leading to the Texas-Mexico border were regularly "congested with returning repatriates."[18]

Ultimately historians have not been able to provide the exact numbers of Mexicans pushed out of the United States. In July 1932, the *New York Times* noted the recent repatriation of an estimated 250,000. In 2004, the California legislature debated Senate Bill 427, a measure to establish a privately funded Commission on the 1930s "Repatriation." Authors of the bill asserted that between 1929 and 1944, 2 million Mexicans, including 1.2 million born in the United States, were the victims of "unconstitutional removal and coerced emigration."[19]

Whatever their exact number, when all these people arrived "back home" in Mexico, what did they find? Reports from the 1930s were grim. A Texas newspaper observed, "Those who go to Mexico will be no better off. Most of them have no other occupation than working in [coal] mines. They have been away from Mexico for fifteen or twenty years and are completely out of touch in that country. They will actually go there as foreigners." Journalist Emma Stevenson sent back an eyewitness account in 1931, vividly illustrating the desperation. She saw women who "swarmed about the warehouse picking up one by one the beans which spilled through the holes in the sacks."[20]

When we picture these women today, we can we imagine their reproductive lives under these pitiful, scavenger conditions. First of all, we might consider that during the time of repatriation, many Mexican women had to leave American cities where modern hospitals like Los Angeles General did serve many Mexicans. Others were sent away from towns where they had given birth under the supervision of respected midwives, most of whom were themselves Mexican-born. By tradition, these midwives were highly trained and skilled. Many had received additional training under the federal Sheppard-Towner Act in the 1920s, and after that, under public health programs funded by the Rockefeller Foundation.

For as long as Mexicans had migrated north, traditional midwives were crucial to Mexican communities in the United States, especially since these were communities in which parturient women (that is, women about to give birth) were so often overworked, underfed, and at risk for pregnancy-related complications.[21] An Anglo public health nurse remembered the key role of the midwives: "When I came [to Arizona] in 1936 the midwives were very important people in their villages and they helped with many other things besides births. Lots of places they were called *medicas.* We might ask for the *partera,* the midwife, when we went into a village, and in the conversation the word *medica* would come out. . . . The midwives often dispensed herbs for different complaints and also played the part of a counselor to the villagers. The midwife was the only type of leader in a village community except for the men who were politically inclined, and of course, except for the religious leaders. People would go to the midwife because there was no other woman leader. It was the only profession open for women, unless they go to town and be a teacher. So, the midwife was a very special person, especially for the other women."[22]

Under the conditions of "forced migration"—a more accurate term, many have argued, than what U.S. officials generally called "repatriation"—Mexican women must have encountered many of the impacts that we now know afflict dislocated populations. For example, migrating peoples, particularly those leaving home under pressure, generally lack adequate food, shelter, and sanitation. Typically women are more vulnerable to violence when families are stressed and when they move across the countryside unprotected by male relatives and without the ability to earn money in nonexploitative ways. The thousands of Mexican women in the 1930s who were pushed out of the United States probably experienced family separation, delayed marriage, and the need to postpone childbearing. At the same time, they lost access to folk contraceptives that many had been used to having at hand.

When Mexican women arrived in the jammed Mexican border towns, or in the cities, or at unsettled tracts in northern Mexico, or at remote haciendas abandoned during the Mexican Revolution, they may have found no birthing assistance whatsoever. One woman observed that in Arizona in the 1930s, Mexican American women looked after each other: "Just as people assisted each other in building irrigation ditches or digging wells, neighbors and friends rallied to help women give birth."[23] But away from home, things were different. In the larger cities and towns, hospitals may not have been prepared for the influx of new populations. Migrants, possibly suffering varieties of traumas, may not have known where to turn for health care or birthing assistance in any case. Many who had lived in the United States for years, or who had been born here, may not have spoken Spanish; receiving maternity help from someone speaking a foreign language is traditionally a difficulty.

Under the conditions of forced migration, public health workers typically report encountering increased incidence of abortion, and since many are self-induced or performed under nonsterile conditions, they see high rates of death among aborting migrant women. They see higher than average numbers of women who have received little or no health care during pregnancy and, consequently, more women who are ill, who have complications during delivery, and whose pregnancies do not lead to live births. They report low-weight babies, babies with congenital deformities, and high rates of women who cannot follow traditional practices of breast-feeding when their lives have been disrupted by forced migration.

Of course historians today do not have access to data from the 1930s that would prove these reproductive impacts on the women of the Mexican "repatriation." No such data were collected or preserved. Depression-era observers did not take testimony from Mexican women about the quality of their prenatal care while they were struggling to find homes for their families in Coahuila. Yet today, because of new studies focusing on the ways that forced migration takes special, harsh tolls on reproducing women around the world, we can think about how the U.S.-imposed migration of Mexicans must have shaped the lives of thousands of Mexican women during the Great Depression.[24]

There were other vulnerable populations in the United States that could not be geographically relocated or expelled. Some eugenicists in the United States turned to Germany in the 1930s for inspiration about what to do with these groups. They looked at how the Nazis were dealing with "undesirable" populations beyond the reach of immigration policies and practices. (Nazi officials themselves had, from the first, been inspired by racialist policies in the United States.)[25] Legal scholar Dorothy Roberts quotes an Alabama health officer who in 1935 shared his enthusiasm for Nazi sterilization laws with the Alabama state legislature, suggesting that Alabama may want to adopt these laws, too: "With bated breath, the entire civilized world is watching the bold experiment with mass sterilization recently launched in Germany. . . . It is estimated that after several decades, hundreds of millions of marks will be saved each year" by these policies.

This speaker reflected a shift in the 1930s among some eugenicists, from a focus on southern and eastern European immigrants to a focus on African Americans. These eugenicists aimed to reduce the Black birthrate and to stamp out mixed-race sex and reproduction, a centuries-old target of whites devoted to the ideals of racial purity and white superiority. In this context, antimiscegenation laws on the books in every southern state performed as eugenic laws, important to whites as a strategy for "preserving" the white race.[26]

For many conservative-minded people in the South and elsewhere in the 1930s, public distribution of contraceptive materials was distasteful and violated traditions of sexual secrecy. But as historian Johanna Schoen found, when race was a factor, local officials could be persuaded to forge a new tradition: public provision of birth control. In North Carolina, for example, one local health officer did not think his county needed contraception. Eugenicists working to create "selective" population control programs on eugenical principles asked the health officer to check his vital statistics. "When he discovered that Negroes were accounting for eighty-five percent of the births, he quickly changed his mind." Under the guidance of selective population-control experts in these years, local officials in the South taught women across the region, "on tobacco road and mill village alley," how to use birth control. Once again experts made the reproducing bodies of certain women the objects of public concern and the targets of public intervention, for "the public good."[27]

At the same time that racialist demographic politics of the Nazi regime inspired and infected some American social planners in the 1930s, eugenicists also borrowed from fascist politics to warn what America would become if population curbs were not employed. Prominent eugenicists proposed that excessive reproduction among "the lowest elements" could "destroy our liberties."[28] Historian Wendy Kline describes the American Eugenics Society's paradoxical solution: "to develop a mainstream following that believed in the concept of reproductive morality and accepted [the AES] mandate to sacrifice personal liberty in order to strengthen the community."[29]

In the 1930s such ideas were potent in part because of their association with the ancient and admired cultures of Germany and Italy. They also appealed to many whites as a way to subdue the "race problem" in America. And these ideas attracted many people because selective pop-ulation control—racist pronatalism—based on ideas about race, class, and human "value," seemed to promise a way out of the Depression. Here we see the construction of modern, public arguments that stretch forward into our own time. This Depression-era claim, so often pre-sented without evidence, or against the evidence, has endured: that when socially and economically disadvantaged women reproduce, they—and their offspring—are the *causes of social and economic problems for the whole country.* The Depression-era claim and its more contempo-rary versions promote this idea: only if public policies convince or co-erce such women to curb their reproduction will the country be safe (again). Only then can the country move forward. This argument was particularly harsh in the Depression, when the lack of jobs, the collapse of banks, and the other causes and consequences of the economic dis-aster clearly had the greatest impacts on the health of the country. Nev-ertheless, the argument was very effective.[30]

Welfare workers and members of the local PTA and others con-cerned about "degeneracy" (that is, the degradation of the population) were not thinking only about the unfit or about racial minorities when they imagined "degenerates" breeding. They were also thinking about the various forms of family dislocation visible all around them during the Depression—"illegitimate" pregnancies and "bastard" children and divorce—all of which, many argued, were traceable to promiscu-ous sex and low, ignorant women. Eugenicists and an increasing pro-portion of the public claimed, "[P]romiscuity not poverty was at the root of family pathology."[31]

As a remedy—one that would improve "the race" and reduce the cost of welfare, but refrain from offending Catholics—the American Birth Control League joined with the American Eugenics Society to pro-pose "all families on relief shall be informed where they may best ob-tain medical advice in a strictly legal fashion as to the limitations of fam-ilies by methods in accordance with their religious convictions."[32] But many eugenicists despaired, believing that poor women were too igno-rant to use birth control properly. A North Carolina official explained, "Some of these people, particularly the colored people, are apt to mis-interpret the procedure and conclude that the method used once be-comes effective for all time."[33]

Sometimes eugenicists attempted to soften their message. In these cases, they took the spotlight off the bodies of poor mothers and shined it on unborn babies. As an interesting precursor to antiabortion arguments emerging in the 1970s, eugenicists defined the child who did not yet exist as a precious, deserving little person who should be spared "the affliction of being born to unqualified parents." As a doctor addressing the New Jersey Health and Sanitary Association in 1937 put it, we must recognize "the right of all children to have competent parents."[34] Thus, incompetents should exercise restraint. They should not reproduce.

And always in the 1930s, class was the trump card, the surest way to appeal to the worried middle class, the new urbanites and suburbanites, the new property owners, the recent immigrants settling in to pursue the American dream, worried about the future. These groups included people vulnerable to images of class warfare. Reflecting an understanding of how class politics meshed with population or reproductive politics, the American Birth Control League warned that "overproduction" by people who shouldn't reproduce "is driving the middle class out of existence." League literature added, "Most serious of all, in the cradle of that second baby that many intelligent, middle-class parents hoped some day to have lies the dependent child of the prodigal proletarian."[35]

In all these ways, in a time of uniquely heightened economic, social, and political anxiety in the United States, many Americans saw reproductive control as an important remedy for everything that ailed that country. In this context, the courts' solutions in the 1930s did create new access to contraception. The Catholic Church and eugenic organizations stepped in with solutions that slighted or denied the dignity of women, depending on their race and class, while simply targeting the fertility of *some* women for control. In the meantime, under the hard conditions of the Great Depression, women of all classes and races negotiated their way through the complicated terrain of fertility, making their reproductive lives as best they could.

WOMEN BREAK THE LAW

Public health officials in the 1930s and historians who have gone looking for the evidence have agreed: huge numbers of women obtained abortions in that decade, apparently because they figured that they could not afford to have a baby, or another baby, under such terrible economic conditions. Studies early in the Depression showed that up to one million abortions were being performed annually in the United States. This meant that between 25 and 40 percent of all pregnancies were terminated, a steep increase over the prosperous 1920s. What's more, the numbers were increasing across the 1930s.[36] Historian Jesse Rodrique cites a striking and consistent 1938 figure: 28 percent of the African American women interviewed for a study of reproductive experiences admitted to "one or more abortions."[37]

Although their abortion services were completely illegal and undertaken at great risk, private doctors along with other specialists such as chiropractors and naturopaths sometimes had ample resources that they could use to protect themselves. With a steady stream of paying clients—Leslie Reagan estimates that the average cost of an abortion was sixty-seven dollars—people who performed abortions made good money, and many turned over hefty wads of cash each month to law enforcement as insurance against arrest.[38] A skillful practitioner providing high-quality services to elite white women and sometimes other women was unlikely to damage an abortion patient or cause her death. Police and district attorneys considered this kind of practitioner a public health asset who protected the well-being of women in their town. Law enforcement agents were happy to protect a good abortionist *and* get the payoff.

The women who flocked to these practitioners almost always obtained quick, clean, abortions. (We have few accounts referring to the race of the women who showed up in these offices, usually a sign that the clientele was white.) Ruth Barnett, a naturopath who performed abortions for about forty years in Portland, Oregon, described how it was for the ones who came to her office: "We had no secrecy in those days [the 1930s]. Women came and went at my clinic with scarcely any more fuss than there would be in keeping an appointment at a beauty salon. Many girls came to me during their lunch hour and returned to work the same afternoon with no distress."[39]

Ruth Barnett's practice was like others around the country: the evidence shows that in the 1930s death from professionally administered abortion was rare. As Reagan puts it, "Most women survived their abortions and never had to tell anyone unless they chose to do so."[40] Even within the world of criminal abortion, we see that the resources and privileges associated with class could enable privacy, safety, and life itself.

Sometimes women who lacked money but possessed contacts or other personal resources could convert these into abortion services. For example, several accounts from the 1930s describe how women who "impressed" the staff at one of Sanger's birth control clinics moved staff members to facilitate a criminal abortion. In 1932 one clinic employee noted a visit by "Miss Eide . . . a Norwegian, without relatives, who is unmarried, and is five weeks pregnant. Expected to be married in March, but when her fiancé discovered her condition, he deserted her. She is a woman of education, came here wanting termination. . . . Then arranged with Dr. Appel for a D&C. . . . We explained to her the confidential nature of our assistance and she promised not to violate our confidence. Was not charged for conference."[41]

Miss Eide was unemployed when she appeared at the clinic. Like many women, she probably thought she did not have enough money for a private doctor and was scared to go searching on her own for an abortion practitioner. But other women caught by pregnancies they could not manage were aware that a large number of doctors, themselves financially needy in the Depression, had turned to practicing abortion or had developed referral lists of dependable, skilled practitioners who performed abortions day in and day out for a steady stream of clients. According to Leslie Reagan, "Most cities had several physicians who 'specialized' in abortion, and many small towns had at least one physician-abortionist." Reagan makes the extremely important point that all the historical evidence points to the fact that a skilled abortionist was a valuable colleague for a physician in the 1930s: "Hundreds of physicians trusted established abortionists and relied on them." Also, these abortionists did not typically work in the infamous (and often mythical) "back alley." Rather, they had permanent practices, business cards, telephone numbers that appeared in the telephone directory. They had signs on their office doors. When women demanded abortion services, their private doctors often complied with these demands or sent their clients to someone who would, a practitioner who could be counted on to do a good job.[42]

At the same time that Miss Eide was applying to the birth control clinic for an abortion, a prominent researcher was tracking the outcomes of criminal abortions for women like the Norwegian immigrant. The resulting study showed that when women had the resources to pay for private services, the outcomes were generally excellent, especially considering that abortion is an invasive procedure and in this period antibiotics had not yet been developed. The study showed that 91 percent of the doctor-performed abortions and 86 percent of the abortions performed by midwives were completed without complications.[43]

Not surprisingly, young working women in the 1930s were aware of the benefits of skilled practitioners. Apparently some sexually active young women who thought they very well might get pregnant when they didn't mean to used their resources to create a group abortion-insurance policy. Abortion historian Reagan's most amazing finding was a news report about "girl clerks" working in downtown Newark offices in 1936: "New Jersey police uncovered a 'Birth Control Club' of 800 dues-paying and card-carrying members. Membership in the club 'entitled' them to regular examinations and to illegal operations, when they needed them, at a further fee of seventy-five dollars and upward."[44]

Here we see the meaning of privacy expanding and vibrant. Even working girls with little previous claim to personal privacy figured out how to build a protective structure for themselves, privately and collectively, perhaps using information about labor union structures or ethnic benevolent societies as a model.

But historians of the illegal era know all too well that women lacking the resources to pay a professional were likely to induce the procedure themselves. In acts that showed utter desperation, they tried to give themselves abortions, even though they knew it was dangerous. Dr. Edward Keemer, an African American physician, a graduate of Meharry Medical College, and an intern at the Freedman's Hospital in Washington, D.C., in the 1930s, gradually turned to abortion practice, in part because of the horrible situations he encountered during the Depression. Keemer describes this world: "I had treated a woman whom we had rushed hemorrhaging into the emergency room. She still had the straightened-out coat hanger hanging from her vagina. Some obtained rubber urinary catheters and died from air embolisms or infection. Over the years, I was to encounter hundreds of other women who had resorted to imaginative but deadly methods of self-induced abortion before they came to me. Some would swallow quinine or turpentine. Others would insert a corrosive potassium permanganate tablet into their vaginas. I recalled a sixteen-year-old girl who died after douching with a cupful of bleach."[45]

We know that the poorer a woman was in the 1930s, the less likely she was to have access to private medical care and the more likely she was to attempt self-abortion.[46] The same study that clearly established the safety of abortion-performing doctors in the 1930s found that 76 percent of self-induced abortions caused complications.[47] So common was the problem that a textbook for coroners written in this period created an alphabetical compendium of substances and methods that desperate women turned to when they lacked professional medical care: "Aloe. Alum. Ammonia. Apiol. Bicycle riding. Catheters. Colocynth. Cotton root bark. Croton oil. Darning needles. Ergot. Camboge. Hot baths. Imitation oil of bitter almonds. Jumping up and down stairs. Laburnum. Lead. Lysol. Methyl salicylate. Nitrobenzol. Oil of nutmeg. Oil of savon (juniper). Oil of pennyroyal. Oil of rue. Oil of tansy. Oil of thyme. Olander leaves and bark. Oxytocin. Phenol (carbolic acid). Quinine. Saffron. Salts of arsenic. Slippery elm sticks. Soapy water. Spanish fly (dried beetle . . .). Sponges. Turpentine. Umbrella ribs. Urethral sounds. White phosphorous (scraped from the tips of kitchen matches). Yew. Zinc sulfate (white vitriol)."

The textbook also listed the gruesome results of these treatments, including acute suppurative peritonitus, central nervous system depression, chills, coma, convulsions, death, delirium, oil embolism, perforated intestine, septic endometritis, stupor, and suffocation.[48]

Indeed, a Children's Bureau study in 1938 found that more than one-quarter of the women who died at some point during pregnancy had had illegal abortions. Most of these were poor, self-aborting women.[49] We also know, through Leslie Reagan's work, that in hospital emergency rooms around the country, as at the Freeman's Hospital in Washington, D.C., doctors, interns, residents, and staff treated "a continuous stream" of women after botched, usually self-induced abortions.[50] A tiny number of physicians spoke out against the laws that caused this result. The rest focused on villainizing the "back-alley butcher," even when doctors knew that most of the damage was self-administered.

Many hospitals, including Harlem Hospital in New York, opened "abortion wards" to respond to the mayhem from self-abortion.[51] Many doctors, along with Dr. Keemer, justified their abortion work then and in retrospect by telling the stories of the lacerated women they encountered and dealt with in the 1930s. Dr. Keemer was an unusual doctor for many reasons, including his clarity about the fact that the women he saw, perhaps most such women, were not victims of the so-called abortion butcher. His patients, desperate and determined, had harmed themselves trying to end pregnancies they felt they couldn't manage.

Over the course of his career, Dr. Keemer performed thousands of abortions. In his autobiography Keemer described how his race and the race of his clients structured his work: "It was one thing for a black doctor to perform abortions on black women—the white authorities might wink at that. They . . . would be grateful that one less black child would grow up in their town. Performing an abortion on a white woman, however, might even lead to a hanging."[52] Dr. Keemer sums up here an ironic advantage black women may have derived from having their reproducing bodies defined by whites as beneath the law.

Ironic advantage

During the Depression, federal poverty policies and local racism created conditions that pushed many poor women to seek out and rely on community resources. For example, in San Francisco, many Chinese women were determined to curb their fertility when their families lost welfare or "relief" benefits, and their cases were transferred to federal Works Project Administration (WPA) work programs. The family member employed by the WPA—usually the man—was confined to very low-paying jobs because he was Chinese, and the family's monthly income was now considerably less than it had been under "relief." Worse still, WPA workers were excluded from supplementary benefits that had been available earlier, such as medical coverage, surplus clothing distributions, and cash payments.

In this context, most Chinese women could no longer stay home to take care of their own children as they were "virtually forced to seek gainful employment to supplement [their husbands'] WPA wages . . . leaving their babies at home alone or with older children."[53] Clearly, under these circumstances, another pregnancy would be a disaster.

Jane Kwong Lee, a community worker and schoolteacher in San Francisco, told this story about how relieved one Chinese-born woman was when she managed her fertility during the Depression. Lee also comments on her own uncertainty regarding how to respond to this woman's solution. "[D]uring the depression years," wrote Lee, "I personally felt the trauma of my poor neighbors and friends, not to mention myself. Those who had big families suffered the most. Money, money, money! Where was there money for expenses and food? . . .

"A poor family with six small children could subsist, but if a seventh child came along, could the mother cope with the family's wretched situation? I doubted it, and I have an example to illustrate my point. Mrs. T. had six small children, ranging in age from one year six months to nine years. Her husband had been a store clerk, but recently was unemployed because of not enough business. She was getting groceries through the allotment card. Whenever a child had a cold, she just concocted some Chinese tea and forced the child to drink it; there was no money to pay for an herbalist.

"One day she came to me and talked about being pregnant. She complained that she did not know what to do if she had another child. We sat and talked for a long time, but no solution arose; all I could offer was sympathy and advice for her to do the best she could to keep the family's health. In a week she came back to see me as if she had a solution to her dilemma of whether she should have another child or not. She did not tell me her decision, but asked me for $5.00, which I gave her as a token of goodwill; I never expected her to pay me back. I thought to myself, 'Poor Mrs. T., I wish I could help her more.'

"Surprisingly, I was astonished a few weeks later that she returned to me the borrowed money. Without my coaxing, she confided to me that she had an abortion. She explained that after seeing me the last time she went to see a Mrs. So and So who knew how to direct pregnant mothers to have their wombs washed. It was very safe and easy, she said. She just stayed in the doctor's office for a few hours and then went home without any ill-effects.

"I listened with interest but could not utter any dissident opinion. She seemed happy to have solved her family problem and said, 'It is better this way. I cannot afford to have another baby.' What could I say? Should I show moral or religious indignation, or should I show her that I sympathized with her for her right action? I could do neither because I was a worker with a prestigious organization which also had the duty to help the unfortunate. Abortion was illegal then and is still a moot question."[54]

Abortion was the only measure some women took to limit fertility; they had no other form of birth control. But where birth control did become available to ordinary women in the 1930s, in Sanger's clinics, for example, or at the meetings of women's auxiliaries attached to male labor unions, women were eager. Julia Ruuttila, a Portland, Oregon, labor organizer, active in the Federation of Woodworkers in the 1930s, remembered that during a lockout, the women's auxiliary tried to raise money for layettes because, as she put it, "the people that were locked out had no money to buy clothes for babies." But the women rapidly moved beyond that strategy. "We got the idea," she said, "that we should have someone come and speak to our auxiliary meetings on birth control because it was no time to be bringing any more children into the world when we couldn't even feed the ones that we had. I had heard that Dr. Lena Kenin was interested in birth control. . . . [She taught us] different methods of birth control, something that most of our members knew absolutely nothing about. It was the largest meeting that we ever had."[55]

In San Francisco, Jane Kwong Lee took women to the Planned Parenthood Association to help them before they got pregnant. She remembered, "Sometimes a public nurse would call me up saying that a Mrs. So and So seemed to need birth control information and would I be able to take her to the clinic for help, since she herself, being a public health nurse, was not permitted to act in this capacity. [A public health nurse was not permitted to advocate contraception.] I answered that I would gladly do whatever was helpful to the woman."[56]

In the rural South, a woman might find out about birth control at a maternity and infant center. In 1939, a doctor working in a Black county in North Carolina described how "[t]hese centers are visited not by one, five, or seven women, but by crowds. They come from far and near; a few in cars, others in carts drawn by mules and many on foot. They keep coming, bringing their friends." The doctor asked rhetorically, "Why do they come?" Historians have explained these pilgrimages in both rural and urban settings as partly a response to economic hardship, partly a result of receiving decent care at these facilities, and, in the case of African American women, partly an expression of growing racial pride. An African American journalist, echoing eugenical concepts (while rejecting eugenical tactics) called birth control "vital" for the Harlem community in New York because it could bring residents "to a higher standard of physical fitness, mental capacity and financial stability."[57]

Quite strikingly, women without middle-class resources began in the 1930s to construct and patronize facilities and services that defined reproductive privacy as their due, regardless of their class position. In Washington, D.C., for example, the Lend A Hand women's club decided to build a place for the "unmarried colored mothers" who deserved to be sheltered from "the hard and cruel public." These young women, club members believed, deserved a chance to emerge from their ordeals, and to go back into public as "strong" girls, "good" mothers, and "honest" citizens. The Federation of Colored Women's Clubs of Georgia, as well as similar groups in Tennessee, Kansas, and probably elsewhere too, were involved in projects like this one to protect the privacy of "their girls."[58]

As we've seen, poor women across the country wrote to government offices, using the mail as it was intended, for private communication. Here a woman living in the rural South writes to an unknown federal bureaucrat in Washington about the most private facts of her existence, apparently believing she will receive a private response: "I have done nothing but . . . keep house and do the routine work that goes with that. . . . I'm completely shut in. I never go to church, Sunday school, visiting, shopping, or anywhere except occasionally to see my mother and father who are very old and feeble. . . . I have never rebelled at motherhood and no one on earth is more devoted to their home and children than I am. I feel like I've had enough children. My husband is 52 and his health is failing fast. He has no income except for the farm which is so uncertain and a failure some years. I do know that at my age I'll have several children yet unless a preventative is used. . . . We are not able financially to have more babies, as it's a terrible time to make 'ends meet' as it is."[59] Ironically, this letter is now in the public domain, published in at least two books.

Moving away from failing farms and into cities across the country, hundreds of white women began in the 1930s to go to urban neighborhood clinics, privately asking for and receiving information and materials to control their fertility. In 1934, the typical patient at one New York clinic was thirty years old and the wife of a laborer in the manufacturing trades. To get the help she needed, this "typical" woman forsook the old traditions of home remedies, grapevine information and gossip with other women, and the ugly prospect of self-abortion, all shrouded in secrecy. Instead, she put on her hat and went to a public clinic for a private consultation. In 1932, there were 145 such facilities in the United States. Five years later there were 357, more than twice as many. In Virginia and West Virginia, Black women, presumably feeling underserved by these public facilities in their areas or not served at all, sponsored birth control organizations. In Oklahoma, a coalition of fourteen Black women's clubs underwrote a clinic. In Nashville, Black nurses visited women in their homes, dispensing information and devices, privately.[60]

Women living in the countryside in the 1930s still had the "luxury" of peddlers coming to their private doorways, house by house, now offering "metal contrivances . . . representing them as solid gold and as having been sanctioned by Mrs. Sanger."[61] City women answered their doorbells to find lady sales representatives hawking birth control, selling ten-cent pamphlets explaining how to use a diaphragm. Both urban and rural women looked in the Sears Roebuck catalogue, now advertising "preventatives." They patronized the five-and-dime store, "the leading distributor of female contraceptives" in the 1930s, including the huge-selling disinfectant douche, Lysol. All these activities tied birth control to consumerism, a powerful, emergent force, slowed but steady during the Depression. And each of these activities illustrates the ways that women were no longer depending on the kindness or discretion of the local pharmacist, friends, and family. Now, privately and as individuals, they increasingly entered into neutral, cash transactions with strangers.[62]

As consumers, fertile women also bought magazines targeting them in the marketplace. They bought all kinds of publications—romance, crime, movie magazines, and homemaking monthlies. Andrea Tone shows us that manufacturers of contraceptive devices understood this readership and invested accordingly: in 1933 alone, various contraceptive makers spent $400,000 on advertising in women's magazines. The returns were spectacular. The business magazine *Forbes* revealed that contraceptive firms were raking in $350 million a year in the midthirties, with profits to manufacturers as high as 30 percent of retail sales.[63]

In New Mexico, one woman, Esperanza Salcido, remembered how she moved from thinking about birth control as a secret to treating it as a product. Mrs. Salcido's story about the first time she spent money on contraceptive materials shows that many different people over the first years of her married life—close family members, then a friend and a merchant outside of the family circle—helped her make this journey. Mrs. Salcido's story suggests that as she became a consumer of contraception like millions of women in the 1930s, she developed a new independence in relation to her husband and to her own life generally. Thinking back to the beginning of her sexually active life, she remembers, "I was so green when I got married. I didn't know anything. In those days you just didn't let the world know you were practicing birth control.

"We weren't real religious, but of course we were Catholics, and it wasn't your best friend that told you anything like this. When we'd been married about a year, Donna was born. We were living on the farm with Joe's family, and it was Joseph's mother, Grandma Lina, she took me right under her wing. She knew I didn't want a large family, and she told me I should make Joseph take care of me. So he did. Then, a few years later, when we moved to town, the wife of the president of the Downtown Merchant's Bank helped me out. She was an educated woman. She knew all about birth control, and she wrote down a list of what I could use and what I could get. Then we went into the drug store. It took me all afternoon to look for the stuff. She'd watch the door. When she saw somebody coming that we knew, she'd say, 'Here comes somebody,' and I'd drop everything. It was worth it though. Now we have just the three children, two girls and a boy, and only one of them was a surprise."[64]

By the end of the 1930s in the United States, reproductive politics was still structured by class privileges and class- and race-defined constraints. It is true, however, that market-driven and legal developments in that decade enabled many women to claim reproductive privacy, including many who could not claim middle-class entitlement.

Privacy w/o middle class status.

MANAGING FERTILITY AND MODERN AMERICA

In some respects, even during the Great Depression, consumerism was an emblem of a culture more strongly committed than ever to the idea of individualism and to the notion that we make our own lives. The new American psychoanalysts focused on individual behavior, motives, and feelings, all based in individual childhood experiences, to treat adult neuroses. Many focused particularly on "neurotic" women whose sexual and reproductive lives were defined as less than normal.[65] New sex education programs and family and marriage counseling opportunities in the 1930s stressed individual capacity for change, for happiness, and for sexual and reproductive fulfillment.[66] Many doctors and the new sexologists promoted sterilization for middle-class women as a modern method of contraception: the "liberated" woman could curb her fertility as a way of bolstering democracy and "the race" while pursuing sex for her own enjoyment.[67]

Some physicians began to acknowledge in the 1930s that when a sexually active patient claimed she did not have the money to have a child, the patient was correct.[68] Women pushed doctors to accept their individual reasons and private claims for contraception and even abortion. When the AMA endorsed birth control in 1937, physicians were responding to the need most women experienced during the Depression to limit their fertility. But the organization was also recognizing the centrality of individualism in modern life, even for women. In the 1930s, signs were everywhere that women were making claims to own and manage their own persons, their bodies, and their status as citizens.

There were other signs of the special status of reproductive individualism in the thirties. The "positive" eugenics campaigns—which aimed to encourage breeding by the "best" couples—depended in part on an individual woman's capacity to understand the goals of eugenics. Her job was to discriminate between suitors and to be able to select the highest-quality match. Child-spacing campaigns—efforts to educate Americans to have fewer, higher-quality children—again depended on individual responsibility (and on the specter of individual failure), as well as on access to birth control.[69]

A close look at each of these seemingly positive developments reveals problems that dangerously marked the reproductive lives of many women. For example, when the AMA endorsed birth control, it placed final authority over its use, in any and all individual cases, in the hands of doctors. This move extended and formalized doctors' authority over women's reproducing bodies, still a contested issue at the beginning of the twenty-first century. Positive eugenics campaigns promoted individual judgment but also laid the groundwork for the racist pronatalist campaign of the 1950s, which pushed white women to stay at home and have lots of babies, if they wanted to be viewed as "normal."

We can see the limits of privacy and the dangers still faced by many thousands of reproducing women at the end of the 1930s when we consider the horrors brought into the lives of some women because of their class and race in combination with their fertility. Consider, for example, the security system at the Phoenix, Arizona, Crittenton home for female juvenile delinquents and unmarried mothers: "A seven foot woven wire fence, mounted with three strands of barbed wire sloping inward, surrounds the institution, with a padlocked iron gate, kept locked day and night."[70]

Consider, also, the plight of a young Black woman who was brought to Dr. Keemer in the thirties. She had been raped but had never reported the crime, believing she had no chance for a hearing, much less for securing justice.

Then she found she was pregnant. Keemer describes meeting the girl: "Alternating between short seizures of sobbing and longer moments of gripping anger, the young woman explained to me that she had been gang-raped by a pack of white teenagers on a desolate country road. They had been drinking and careening down the road in a beat-up panel truck, and when they spotted her walking alone, they jumped out and chased her into a clump of leafless bushes. There, on the cold winter ground, they sated their drunken desires in her shivering young body. And when they were finished, they urinated on her for good measure. The embryo of one of those slobbering animals was now growing in her womb."[71]

4

Central Planning

*Managing Fertility, Race, and Rights
in Postwar America, 1940s to 1960*

IN AUGUST 1938 President Franklin Roosevelt invited Mr. and Mrs. America to sit down by their radios and join him in "a long look backward" at the beginnings of the Social Security system three years earlier. FDR, always warm and fatherly on the radio, invited Americans "to cast an appraising eye" over this most important piece of New Deal legislation. He wanted Americans to consider how the Social Security Act of 1935 had changed the United States. The president especially wanted to remind his listeners that the Social Security system was a powerful sign of the government's obligations to all citizens.

In this time of economic disaster, Roosevelt said, "The government must now step in and help [ordinary, struggling Americans] lay the foundation stones [of their economic security], just as Government in the past has helped lay the foundation of business and industry." The presidential message defined *potent* government: only the federal apparatus could solve a national problem as grave and far-reaching as the Great Depression.

In the middle of the Depression, a great many Americans endorsed the strong central government that the president described. One journalist explained, "There is a country-wide dumping of responsibility on the Federal Government. If Mr. Roosevelt goes on collecting mandates, one after another, until their sum is startling, it is because all the other powers—industry, commerce, finance, labor, farmer, and householder, state and city—virtually abdicate in his favor. America today literally asks for orders."[1]

For the remaining six and a half years of his life, Franklin Roosevelt steered the country through the Depression, through wartime mobilization, and through World War II, relying on the rhetoric of government potency and on principles and programs based on central planning. Roosevelt said again and again that centralized planning was necessary for preserving democracy and restoring progress in the United States.

From 1932 into the 1940s, federal programs aimed to protect, restore, regulate, manufacture, distribute. Targets ranged from wages to wheat, from water to armaments to education. Among the government's multiple efforts to protect democracy and restore progress, the Social Security Act of 1935 stands out for many reasons. For our purposes, the act is important because through what FDR called "this piece of intelligent planning," the government reached down into the American family and responded to the reproductive activity of some resourceless women.[2]

Before 1935, many states had funded mothers' pension programs. These efforts provided meager assistance for poor and "worthy" mothers and their children. Most often the mothers were white widows.[3] The Great Depression finally pushed the government to create a partnership with the states in order to expand aid to a larger, though still restricted, group of poor mothers. Central planning had penetrated the family, beginning with the families of some women whose husbands were dead or gone. The Aid to Dependent Children program (ADC) (established by Title IV of the Social Security Act and popularly known as relief or welfare), distributed still-meager sums of money to women of whom social workers approved. These mothers were selected for relief because they were viewed as morally "pure." They had been married. They promised not to work outside the home. They were almost always white.

Even as the ADC program grew and the United States entered World War II, federal officials in charge of the welfare program—and the ones at the War Manpower Commission in charge of deploying the wartime workforce—insisted to local welfare agencies that poor white mothers had the right to choose welfare. If these women took war-related jobs, officials argued, their children might be neglected. During this period unwed mothers were denied aid on moral grounds. Mothers of color were found unworthy by definition, or they were defined as more suitable for waged work than for raising their own children.

But officials were likely to define a poor white mother who met ADC qualifications as a *legitimate mother.* Based on her race, officials certified this mother as deserving aid *and* deserving the right to take care of her children. One federal welfare official in the early 1940s noted that some mothers applied for day care services for their children so that they could take jobs. This, she warned, was a sign that (white) women needed ADC so that they could stay home and care for their children.

By the end of World War II the federal government, in partnership with state and local social welfare bureaucracies, had been assessing "the family" as a target of central planning for a decade. The government had developed and disseminated ways of answering these questions: Which mothers are legitimate? Which ones are worthy of taking care of their own children? Which children are worth government support? The states did not always accept the federal government's definitions of worthiness, but the point was clear: the federal government was taking responsibility for the reproductive activity of certain mothers in the United States.

At the end of the war, though, central planners were not prepared for a number of demographic developments that ended up expanding the involvement of government in family matters, including in the reproductive lives of millions of American women in the 1940s and 1950s. This chapter will briefly describe these major demographic shifts. Then we'll see how these changes in women's work lives and reproductive lives occurred in the context of another dramatic and historical postwar development: the new and widespread appearance of *human rights or civil rights claims* in the United States after World War II. In many cases, these claims and the ways various speakers made them explicitly or implicitly expressed the reproductive needs of the ever-growing number of women who were earning wages during their fertile years.

Finally, this chapter will explore three different centrally managed strategies that federal, state, and local governments and community institutions turned to in efforts to oppose women's more independent postwar statuses. These centrally managed efforts involving welfare, adoption, and abortion also aimed to blunt the impact of rights claims, particularly the claims that involved female reproductive autonomy. The government's efforts most pointedly targeted the reproductive lives of women of color.

DEMOGRAPHIC SURPRISES

From 1900 to 1940, female labor force participation had increased by an average of 6 percent a decade. And then, during World War II, women streamed into the paid workforce. Historian Alice Kessler-Harris estimates that after 1941, approximately 3.5 million women entered the workforce for war-related jobs. In the absence of war, many of these women may not have taken paying work. As it was, by the end of the war more women worked for wages than ever before. Three-quarters of them were married. Most were mothers. The demographic surprise was that after the war, after many women left or were pushed out of the labor force when American soldiers came home, huge numbers of women returned to wage-earning jobs.

By 1950, one-third of all women worked for pay. In the 1950s, far fewer women quit their jobs when they married. More worked full-time instead of part-time. More returned to work after their youngest child began school rather than ending their paid work life when they became mothers.

As usual, white women and women of color had very different experiences in the workforce. Since employers paid white men higher wages than they paid men of color—and white men had access to higher-paying jobs—many white women didn't have to work for wages. Plus, their husbands didn't want them to go out to work. After the Depression, having a wife at home was a powerful emblem that a family had made its way into the burgeoning middle class because the husband was a good earner.

In the early 1950s, more than 30 percent of African American married mothers with children under the age of six worked for wages. The figure for all married mothers with children in that age range was approximately 15 percent. For all women with children between six and seventeen, the waged-work rate was about 30 percent. For Blacks, it was more than 50 percent.

After the war, many white women and most women of color came back to paid employment, and they stayed. What's more, many began to show "a new impatience" about employment-related "constraints of gender." Kessler-Harris writes about these demographic and activist developments: "Everyone was astonished" by the persistence and audacity of women workers.[4]

Disliked emp. discrim.

As we would expect, during the war and after, when so many women tapped into their own earning power to bolster the family budget, birth control was crucial. Birth control was just as crucial, in fact, as it had been during the Depression, when millions of American parents knew they did not have the resources to feed another child. Then, as we've seen, so many women did what they could legally and illegally to control their fertility that even the American Medical Association changed its position on contraception in 1937.

There is plenty of evidence that by the early 1940s, woman all over the country—many of them holding down jobs—were eager for birth control. A Gallup poll at this time reported that 77 percent of Americans approved of public health clinics distributing contraceptive materials. When the wartime rubber shortage caused difficulties for people trying to buy condoms, a nurse in a southern clinic, invoking a wartime sin, told a visitor, "I wouldn't be surprised if our patients aren't hoarding them."[5] Medical schools began preparing future doctors for a world in which the vast majority of married couples wanted to separate sex and pregnancy, and for a world in which wives could not afford to lose their earning power to an unplanned baby. A 1944 study showed that almost three-quarters of doctors trained in the late 1930s and later had received instruction in birth control, compared with only 10 percent of those trained before 1920.[6]

In 1942 the Birth Control Federation of America, the organization founded by Margaret Sanger and by then sponsoring more than two hundred clinics around the country, changed its name to the Planned Parenthood Federation of America. (Resonating with the theme of this chapter, the 1942 name change signaled a shifted from a focus on the connection between the sex act and a potential child to a focus on re-sponsible—planned—adult behavior.) During the war, Planned Parenthood, newly empowered by mainstream acceptance of birth control, distributed pamphlets that associated use of contraception with patri-otism, national strength, and military victory. Above all, Planned Parenthood identified birth control as a crucial element in a centrally planned, successful, postwar America. One pamphlet, "Planning for Victory," read in part, "The American people today need no further ev-idence on the necessity for quality in man power and materials to win the war. It seems, at last, that victory cannot be won without planning. . . . Planned Parenthood, with your understanding and support, can, in

1943, be made to mean that more healthy children will be born to maintain the kind of peace for which we fight."[7]

Other central planners believed that birth control would have a different impact on the war effort. The Connecticut labor commissioner called contraception "a direct assault on our strength as a nation." He exhorted Americans to "propagate the family" and decreed, "There should be no rationing of babies." Those who used birth control, the commissioner argued, were indulging in pleasure, not thinking of their country.[8] But both those in favor of contraception and those against it thought about birth control as an important feature of postwar family life. And both sides suggested that "rubbers" and diaphragms would have an impact on the war's outcome and on the character of postwar America. Contraception had arrived as a force to be reckoned with.

The combination of birth control's popularity and the huge number of mothers in the paid workforce in the 1940s and 1950s challenged traditional sources of male supremacy: many women gained personal dignity from limiting their fertility and earning money. Many gained social status. At the same time, these developments encouraged some men to feel less responsible for supporting their families and less responsible for their sexual behavior. In this era when many women wanted "to be something besides reproducers," old traditionalist social commentators —and ordinary people—worried about the consequences of change. They looked at wage-earning, contracepting mothers and worried about a gender-poisoned nation—a country in which "woman" and "man" had lost their distinctive meanings—a county on the verge of ruin.[9]

Speaking to many Americans confused about the meaning of these developments, the best-selling book *Modern Woman: The Lost Sex* (1947) unambiguously resolved the dilemma: the woman who combines work and motherhood "must of necessity be deeply in conflict . . . her work develops aggressiveness, which is essentially a denial of her femininity."[10] The authors, one of whom was a female physician-psychiatrist, wrote that when women worked for pay, they became masculine. A woman who split her life in two—mother and worker—was in a "dangerous position of having to live one part of her life on the masculine level, another on the feminine." The result: modern women are on "the path leading to discontent and frustration and resultant hostility and destructiveness."[11]

In *Modern Woman,* the evil twin of a working mother is a woman who limits her fertility. "A child," wrote Farnham and Lundberg, invoking a very traditional mandate just as the mandate was fraying, "is the woman's power in the world." Women who spurn procreation are "almost invariably" victims of "emotional disorder." They make themselves strangers to pleasure. In the presence of a nonreproducing woman, Farnham and Lundberg descriptively suggested, pleasure "limps, sags, fails, disappears, or converts itself into active displeasure." Farnham and Lundberg wrote that a contracepting woman is breaking "a deep primordial rhythm."[12]

At a historical moment when more American women than ever before were working for wages and using contraception, *Modern Woman: The Lost Sex* and other like-minded jeremiads were efforts to recapture rigid sex and gender roles, to turn back the clock, to stop change. Being a woman after World War II often meant being in reproductive conflict: knowledgeable about contraception, in a position to get it, and determined to use it, on the one hand. On the other hand, for good reason, many women still felt the heavy hand of the cultural mandate that pressed them to reproduce, to be mothers, again and again. The mandate insisted that reproduction was white women's most valuable gift to the family, the community, and the nation.

RIGHTS CLAIMS IN THE POSTWAR ERA

After World War II, Americans were indeed "astonished" to realize how many married women were using birth control and working for wages. Equally astonishing and equally relevant to the history of reproductive politics was the blossoming after the war of powerful human rights rhetoric and human rights claims. Focusing on this aspect of postwar America is particularly important since, in the years after Martin Luther King Jr.'s death in 1968, American schoolchildren and even their elders have received lessons about the "civil rights movement" that foreshorten and thin out its contours, its content, and its consequences.

The most typical lesson about the civil rights movement begins with Martin Luther King Jr.'s "I have a dream" speech before hundreds of thousands of dedicated and peaceful marchers in Washington, D.C., on August 28, 1963. The lesson continues across the Edmund Pettus

Bridge in Selma, Alabama, in 1965, when more peaceful marchers, demonstrating for the right to vote and led by King, start out a second time for the state capital, after a violent phalanx of state police beat them back the first time. In this story, the "movement" ends less than five years after it was born, in Memphis, Tennessee, on April 4, 1968, when King was assassinated.

When we bring a fuller and more complicated history of the civil rights movement into focus, we can, for one thing, build a context for understanding reproductive politics in the decades right after World War II. A number of excellent historians have looked carefully at this period when American soldiers, inspired by the promise of democracy, defeated totalitarian-expansionist governments in Europe and Japan and then came home to racial segregation. Historians have captured how critical masses of African Americans and other oppressed groups in the United States spoke publicly, using the potent language of democracy and human rights, to claim rights and full citizenship status for themselves.[13] Walter White, the head of the National Association for the Advancement of Colored People (NAACP), declared after the war, "Those who believe in democracy are now on the offensive and have put the enemies of decency on the defensive as they have never been before."[14]

Reproductive rights were often central to the claims of those who believed in democracy. During and after World War II, American society grappled with mothers who worked for wages and women who controlled their fertility in the context of a society witnessing persistent and increasingly visible outbreaks of rights rhetoric and rights claims. And these outbreaks deepened the threat against male supremacy and white supremacy in the United States. Rights claims, interacting with women's challenges to traditional gender roles, stimulated "central planners" to tighten the legal and social constraints on fertile women.

Legal historian Mark Tushnet and others have shown how civil rights activism, often coordinated by future Supreme Court justice Thurgood Marshall and the staff at the NAACP, ranged across multiple terrains in the 1940s and 1950s. Marshall and the staff raised legal challenges against discrimination in employment, housing, transportation, and education. They challenged the use of "kangaroo courts" that denied people of color fair trials when they were accused of crimes. They also challenged practices that excluded people of color from voting.

They challenged the "white primary" system in the South.[15] Lawyers developed and pursued these cases along with willing, if deeply wary, plaintiffs—and with the profound, if often quiet, support of communities of color. Many of these communities, after all, still—or especially—lived in the 1940s in the midst of whites, who as Tushnet puts it, "maintained political power in the south by means that the legal challenge could not reach, such as physical terror."[16]

After the war, federal courts were beginning to support human rights claims. In the mid-1940s, the U.S. solicitor general of the United States decided that the government must argue that *Plessy v. Ferguson,* the 1898 Supreme Court decision validating the so-called separate-but-equal doctrine, should be overruled. Taking action, the solicitor general filed amicus curiae briefs in support of NAACP-led cases to integrate graduate schools in Oklahoma and Texas. Most Supreme Court justices in this era were also sympathetic to the aims of Marshall and the NAACP. By 1954, of course, the Court unanimously and finally outlawed state-sponsored school segregation with its decision in *Brown v. Board of Education.*[17]

In December 1946, President Truman, allying his office with the idea of racial equality, appointed the Committee on Civil Rights. In the fall of the following year, this group issued a report entitled "To Secure These Rights," which expressed the members' conviction that democracy and human rights were tightly related to each other. In 1948, *Time* magazine noted that the white South's "revolt" against growing support for equal rights coincided with the publication of this report. *Time* said that the report "dropped a match into the dry and prickly underbrush of Southern pride and fear." Leaders of this revolt morphed the *civil rights* language that they hated into the white supremacist language of *states' rights* in an effort to stem the tide of change.[18]

Soon Americans were encountering rights language in many venues. When Senator Robert F. Wagner of New York opened hearings on the Full Employment Act in the mid-1940s, he declared, "[T]he right to work is synonymous with the inalienable right to live." Several years later, a federal welfare official published an influential article in the *Harvard Law Review* arguing that the federal government owed public assistance to poor people because welfare supported "the individual's right to life in economic terms."[19] The rights language and the rights claims, colored by visions of racial justice, were steadily reshaping mid-century American politics and culture.

Right discourse + thought

In 1942, the Supreme Court moved away from its harsh "three generations of imbeciles is enough" decision in *Buck v. Bell* (1927), described in chapter 2, when it issued an opinion that tied reproduction itself to human rights. In *Skinner v. Oklahoma,* a white man convicted of stealing chickens was sentenced to be sterilized under that state's Habitual Criminal Sterilization Act of 1935. In voiding the punishment, the Supreme Court defined sterilization "as an encroachment on basic liberty." Justice William O. Douglas, writing for the majority, clearly began to define a concept of *reproductive rights.* He wrote, "This case touches a sensitive and important area of human rights. Oklahoma deprives certain individuals of a right which is basic to the perpetuation of the race —the right to have offspring."[20]

This first association of "reproduction" and "rights" tied reproductive rights to the person of a man—a white man. And Justice Douglas is concerned in *Skinner* with the plaintiff's right to have children, not with Mr. Skinner's or anybody else's right to take steps not to have offspring. Nevertheless, *Skinner* represented a milestone. The decision implied that the right to reproduce is a basic civil right. Therefore, the three written opinions in the case suggest, laws touching on this right ought to be subjected to strict scrutiny, the court's highest standard of review.

Despite these legal and political developments, as historian Alice Kessler-Harris has shown, Americans sustained an intensely "gendered imagination" through the postwar decades: Americans continued to imagine women as wives and mothers, not as rights-bearing workers or citizens. Despite the *Skinner* decision, most Americans in these decades probably would have argued that women reproduced as an act of nature and as a social duty, not as an expression of human or civil rights. White women, especially those who could claim a place in the growing middle class, had their reproductive *duty* burnished with a notion of the *value* of their reproductive output. These women were often portrayed in the media as engines of democracy, generating baby-citizens for the free world. They were also pictured as engines of consumerism, reproducing for the economy.[21]

Their Cold War status tied mid-twentieth-century white mothers back to late eighteenth-century Republican Motherhood: women who fulfilled their duty to the nation by producing—and raising—the next generation of free citizens.[22] Such a woman was a national resource and a national treasure. In the absence of a robust concept of reproductive rights, a reproducing white woman was simply fulfilling the mandate that directed her life. She was reproductively obedient—the most and best that a non-rights-bearing woman could be.

In fact, though, no matter what the mass media and other authorities prescribed, American women displayed astonishing levels of reproductive *disobedience* or insubordination in this era. In the postwar decades, individual women rampantly disobeyed the rules of reproduction. Millions showed an ad hoc determination to personally claim reproductive rights in the 1940s and 1950s.[23] The behavior of millions of individual women foreshadowed the time when women collectively and publicly would claim the right to be a mother or not—reproductive rights—as a keystone of their citizenship status.

Even as the civil rights movement gathered force in the 1940s and 1950s, however, women of color faced particularly tough resistance to any reproductive rights claims they might make. There were three especially insidious sources of white resistance. First, some influential white intellectuals continued to define the least powerful women in the United States as the "most sexualized." Historian Nell Painter has shown how historian Wilbur J. Cash, in his prominent 1941 volume, *The Mind of the South,* continued and underscored the tradition of reducing "'the Negro Woman' to nothing but sex." Cash defined this figure as "all-complaisant . . . to be had for the taking." According to many whites, either sexual rights—including freedom from rape—or reproductive rights for such a woman would be a contradiction in terms.[24]

Second, the most visible mainstream proponent of contraception in the 1940s, Planned Parenthood Federation of America, began to bolster its public education work with arguments that "a family's economic status [was] a paramount criterion regarding the desirability of reproduction." A staff member chided the organization in 1943 for "implying that people without wealth have no right to have children."[25] In 1948, William Voigt, soon to be the national director of Planned Parenthood, wrote an international best seller, *Road to Survival,* in which he proposed paying poor people modest sums to refrain from reproducing. This plan, Voigt explained, would spare the country the need to support "their hordes of offspring that, by both genetic and social inheritance, would tend to perpetuate their fecklessness."[26]

In this way, Planned Parenthood and other organizations contributed to early efforts to define motherhood as a class privilege. Purposely or not, these groups gave force to the idea that poor women, especially women of color, should be targets of centrally planned reproductive control, not bearers of reproductive rights. At the same time, state and local administrators of the Aid to Dependent Children program routinely denied public assistance to mothers of color, and apartheid-like labor practices guaranteed poverty for these women raising children. Both public policies and private practices guaranteed that many females would certainly fail to meet the "paramount criterion."

Third, girls and women of color faced another grave obstacle to reproductive dignity after World War II: white resistance to the growing call for civil rights often took the form of claiming that mothers who weren't white couldn't or shouldn't be raising future citizens. Indeed, white resistance to civil rights for minorities often took the form of targeting nonwhite children. Angry about developments such as federal legislation that lifted race-based qualifications for immigration in 1952, and the Supreme Court's *Brown* decision in 1954, many whites claimed that the children of newly entitled immigrants and the children of African Americans could not be molded into American citizens. Surely, they claimed, the mothers of these children were not equal to the task of training them for citizenship.

Efforts to obstruct the enforcement of civil rights typically targeted nonwhite children as unworthy of welfare assistance and unworthy of attending formerly all-white schools. White resisters looked to state governments to design ways of preserving white supremacy. They advocated for strategies that degraded the motherhood status of mothers of color and the citizenship potentiality of their children.[27]

Nevertheless—and not surprisingly—many people of color in this era of rights claims showed how strongly they felt about managing their own fertility. The National Council of Negro Women established the permanent Committee on Family Planning in the mid-1940s; its chair, Dr. Dorothy Boulding Ferebee, was a longtime advocate of the idea that the committee's beneficiaries should have a hand in planning the fertility-control programs that served their communities.[28] E. Franklin Frazier, the great African American sociologist, pointed out in the 1940s that being able to plan a pregnancy was "no substitute" for a job and a good wage. But, he insisted, reproductive planning was "equally important to the family of a sharecropper or a president of a university." Frazier was not free of the impulse to associate poverty with promiscuity. Like others in the 1940s, he championed "planning," not rights, as the antidote to "uncontrolled impulse." Frazier also believed that "planning"—the use of birth control—was the best way to ensure the end of white exploitation of "the masses of cheap, unlettered labor." If African Americans planned their fertility, Frazier argued, white employers could no longer mistreat their workers under the theory that "there are plenty more where they came from."[29]

Other African American commentators took what seemed like the opposite position, arguing that the relatively high birth rate among African Americans was the race's "greatest factor of safety." In this view, birth control clinics would harm the Black race at the same time that they helped whites maintain their demographic dominance. African American physician Julian Lewis, a proponent of this perspective, urged Blacks to work for the kinds of economic, medical, and educational reforms that would lower the Black death rate. He counseled that African Americans should "look askance at any proposals that threatened to reduce their birth rate."[30]

The combination of major changes in the employment and reproductive lives of American women—and the widespread emergence of rights claims—stimulated central planners of many varieties to support policies and practices that would shore up traditional but fraying gender and racial roles in American society. Frequently these policies and practices identified women's reproductive capacity as the appropriate site for this project. By managing the reproductive capacity of different groups of women differently—according to race—social relations could be maintained as they "always" had been.

Revitalizing male supremacy and white supremacy and underscoring the importance of racial purity would be difficult to accomplish in a society changing rapidly in the postwar era. It would be hard to hold back change in a society where many women and minorities were defining entitlements and rights for themselves and against tradition.

But the state at various levels (federal, state, local), in partnership with a range of religious and voluntary organizations, did step in, aiming to forestall or even reverse this revolution in rights and relationships, in part by restraining female reproductive decision making. The rest of this chapter will describe three different policy initiatives—all related to female fertility, all designed in one way or another to squelch female independence, all associated in one way or another with protecting white "superiority" at the opening of the civil rights era.

These initiatives did not add up to a neat package of coordinated, centrally planned policies. Rather, the three initiatives cropped up at various levels of government and in voluntary organizations around the country simultaneously, overlappingly, reinforcingly, sometimes independently, sometimes not. Each of these initiatives—and all three of them together—does show us some of the ways that public and private programs designed to respond to female fertility ended up ensuring racial difference in this era. The initiatives illustrate some of the ways that racism was institutionalized and extended in American society in the postwar decades. Each of these initiatives intersects with the others as a political strategy for blunting the rights claims of women moving to control their own reproductive lives.

DEPLOYING WELFARE

In 1940, five years after the Social Security Act became law, not many Americans could have predicted that the Aid to Dependent Children program would become and remain one of the most viciously debated domestic political and policy issues of the twentieth century. But by the end of the 1940s, the subject of welfare assistance had become sharply politicized. Policy experts and ordinary Americans were increasingly split and vocal. On one side were those who focused on the needs of poor mothers and their children—and on how ADC could address those needs. On the other side were people who focused first on the bad behavior of ADC recipients and potential recipients, and then on ways to make sure that ADC payments were reserved for the "worthy poor."[31]

In 1944 President Franklin D. Roosevelt, endorsing the goals of the Social Security Act, referred in his State of the Union address to an economic "bill of rights" for the American people, a guarantee of "security and prosperity for all—regardless of station, race, or creed."[32] In the spirit of this vision of democracy, the federal Bureau of Public Assistance worked throughout the 1940s to increase the proportion of nonwhite recipients on the welfare rolls. Between 1942 and 1948 the proportion rose from 21 percent to 30 percent. Still, the gains were not equal. In the 1940s, people of color were much more likely to receive welfare benefits in northern states than in the South. For example, in Illinois, 173 out of 1,000 Blacks were ADC recipients; in North Carolina, despite near-complete impoverishment of the Black population, only 14 out of 1,000 Blacks received benefits.[33]

After the war, when women of color began to apply for welfare assistance, the federal government exerted intermittent pressure on state welfare agencies to accept these applicants onto the rolls. In response, some states intensified efforts to keep their welfare programs as white as possible. For example, state welfare administrators wrote rules to define these new applicants as ineligible. Many southern states used work rules to exclude African American women. Many states also developed rules to exclude children whose homes the welfare office defined as "unsuitable."

As the federal government began to extend the benefits of economic security programs to poor mothers—including mothers of color in the 1940s—many governors, state legislatures, and state welfare bureaucrats asserted the "states' rights" argument against welfare for mothers of color and their children. They argued that states had the right to ignore federal rules and exclude anyone they chose from benefits, even if the exclusion was based on race. Officials used this "states' rights" argument some years before they claimed "states' rights" against federal mandates to integrate public schools.[34]

In other words, at the dawn of the civil rights era, numerous state-level politicians and policymakers relied on whites to approve of state action against subsidizing the reproductive activity of women of color. Denying aid to African American mothers and sending them to work flew in the face of the federal government's intentions, articulated in a 1909 White House conference on the care of dependent children. Conference members had agreed that mothers should take care of their own children, with assistance if necessary.[35] By 1935, in fact, all but two states had created laws helping mothers in this way.

But just a few years later, in 1942, the federal Bureau of Public Assistance found that African American, Indian, and Mexican children were all receiving benefits at rates much lower than white children in the same states. Even though state studies showed unequal treatment, and federal offices encouraged states to fix their practices, nothing changed. Unlike white women, mothers of color were routinely denied both assistance and the right to take care of their own children. Welfare offices functioned as employment centers for these mothers, who were sent by welfare workers to fill the labor force slots tagged for low-wage, menial, nonwhite workers. In Louisiana, for example, the state welfare agency adopted a formal and racially specific rule in 1943 requiring that no ADC applicant would be granted assistance as long as she was needed in the cotton fields. This rule included children as young as seven. Now, in a new, state-sanctioned way, caring for one's own child —being a mother—was again a racial privilege. The Georgia policy targeting African Americans read this way: "Able-bodied mothers with no children under twelve months of age are expected to find employment if work is available, and so long as work is available in the area, their families are not eligible for ADC." White mothers of infants were not expected to find waged work, even those applying for welfare assistance.

The other powerful exclusionary strategy that states used was to define certain babies and children as not worth, or not worthy of, public support because their mothers did not reproduce under state-approved conditions. It is important to underscore here, again, that various states were using the reproductive capacity of women of color to resist implementing federal human rights or civil rights policies designed to extend the "right to live" to poor, resourceless women and their children.

For the purpose of excluding families of color, 40 percent or more of the states wrote "suitable home" laws that barred aid to "illegitimate children." Legislatures accepted welfare rules that threw mothers and their children off the welfare rolls if some official believed that the mother had had sex with a man—whether the father of her children or someone else. This was called the "substitute father" or "man-in-the-house rule." These rules targeted poor African American mothers, who were instructed to stay away from men and punished if they disobeyed. These rules demonstrate the development of a set of state-sanctioned policies resting on the premise that sexual relations could be treated as a class-and-race-and-gender privilege.

The man-in-the-house rules, which remained in effect for decades, also insisted that the state had the right to define a poor African American woman who had given birth as, in essence, a prostitute. The fact that she had given birth meant that any future sexual partner had to pay. If he had sex with the mother, he had to pay by supporting her children. Unlike a white woman, even a poor, unmarried white woman who gave birth, as we shall see, a poor, unmarried African American mother or other woman of color had to be a wage earner in order to earn the right to have sex free from government surveillance. She had to be a wage earner in order for the government to treat her as if she had the right to have sex with a man without being officially forced to enter a relationship of financial dependency on that man. As welfare officials pressed their poor clients of color to name the fathers of their babies in exchange for the welfare check, sexual and reproductive privacy were also stamped as privileges of race and class at midcentury. Once the federal ADC program granted states the job of administering the national welfare program for mothers and children, central planning for welfare distribution became an efficient and popular way for unwilling states to resist.

Winifred Bell, the great scholar of welfare provision and tactical exclusion in this era, showed how in the late 1940s many states established special investigative units to help public assistance workers gather evidence that "needy mothers were consorting with men." These units showed up in the middle of the night, pawed through closets and drawers, and peered under beds looking for "substitute fathers." The units not incidentally re-created the right to be free of unreasonable "search and seizure" as a race-and-class privilege as well.[36]

The "suitable home" rules were supposed to indicate that as an unwed person, the woman of the house was an unfit mother. Welfare officials routinely excluded such women and their children from benefits, but officials did not remove children from the care of their "unfit" mothers. Once a woman's ineligibility was established, the children were no longer objects of interest to the welfare department. (Winifred Bell found that welfare workers did threaten to remove children from their mothers, but only in cases where the mothers hadn't withdrawn their welfare applications.) Bell reported that in this era, resistance to providing public assistance to fertile, reproducing African American women was so fierce that in many states, including Arkansas, Georgia, Michigan, Mississippi, and Texas, "the responsibility of public assistance workers seems to have been virtually limited to denying or discontinuing grants if mothers became pregnant out-of-wedlock after receiving a welfare check."[37]

Years before contraception was publicly available to most American women, poor African Americans discovered that birth control was a racialized opportunity. Northern proponents of birth control established the Negro Advisory Council and other vehicles for championing limited births, not welfare, for this population.[38] Sometimes tactics for limiting the reproductive "output" of poor mothers of color included sterilization. Historian Johanna Schoen connects the rise of this "solution" with the "desire" of welfare officials "to control rising expenditures."[39]

In many states, public officials defined poor mothers of color as re-productively expensive and as producers of worthless children. Their race, their poverty, and their gender, and all the vulnerability inherent in those statuses, cast the reproductive capacity of these women as the source of social problems and the site of solutions to a number of post-war social ills. First, many federal and state officials began to argue in the 1940s and 1950s that African American woman were reproductively unnatural. They didn't have babies out of maternal feeling or out of the desire to make a family, or even because they lacked contraceptives. They had babies in order to get welfare. If we deny them welfare, offi-cials argued, we will halt their reproductive adventures. We will reduce welfare costs, reduce taxes, and slow the population growth of minori-ties in the United States.[40]

Second, proponents of school segregation, restrictive public hous-ing, and enforced sterilization—as well as exclusionary welfare policies —all used the issue of relatively high rates of out-of-marriage pregnan-cies and childbirth among African American women to support their campaigns. White supremacists in Mississippi, Louisiana, and else-where strategically timed legislation to punish or exclude these women from public assistance. Some states passed laws right after the Supreme Court's *Brown v. Board of Education* ruling to end school segregation. Others passed or revitalized older laws as the federal government en-forced school integration. In 1956 the *New York Times* reported on a hear-ing in the U.S. House of Representatives on the desegregation of schools in Washington, D.C. The prevalence of unwed mothers among Black schoolgirls was an immediate rallying cry for southern segregationists, the paper observed. And the House subcommittee majority tri-umphantly wrote its report recommending that segregation be re-stored.[41]

Third, into the 1950s, as "overpopulation" became a policy preoc-cupation, the "excessive breeding" of poor women of color in the United States was folded into the panic that policymakers expressed about the politically explosive potential of "hungry people" here and around the world. Hungry people, argued influential demographer Hugh Moore in the mid-1950s, could be easily manipulated by com-munists and others who could hurt the interests of the U.S. govern-ment. Moore wrote that birth control was far less important for its "so-ciological or humanitarian aspects" than for its ability to curb repro-duction, hunger, and destabilizing aggression.[42]

Treated as welfare prostitutes, as ugly emblems of desegregation, and as explosively and aggressively fertile, poor women of color got pregnant and had babies in a hostile America after World War II. Here is a letter that a young African American woman in Philadelphia wrote to Harry Truman, the president of the United States, in 1948. This young woman was bereft, resourceless, and desperate enough to turn for help to a remote figure of authority. But she turned to President Truman with dignity and a sense of her rights. At the end of her letter, she shows her clear understanding that a woman in her position had standing as a citizen and deserved help: "I am a girl expecting a baby . . . an unmarried girl. And I have been to Public Assistance here also to Municipal Court and Public hospital and they won't help me and I want to know if you could write them . . . because I need help bad and can not work because I'm not well and every time I go to them, they tell me to found my friend and I don't know where he is and can't found him and I don't have any one to help me at all. Please write them right away because that is their job public assistance for the public."[43]

This woman in Philadelphia defined her claim in terms similar to those that would catalyze a generation of poor mothers twenty years later. As part of the welfare rights movement in the 1960s, poor mothers of color and others would boldly define themselves, like this woman, as rights-bearing fertile persons whose reproductive lives did not disqualify them from citizenship-based entitlements. Their reproductive lives, they argued, in fact, constituted their core qualification.

INVENTING ADOPTION

Between approximately 1945 and 1973, unwed mothers, both Black and white, were defined as deviants.[44] But families, communities, and social agencies treated white and Black unwed mothers in racially distinct ways. After the war, a Black single mother typically stayed within her family and community and kept her child to raise herself, often with the help of her family. As larger numbers of these mothers (most shut out from well-paying employment opportunities) became eligible for public assistance in the late 1940s and early 1950s, and the civil rights movement was emerging, as we've seen, white politicians and policymakers went to extreme lengths to portray them as sexually and maternally irresponsible. More and more often, politicians said in public that these mothers were only interested in having babies to get welfare checks. As we've seen, politicians routinely promoted policies that used the out-of-wedlock childbearing of some women of color to shore up racial segregation in general. Specifically, they made it difficult for these mothers to get public housing, public assistance, education, and jobs.

Not surprisingly in a racially divided country, the postwar experiences of white unwed mothers were quite different. Their experiences were, however, equally cruel. As Freudian theory began to shape the ways that social services were delivered to agency clients, white single mothers were, for the first time, diagnosed as psychologically disturbed on the basis of their nonmarital childbearing. Unwed pregnancy was constituted as evidence that they were unfit to be mothers. The new treatment for these girls and women involved temporarily banishing them from their families and communities and placing them in maternity homes or other remote locations and coercing them to relinquish their babies.

The new psychological explanation of white single pregnancy replaced the earlier explanation that girls and women who became pregnant while unmarried (and had no prospects that the father would make them "honest women") were products of poor environments and the weakened moral and physical fiber that resulted from growing up in the urban slums with, for example, alcoholic parents and subnormal IQs. Unwed mothers from such tainted environments were understood to produce similarly tainted babies. Before World War II, there were no hordes of childless white couples vying for selection as adoptive parents of "bastard" babies. The white biological mothers of illegitimate babies were "fallen women," but they were still the mothers of children they bore. These women were often consigned to live out their ruined lives on the fringes of society. But rarely did anyone question their status as mothers.

The psychological explanation of white single pregnancy had a number of dramatic and swiftly applied implications. First of all, this explanation was an important ingredient in the postwar cultural consensus that broke the relationship between biology and motherhood. After the war, those who made and implemented public policy, along with large segments of the public, came to believe that for whites, motherhood was determined not by biology, by giving birth, but by marriage. A white girl or woman who had a baby outside of marriage was diagnosed as mentally disturbed. The fact that she had no husband to protect and love her was proof of her neurosis and her unfitness for motherhood.

Second, the psychological explanation of white single pregnancy was crucial to defining white illegitimate babies as valuable and adoptable. The women who had given birth to them, experts now argued, were not marked by fixed traits of biological inferiority. They were seen, rather, as nongenetically, temporarily, and treatably *neurotic*. Consequently, unlike bastard babies born of "tainted" mothers in the early decades of the twentieth century, illegitimate white babies born after the war were defined as free of maternal taint. These two innovations supported, naturally, the third innovation: that white unwed mothers must give their newly valuable illegitimate babies up for adoption.

These developments describe the beginnings of an informal but rigidly enforced white adoption mandate in the United States. But why did these practices—banishing and hiding away the pregnant young woman, making her surrender her baby to strangers, unmaking her as a mother—become so widespread in the postwar decades? There were, in fact, several "social problems" that the white adoption mandate addressed and appeared to resolve.

To begin with, the white adoption mandate appeared to provide a practical solution to the problem of infertility at a moment in American history when the inability to reproduce may have been most stigmatizing. Like all good "solutions," adoption seemed to create a win-win situation. Through adoption, white, unwed mothers achieved a humane resolution of their terrible dilemma. Girls could pass their babies over to deserving couples. Having been "prematurely sexually active" (especially before birth control was available to unmarried females), unwed mothers no longer had to live out their lives as fallen women, raising bastard children. Postwar ideas about the *malleable self* encouraged social workers, parents, clergy, and others to believe that having disappeared from the community and having surrendered their babies in secrecy, the white, former unwed mother could reemerge with a clean slate. If no one knew about the illegitimate pregnancy, the event never happened. The girl herself would forget what had happened.

Providing a child to a childless couple was the key. According to the adoption experts, with this act, the girl redeemed herself, resolved the psychological disturbances that caused her pregnancy, and in some remarkable way restored her virginal status. She could once again look forward to dating, to marriage, to real motherhood. All this was guaranteed if she helped a childless man and woman or an infertile couple make a family. This was a stiff bargain, but one that thousands of young white women entered into, willingly or not.

The white adoption mandate also resolved an additional problem: preserving or restoring the "look" of an unmarried white girl's chastity. With a baby but no wedding ring, a young white woman could become an object of her own parents' fear and disgrace in the era of "family togetherness." An unmarried pregnant daughter, particularly one who turned up in the postwar decades in one of the millions of newly middle-class families, was a serious threat to her family's social status. Mothers and fathers panicked. They threatened and begged. They forbade their daughters to leave the house or see their offending boyfriends. They tried to get the boys to marry their daughters or, alternately, they tried to get the boys arrested and thrown in jail. Parents frantically arranged to have daughters leave town, go underground, as it were, until the "evidence" was no longer visible.

The lengths that white families went to in this era to efface their daughters' sexual misconduct—including giving away a grandchild/child, and in many cases refusing ever to talk about the ordeal as soon as it was "over"—suggest how much white families had to lose when their daughters were publicly associated with *unchastity*. Willingness to enter into this family-rending trauma also shows the danger and the power of the reproductive capacity of daughters. It illustrates the story that the "white community" believed in, the story about the value lost when a girl's reproductive capacity was not deployed under conditions prescribed for white females.

As we've seen, politicians and policymakers argued for preserving segregated schools because "Negro girls" had babies out of wedlock, and this behavior might be "catching." Also, politicians and policymakers tutored the white public: welfare is a bad program. It rewards "Negro girls" with dollars for what their kind does every day: have babies without having husbands. When "white girls" did the same thing, they were not simply shaming their parents and inviting neighbors to rank the tainted family as insufficiently middle-class. The unwed pregnant daughter stood out as insufficiently white.

In an era in which most whites were beginning to realize that traditional American racial boundaries might not hold forever, many whites depended on their daughters' sexual propriety, or at least the girl's abil-

Sexuality→define racial difference

ity to keep her sexual impropriety *invisible,* as a firewall defining racial difference.

The maternity homes to which so many white parents sent their offending daughters for hiding during the pregnancy served as weird, racialized finishing schools. The postwar curriculum aimed to strain out impurities. The white, pregnant girl was rehearsed, until the day she left the home without the baby, in the norms of white womanhood, as defined by maternity home staff: domesticity, femininity, chastity, obedience, self-sacrifice. Girls were tutored to understand that when a white girl broke the rules governing her sexual behavior, the social cost could be, as more than one former maternity home inmate put it, "worse than death." Many young women caught in the regime of the maternity home reported later that they learned this core lesson: that they were different from the black girls they glimpsed pushing baby buggies outside the gates of the home. The ones outside were not locked up, and they got to keep their babies.

The "invention of adoption" underscored the differences between white unwed mothers and unwed mothers of color. Postwar adoption practices also underscored the difference between the "value" of white babies and the "value" of babies of color. Politicians, the media, and other cultural forces defined "illegitimate" babies of poor women of color as lacking value and as creating expense for white taxpayers. These infants were consigned to their own poor mothers. White babies born to unwed mothers were, at the same time, defined as prizes, worth great sums of money and great quantities of love to thousands of white couples competing with each other to have such a child for their own, to complete their family.[45]

Value of white v. black babies

White babies as prizes

MANAGING ABORTION

No official of the federal government publicly mentioned abortion in the postwar decades. No laws were proposed or passed to respond to the extremely high rates of illegal abortion all over the country. But in the 1940s and 1950s, in another form of centrally planned response to women's reproduction-related activity, this changed. Politicians and law enforcement officials in cities and towns nationwide mounted aggressive campaigns to arrest abortion practitioners. And doctors, in yet another centralized strategy, set up hospital abortion committees to decide which women had "good reason" to end a pregnancy and which did not. In the last section of this chapter, I will show how abortion became a public issue in the postwar decades and consider what kind of an issue it became.[46]

In our own times, abortion practitioners in the United States have been targeted and reviled by radical anti-reproductive-rights activists and sometimes isolated by their communities. In the 1990s, many wore bulletproof vests in public, and most had unlisted home telephone numbers. Abortion practitioners in the immediate postwar decades took no such precautions. They operated with varying degrees of secrecy, but did not fear for their lives. In fact, a number of abortionists in the illegal era provided their services for years—twenty, thirty, forty years, and more—completely unimpeded by the law. In many communities, the local abortion practitioner's name and address were well known not only to women who might require the service but also to police and politicians, who generally regarded a good abortionist in town as a public health asset. As we've seen, in most communities, an unwritten agreement prevailed between law enforcement and practitioners: no death, no prosecution.

But after World War II, in the context of women's massive reproductive disobedience and rights claims, the old agreement was rather suddenly canceled. Now practitioners were arrested, convicted, and sent to jail in unprecedented numbers, even when there was no evidence of a botched abortion. Many of the arrested abortionists were highly skilled, having performed twenty or more abortions a day, year after year.

If we look at when and how these arrests were carried out and at how abortion trials were conducted, we can get a sense of what was at issue. We can begin to understand the agendas of the district attorneys, judges, and politicians who managed the postwar crackdowns. Often scandal-tainted mayors and police forces used abortion prosecutions to show that municipal governance and law enforcement were not corrupt or negligent, as charged. In many cities what stands out is that everything about these prosecutions—as seen through the sensationalized media coverage of police raids, arrests, and trials—transformed abortion from the everyday, if semisecret, event that it was during the Depression into a crime.

Many police chiefs, together with a DA's office, an eager crime-busting reporter, or a group of city fathers concerned with restoring their city's reputation, scouted for ways to make their case. They chose a Cold War strategy: expose the "hidden" enemy and "cleanse" the city in the process. In Los Angeles, San Francisco, Cincinnati, St. Louis, Trenton, Portland, and other cities, even though there was no public antiabortion agenda (that is, nobody publicly expressed concerns about unborn babies), abortionists and their clients became targets for arrest. Women abortionists, especially, represented a political opportunity. Few were medical doctors; most were chiropractors, nurses, or naturopaths. They were vulnerable. They did not have dignified professional colleagues who would stand up in court for them. They had almost no chance of making a credible defense.

Also, abortion cases evoked sex and secrecy and other titillating matters, and so the arrests were exciting. The lurid headlines sold newspapers. Through the sensational coverage of arrests and salacious trials, the public learned that their police force and their mayor and others were exposing female misbehavior and, in the process, addressing a crucial postwar question: Who is and who is not a "real" woman? When the female abortionists and their clients were defined in the courtroom as perverse and unwomanly, the qualities of "real womanhood" were clarified and reaffirmed.

Lawyers and judges—the men in charge at the courthouse—conducted the abortion trials quite brutally. They oversaw a courtroom in which both the female abortion provider and the person who had gone for the operation were degraded, humiliated, divided against each other, and exposed. The most private facts of these women's lives were publicly revealed and reviled. It was not uncommon for the lawyer defending the abortionist to hideously humiliate the girl on the witness stand. The lawyer's job, after all, was to save his client, the abortion provider, from going to prison.

The lawyer might calculate that a sexually shamed girl was not a credible witness. In most trials, the lawyer quickly moved to shred a woman's claim to sexual modesty and propriety. A popular tactic was to get the girl to admit that she had slept with a man not her husband, or that she was just plain promiscuous. In the trial of one female abortionist, for example, the defense attorney's tactic was typical. "You have been pregnant before?" he asked Polly Smith, the girl who had gone for the abortion. "And you were not married? You have never been married, have you? Who is the father of this child, if you care to tell, or would you care to tell us if the same man was the father both times?" At this point, the prosecutor objected. Polly, of course, had no lawyer of her own, despite her obvious need for a champion. She was only a witness for the prosecution, though she may well have felt as if she were on trial. But the judge found none of the defense lawyer's questions objectionable. Not surprisingly, Polly did. "Well, I'd rather not answer these questions," she said, but the judge made her respond.

Quite often, prosecuting lawyers seemed to act on the theory that the more sexual references and sexual innuendo they could spread around in the courtroom, the more perverse the case, and the more perverse and guilty the accused. So in the name of cleansing the community of the foul stench associated with abortion, prosecutors spread sex around quite thickly. Over and over, women were forced to describe in open court how they undressed in the abortionist's office. They were made to respond to questions like this: "Miss Smith, when Dr. Jowers examined you—I don't like to be unpleasant about the thing—but I just want to know if he inserted his hand or his finger into your vagina?" And then, "Miss Polly, maybe somebody may not know what you mean when you say your 'privates.' Which of your privates was it that she injected her instruments into? Did she insert it into your rectum?" To which Polly answered weakly, "I know where she put it, but I don't know how to tell you."

In some trials, girls and women had pictures of their "privates" drawn on courtroom chalkboards ("to a pretty large scale, please") for the edification of the audience. They sat in the witness box as the abortion table was wheeled into the courtroom and placed in front of them. They were told to speak up and describe exactly how they were placed on the table ("How far apart would you say your legs were spread?"). They were made to identify the "macabre" tools of the trade, also brought into the courtroom, and tell which ones were placed inside which of their orifices.

The abortion trial "script" allowed for men—doctors, lawyers, judges, journalists, and myriad expert witnesses—to stand up in the courtroom and reaffirm their prerogatives over women's bodies and their lives. The abortion trial was a show that almost always included elements of cryptoporn, that is, it specialized in moments that titillated the crowd while provoking shame and repugnance.

These scenarios were enacted against a backdrop of demands for the redomestication of women after the Depression and war years. Cultural arbiters ordered white women to go "back home," to be proper wives and mothers, to be content with their lot. The incidence of abortion after the war provided distressing evidence that many women were resisting some parts—or all—of this prescription. The trials provided the opportunity to humiliate resisters, to reiterate the injunction, and to clarify an important source of cultural as well as legal authority. These courtroom spectacles announced the danger and the just deserts for any woman associated with abortion.

The prosecutions also carried the message that abortion practitioners in the criminal era were vermin, "back-alley butchers," and horribly dangerous. But as I mentioned earlier, the historical evidence shows that most abortion providers, performing the operation day in and day out, were skilled. Even before the use of antibiotics, only a tiny percentage of abortions were "botched." Contrary to the myths about the illegal era, there is no evidence of high mortality or morbidity rates associated with abortion—except in cases of self-induced abortions.

People who saw the results of antiabortion laws firsthand in the illegal era—the physicians and public health officials who kept tabs on emergency room traffic—were well aware that it was not the physician-abortionist, or the midwife or chiropractor or even nonmedical people trying to make a buck, who caused abortion-seeking girls and women the most physical damage before *Roe v. Wade*. Unquestionably, the greatest damage came from the hands of the unwillingly pregnant woman herself, so desperate and resourceless, so shamed and determined, that she took up a hideous array of herbs and implements, despite the specter of damage and death from self-styled abortions that haunted every woman in those days.

The famous sexologist Dr. Alfred Kinsey and his colleagues in the 1950s estimated that 75 to 85 percent of septic abortions were self-induced. An obstetrician in Washington, D.C., observed in 1958 that attempts to suppress abortion simply raised the self-induced abortion rate and consequently the death rate.

The greatest source of danger to women in this era was hardly the so-called back-alley butcher. The greatest source of danger was *the law* itself—and the cultural and political context in which the law was sometimes enforced, sometimes not. A glimpse into the courtroom when abortion was a crime lets us see how the law placed women in danger. The trials illustrate how danger flows when an activity is simultaneously illegal, culturally taboo, and considered one of life's necessities by women. Under these circumstances, the opportunities abound for exploiting women while enhancing the power of male authority. Anyone in the courtroom could see that enforcing antiabortion laws involved the degradation of women. Here was the core lesson of these trials: every woman, whether she ever had or ever would climb up on the abortionist's table, was endangered by the statutes that criminalized abortion. That was because the law and the prosecutions drove home a powerful message—that women dare not try to claim reproductive self-determination.

Understanding these dangers, many women who could pay for private doctors made appointments to ask or to beg for help ending pregnancies they could not manage. Doctors were accustomed to receiving these kinds of desperate visits. But in the postwar era, many felt new political, cultural, and scientific pressures to refuse. DA's and their unpredictable crackdowns scared doctors. Many doctors themselves subscribed to postwar cultural mandates that defined women's bodies as safe, reproductive containers for the fetus. Many doctors participated in reinvigorating the mandates that stressed women's destiny as mothers. One prominent obstetrician explained women's suitability for this destiny: "Woman is a uterus surrounded by a supporting mechanism and a directing personality."

As doctors adapted their practices to these ideas, the number of hospital-based "therapeutic" abortions—common in the 1930s—plummeted. But women pressed doctors for help in ending pregnancies in ever-growing numbers in the postwar era. All this begging left doctors uncertain about what to do and how to protect themselves. Often, psychiatrists helped out in the crisis, offering obstetricians and gynecologists psychologically based ways of selecting who should and who shouldn't be permitted an abortion.

Even with help from psychiatrists, though, physicians felt a need for something more to strengthen their position as abortion decision makers. After the war they began to assemble themselves into hospital abortion committees that enabled doctors to issue decisions in one "scientific" voice about which women would be allowed to get therapeutic abortions. This arrangement lent doctors legal protection, kept the number of abortions low in any one hospital, and generally satisfied many doctors as a good solution.

But unhappily pregnant women were not so thrilled. The doctor of a physically exhausted mother of three little ones who was determined to have no more children told his patient that abortion was unnecessary and immoral. This woman may have been determined enough to persist and make an application to the abortion committee (a humiliating and coercive innovation, from her point of view, that no one had even heard of a year earlier). Dr. Alan Guttmacher, a great champion of these committees, wrote a description at the time of how his committee worked at Mt. Sinai Hospital in New York: "The director of the obstetrical and gynecological service is chairman of the permanent abortion committee. The other members are the chief, or a senior attending, from the departments of medicine, surgery, neuropsychiatry, and pediatrics. The board has a scheduled weekly meeting-hour and convenes routinely whenever a case is pending. No case is considered unless the staff ob-gyn desiring to carry out the procedure presents affirmative letters from two consultants in the medical field involved. Five copies of each letter must be filed at least forty-eight hours in advance of the meeting. The ob-gyn whose case it is, and one of the two consultants who made the recommendation, must make themselves available at the meeting for further information when desired. In addition, if the chairman feels that an expert from some other department would be helpful in arriving at a proper decision, this specialist is requested to attend as a nonvoting member. The case is then carefully discussed and if any member of the five on the committee opposes therapeutic interruption, the procedure is disallowed."

Many women who went through this ordeal in the postwar decades remember their experience with the abortion committee as among the most awful of their lives. In retrospect, the committees did provide some women with an opportunity of sorts to plead their own cases, to explain their unwillingness to be pregnant. In this way, the hospital abortion board cracked open a space for the individual woman's voice. But many women whose cases went before the committee spoke afterward about having been "on trial" before a group of male physicians who did not pay attention to the cardinal principle of the U.S. legal system. The physicians did not assume the women's innocence. Instead, in many cases, physicians on hospital abortion boards assumed that women applying for permission to terminate pregnancies were neurotic, selfish, vain, or guilty of other terrible gender flaws.

Plus, for some women who put their cases before these boards, the worst was still ahead. Many women who were "successful" with the committee found, to their horror, that they had been granted permission to have an abortion only if they agreed to be sterilized at the same time. One doctor explained, "A serious effort is made to control the need for dealing with the same problem in the same patient twice." One doctor, angry at his colleagues for sterilizing women who underwent abortion, declared, "The fairly common practice of insisting on sterilization if an abortion is permitted may have arisen from dealing with epileptics or feeble-minded women. It carries on as a punishment or a threat—as if the physician is saying, 'All right, if you do not want this baby, you are not capable of having any.'"

Studies conducted at the time showed that abortion-related sterilization had indeed become a fairly common practice in the early fifties. More than 53 percent of teaching hospitals made simultaneous sterilization a condition of approval for abortion, and in all U.S. hospitals, the rate was 40 percent. One doctor, unhappy about the fact that unwillingly pregnant women were being forced to accept sterilization, observed that the practice had the effect of driving women to illegal abortionists to escape the likelihood that dealing with law-abiding physicians would lead to permanent loss of their fertility. He added, "I would like to point out because [therapeutic abortion and sterilization at the same time] is so frequent, I therefore consider them fortunate to have been illegally rather than therapeutically aborted and thus spared sterilization."

The doctor accurately assessed the experiences of many women in the postwar decades. As pregnant women made their way through this nightmare maze of newly conceived psychological and cultural ideas about pregnancy and abortion, many of them declined the opportunity to become supplicants before the abortion panels. Many held fast to the idea that a particular pregnancy could be dangerous or damaging. So while abortion boards were sitting in hospitals around the country, hundreds of thousands of women each year did the only thing they felt they could. They sought out illegal practitioners everywhere.

The postwar era was the last period in this history when cultural (and political and legal) authorities could even semicredibly claim that sex was supposed to be for married people only. Everyone knew that ever-larger numbers of unmarried people, including women, engaged in sexual relations. In the postwar decades, many authorities, including the parents of unmarried females, still preferred to claim that nice women had sex in order to have babies, within loving marriages. But everyone knew that women of all kinds, married and unmarried, now had sex without intending to become pregnant. Without legal access to birth control or abortion, this was a dangerous development.

The 1940s and 1950s were a time when powerful cultural and legal mandates expressed desperate determination to beat back undeniable evidence that women were claiming sexual and reproductive autonomy. These efforts to reassert control over women's sexual and reproductive behavior were exerted in a context where relatively powerless people—women and people of color—were beginning to claim a variety of human rights.

Authorities who issued sexual and reproductive mandates were still formidable in the 1940s and 1950s. Their ability to craft and impose centrally planned laws, policies, and other strategies was still intact. Over the course of the 1960s and beyond, these authorities would lose a great deal of their force and coherence. The capacity of the state and voluntary organizations to centrally plan the outcomes of women's sexual and reproductive experiences would become much weaker—perhaps moribund. Human rights claims—and individual choices—began, here and there, and then collectively, to eclipse the gray central planners in Washington and around the country.

5

The Human Rights Era

The Rise of Choice,
the Contours of Backlash, 1960–1980

IN THE 1950s, nobody was allowed to say the word "pregnant" on TV. The Federal Communications Commission and broadcast executives wouldn't permit it, even when Lucille Ball, the well-loved star of *I Love Lucy*, was visibly *expecting*. "Pregnant" was apparently too strongly physical and too crudely sexual a word to fit into America's living rooms. It wasn't long, though, before "pregnancy" was everywhere.

By the end of the 1950s, concern about the worldwide "population explosion"—and about the way that poor people were making human rights claims—turned the public spotlight on women's fertile bodies, at home and around the globe. The problems and the vocabulary of reproduction became culturally and politically hot. Some experts warned that uncurbed fertility would exacerbate the "mass neurosis" stalking the country. Others prescribed curbing fertility to contain "world chaos." The pope and the Roman Catholic bishops of the United States spoke out sharply against interfering with fertility. The pope especially deplored antipoverty strategies that relied on "erroneous doctrines and pernicious and death-dealing methods" of birth control, by which he meant all birth control.

In 1959 President Dwight Eisenhower, a Republican, gave a major address on the subject of female fertility and foreign policy. The president seemed to be looking over one shoulder toward Catholic voters. Then he seemed to look over the other shoulder at the Republican Party's likely 1960 Democratic rivals, many of whom were in favor of a government role in curbing female fertility. In the speech, Eisenhower barred the use of foreign aid funds to disseminate birth control. He said,

"I cannot imagine anything more emphatically a subject that is not a proper political or governmental activity or function or responsibility."[1]

But in truth, Eisenhower's own administration was already paying for birth control activities in the United States. When state health officers in Alabama, Mississippi, North Carolina, Virginia, Florida, Georgia, and South Carolina had asked for federal money to support contraception programs for poor, largely African American populations, the Eisenhower administration had sent funds.

The late 1950s was a fearful era: the Cold War, the atomic bomb, the specter of race revolution, and the "population explosion" constituted an apocalyptic quartet. Commentators cited all four as forces that threatened to benefit the Soviet Union and harm the United States, perhaps even fatally. These threats, though, were not always represented accurately. By the end of the Eisenhower administration, for example, the rate of population growth in the United States had slowed, raising questions about how worried Americans should be about overpopulation in this country. With larger numbers of women entering and remaining in the workforce, the birthrate was likely to decline further.

Nevertheless, political commentators and others seemed to see the superfertile female body everywhere—and imagined this body as racially, sexually, politically explosive. Experts and ordinary citizens pointed to this fecund female body to explain what was wrong with the world—and how to fix it. "Overpopulation" was an idea that spoke in different ways to different parts of the population, but it always focused on the fertile female body. Doctors and diplomats blamed excessively fertile women in Latin America and other poor regions for creating revolutionary pressures in "the most unfortunate, miserable and devastated regions of the planet." *New York Times* editorialist James Reston remarked, "It cannot be said too often that sexual energy may prove to be a greater menace to the human family by the end of this century than atomic energy."[2] Experts defined the task ahead: stop the female body from conceiving.

The implications of overpopulation were especially dire, experts still claimed, because democracy could not flourish in a society producing "too many" babies. Overpopulation bred hunger and squalor and revolutionary movements under the leadership of men who would turn to the Soviet Union for support. In the mid-1960s, a group of experts meeting at the White House expressed the concern that the consequences of rapid population growth were so serious that the current generation of fertile women could be "the last generation" allowed to deal with fertility "on the basis of free choice."[3] Members of this group raised the possibility of forced sterilization and other government-managed strategies to reduce female fertility worldwide.

Other commentators still committed to central planning focused on the dangers associated with fertility in the United States, where Gallup polls showed Americans increasingly worried about overpopulation and increasingly likely to use birth control.[4] In the early 1960s, policy analysts began to argue that because of the crisis, some unmarried women and girls should be included in family planning programs supported by federal antipoverty funds. In what was less a call for democratic access to birth control than a strategy for reproductive containment, columnists Rowland Evans and Robert Novak, for example, wrote about *certain* fertile bodies, marking them very specifically and enhancing their visibility: "The precise heart of the problem is unmarried women and married women not living with their husbands. The American problem of exploding population is centered in illegitimate Negro births in the slums of the great Northern cities."[5] Going further —and articulating what would become a comprehensive and enduring way to assess the impacts of the reproductive capacities of poor women of color—Philip Hauser, a prominent demographer, claimed that over-population of these cities would "worsen the United States unemployment problem, greatly increase the magnitude of juvenile delinquency, exacerbate already dangerous race tensions, . . . greatly increase traffic accidents and fatalities, augment urban congestion and further subvert the traditional American governmental system."[6]

In other venues, the fertile bodies of white middle-class women were portrayed as beneficial to society. Middle-class marital fertility was a sign of approved sexual pleasure and a seal of family formation. Equally important, when a middle-class woman had a baby, the birth became an occasion for exercising the family's purchasing power. Her fertility was still the engine of the country's powerful consumer economy.[7] Her sexuality was the spark.

What especially marked this period was that now many grassroots and national campaigns for human rights and civil rights defined female fertility as the key to both women's oppression and women's liberation. Women's rights advocates began in the 1960s to define reproductive autonomy as a core requirement of full citizenship status for women. In various ways, different feminist constituencies insisted that women themselves must have the right to decide whether and when to become mothers. These claims expressed women's determination to make female fertility visible—not as a symbol of overpopulation but in order to achieve reproductive rights. These claims were supported by testimonies, grassroots organizing, and marches, by court decisions and legislation. They were opposed by some religious groups, and by "antigenocide" Black nationalists. But in all cases, female fertility was now front and center in the public square. Female fertility became an intense, culture-rending issue. Between 1960 and 1980, sex-and-pregnancy—female reproductive capacity—its uses and abuses became a national issue in the United States as never before, in large part because women themselves claimed a central role in every aspect of the debate.

The rest of this chapter is divided into five sections. First is a consideration of the birth control pill—its emergence, the way it was marketed, and various responses to this new contraception in 1960 and the years after that. I will review the racially specific impacts of the pill on women's lives and on their physical well-being. The next section recounts the last years of criminal abortion in the 1960s and the political and cultural conditions that made the Supreme Court's 1973 *Roe v. Wade* decision likely. Then the chapter moves on to a discussion of campaigns for abortion rights at the end of the 1960s and the beginning of the 1970s and how these efforts were racially distinct. It describes the surprising coalition of organizations—from antiwelfare politicians and population control groups to activist feminists—who believed that the United States needed to legalize abortion. The chapter goes on to look at reproductive politics in the context of the civil rights movement and to assess the impact of post-*Roe* legislation that aimed to make reproductive liberty the right of women who could pay for it. Finally, this chapter considers the rise of the anti-abortion-rights movement and its goals.

THE PILL

In the spring of 1960 the U.S. Food and Drug Administration (FDA) approved the birth control pill as a safe and effective contraceptive. In its statement of approval, the FDA avoided any mention of moral issues the pill might raise. That same spring, Pope John XXIII urged parents to have as many children as they possibly could. Many people at the time believed that with these words, the pope was underscoring the Catholic Church's opposition to contraception. John F. Kennedy, a leading candidate for the U.S. presidency that year, felt compelled, in part because 1960 was the year of the new birth control pill—and he stood to become the country's first Catholic president—to define his vision of America as a country "where no religious body seeks to impose its will directly or indirectly upon the general populace or the public acts of officials."[8] Kennedy's statement and other reassurances placated the venerable family planning advocate Margaret Sanger, who had vowed to leave the United States if the Catholic candidate were elected. On November 10, 1960, a few days after the presidential election, Mrs. Sanger announced her compromise: she would give the administration one year before deciding whether to go or to stay.[9] The pill drew public figures and ordinary people into religious debates, moral conundrums, and watercooler jokes about the fertile female body. Experts and nonexperts recognized immediately that the pill changed everything about sex and fertility.

From 1960 forward, politicians, demographers, and economists issued statements defining the pill as the solution to overpopulation worldwide. Policymakers defined a new relationship between fertility and poverty. With the advent of the pill, pregnancy prevention would become *the* simple, cost-effective strategy to prevent poverty. The pill would ameliorate global and national problems while making life much better for individual women. Now a woman could curb fertility without involving her sexual partner at all. A failsafe method of contraception would, many early analysts also pointed out, allow women to enjoy sex a lot more.

In 1960 everyone knew a woman with a sad story like Francine's. Francine was a girl who had gone to high school in the 1950s, when there was "no contraceptive information at all." Francine got pregnant in 1955, and later, looking back, she said, "It was devastating. It was probably the most difficult thing I've ever gone through in my life. I was a senior in high school. I would have been valedictorian of my class. I dropped out of school—at my mother's request—three months before graduation. I was sixteen. It was devastating because I had already been accepted at two colleges. I had scholarships all lined up. Everybody was devastated; teachers were devastated, my friends, and my family. It was just a very difficult, difficult thing."[10] Now with the pill, many girls and women could imagine a world with no more Francines. The pill would give American women what an essayist in the *Saturday Evening Post* called "a new kind of life."[11]

Not all Americans in the early 1960s wanted to imagine wives and sisters and especially daughters living free, sexual lives. Sociologist and journalist Andrew Hacker soothed fears, explaining, "When a majority of girls state they would like to have the pill available, it does not mean that they are about to embark on a nymphomaniacal orgy. Quite the contrary. It suggests that they wish to catch themselves a husband and simply desire to have both a sexual relationship and contraceptive protection during the period of engagement." Young women, Hacker added, are planning to use birth control pills "sparingly" and "monogamously."[12] All of these various discussions about the meanings and implications of the pill started up in 1960 and continued for decades, and all of them brought women's sexual, fertile bodies explicitly into the forefront of the consciousness—and into the mind's eye—of ordinary Americans as never before.

Very early on, these public considerations of the birth control pill were severely racialized. When experts talked about the pill in relation to white women, focus was on pleasure and an enhanced life. The pill would create "a stronger love between husband and wife." It would make possible "warmer relations between parents and children." It would diminish the pain of menstruation. When public discussion centered on unmarried white girls using the pill, many people did express trepidation about sex before marriage. But over time, the dominant theme was "protection." With the pill, a girl could protect her reputation and her future. Everyone knew that if unmarried white girls could get hold of the pill, they could have sex with their boyfriends and not end up in maternity homes with a baby they had to give away.[13]

When experts spoke publicly or to each other about the pill in relation to women of color—generally African Americans in the 1960s—the focus was on restraint. By the mid-1960s, Democrats and Republicans in Congress agreed: family planning, preferably in the form of birth control pills, was the best way to curb "social discord created by unwanted, out-of-wedlock births" among "Negroes." And the birth control pill was accepted as the best way to solve the welfare mess. The 1967 amendments to the Social Security Act required state welfare agencies to develop programs for distributing birth control. For the first time, the federal government would fund the birth control programs of nonprofit, nongovernmental groups such as Planned Parenthood. As public policy historian Donald Critchlow put it, these programs "brought the federal government gently but explicitly into the business of family planning."[14] Clearly, the government was investing in services where it expected the beneficiaries to be Black.

At the height of the civil rights movement, then, politicians, policy-makers, public officials, and the personnel of many service agencies used racially distinct definitions of birth control. And they deployed the new miracle pill accordingly. The earliest meanings attached to the pill generated new ways of distinguishing between females of different "races."

As soon as the pill was on the market, public discussions turned toward portentous, often racialized questions about the relationship between sexuality, reproduction, womanhood, and good consumer behavior. For example, as we have seen in earlier chapters, concepts of ideal womanhood had historically involved sexual purity, fecundity, and motherhood. In what ways did sex-without-consequences, facilitated by the pill, reshape the meaning of womanhood? Early on, cultural arbiters such as Sarah Gibson Blanding, the president of Vassar College, then a women's school, imagined her students engaging in "offensive and vulgar behavior" in the era of the pill. She imagined girls in serious danger of destroying their claim to good womanhood.

The director of the health center at another college could accept white female students having sex free of pregnancy scares, but only under conditions he approved. Dr. Russell Johnson explained that before he gave a student birth control pills, he wanted to "know why she wanted it." He said, "I want to feel I'm contributing to a good solid relationship and not to promiscuity."[15] As we can see from Dr. Johnson's rationalization of his practices, white college girls and others were pushing mainstream authorities to redefine ideal white womanhood so that out-of-wedlock sex was not a disqualifying behavior. Put another way, both unmarried and married white females, empowered by the pill, redefined sex as a two-track experience. When the pill allowed women to embrace sex as nonprocreative, pleasurable fun, these females were in effect embracing a new definition of ideal white womanhood—a definition that finally turned away from chastity.

Second, with the pill on the market, many authorities raised this question: Could women be rational choice makers? Experts typically described white females as better able to exercise rational choice than women of color, yet most commentators found all women seriously deficient choice makers. Once the birth control pill was available, experts tended to blame all unintended pregnancies on women's "laziness, stupidity and reluctance." In the 1960s Lawrence Lader, a great champion of abortion rights, bemoaned the fact that "[m]any women are still frighteningly irresponsible about birth control and are ignorant or lazy enough to use methods like rhythm and withdrawal, which hardly deserve to be ranked as contraception."[16]

In the 1960s, drug companies launched enormous advertising campaigns to promote birth control pills. But the advertisements did not try to appeal to prospective customers as adult, rational choice makers. Instead, they appealed through the deeply and famously "irrational" traits of females—vanity, frivolity, and femininity. Advertisements sported "lace-and-roses borders." The pills themselves were "sold in 'feminine and fashionable' dispensers that looked like powder compacts and telephone dials." One California doctor, worried about misuse of the pill, imagined women inappropriately and dangerously applying old-fashioned female traditions to the serious scientific business of contraception: "There is certainly a lot of pill swapping [going on], like sugar and eggs."[17] On the one hand, ads for birth control products appealed to white women, using liberatory language: "Are you missing out on the new freedom in family planning?" On the other hand, commentators constantly worried that women who chose freedom would not choose to use it properly. Mary Steichen Calderone, a prominent advocate of sex education and the medical director of Planned Parenthood, expressed her concern this way: "We now have the means of separating our sexual and our reproductive lives . . . and we have a great responsibility to make proper use of both of them."[18]

In this era, the president of Planned Parenthood, Dr. Alan Guttmacher, a great advocate for both teen access to contraception and abortion rights, spoke unselfconsciously about the ways that race and class affected a woman's ability to be a successful chooser and user of the birth control pill. Private (white, middle-class) patients were good users. Clinic (poor, nonwhite) patients were not. Experts typically cast clinic patients as poor choice makers, irresponsible and fickle-minded. When the intrauterine device (IUD) became available in the late 1960s and early 1970s, Guttmacher advocated its use in "underdeveloped areas." He believed that only a fixed implant like the IUD could make up for the lack of motivation typical of females living in these places. Guttmacher particularly liked the fact that "once the damn thing is in, the patient cannot change her mind."[19]

Many analysts and policymakers argued implicitly in the 1960s that choice was a privilege of class. That is, elites took the position that overpopulation and urban poverty and "family breakdown" (and the high taxes required to respond to these social problems) were such dire issues in the United States that poor women simply had to use a technical solution like the pill to cure national crises. One commentator, writing in the *New York Times Magazine,* identified birth control as the correct prescription for neutralizing the "virus of failure" that infected the inner city. The medicine would be delivered this way: "We need to penetrate into the home, as though a plague were raging." This author and others effaced the choice-making poor woman. The situation was too serious for either individual decision making or freedom of choice, generally.[20]

Other analysts relied on rational choice exercised by economists and government-sponsored clinics, not by women. Here is how one prominent expert calculated the role of family planning in the reduction of poverty: "Using conservative assumptions, the costs of family-planning programs are estimated to average $300 to prevent every unwanted birth that would otherwise have occurred. Over the years, however, the avoidance of an unwanted child would save the family an average of $8000 in the costs of child care. . . . When all of these earnings are discounted to the year in which the unwanted births were prevented, the total economic benefits average $7,800 for every three hundred dollars spent on family planning services."[21] Clearly, this calculation relied on cost-benefit analysis, not women's rights, as the route to fixing overpopulation.

Ultimately, American women posed and answered their own questions about the pill. Between 1960 and 1962 the number of new prescriptions for the Enovid birth control pill increased tenfold, from 191,000 to 1,981,000. A 1960 Planned Parenthood study of contraceptive use had found that whites preferred condoms, African Americans the douche, and Mexican Americans the diaphragm. By 1968, even though a higher percentage of whites had switched to the pill than other groups, American women of all races and classes—and religions—constructed their own systems of rational choice. Millions chose the pill. At the end of the 1960s, American women spent $150 million annually on birth control pills, the same amount that Americans spent on all birth control methods combined in 1958.[22]

Many poor women, however, could not afford to use the pill. African American women in some areas of the South, for example, where poor people, working as sharecroppers and household workers, had little or no access to cash money, did not have the one dollar a month that health clinics were charging for birth control. In some northern cities, there were other obstacles, such as pharmacists who would sell only one month's worth of pills at a time to women on Medicaid, since government reimbursements were so slow.[23]

A study in the late 1960s of attitudes toward birth control among Black women in Chicago found that 80 percent approved of its use and that 75 percent used some form of birth control.[24] Despite high approval rates, many poor women in communities where educational and employment opportunities remained bleak still found that motherhood was the most accessible route to adulthood. Often it was the only track that young women could identify. As sociologist Joyce Ladner observed at the time, "The ultimate test of womanhood . . . is one's ability to bring forth life," and do the same things that your own mother has done. Ladner interviewed one sixteen-year-old young woman who explained how becoming a mother could change someone's life: "First of all, they consider themselves grown and then they just start acting like grown women. They don't think they're children anymore. They won't listen to anybody."[25]

Historian Rivka Polatnick described how in Mt. Vernon, New York, outside of New York City, African American girls and women experienced motherhood as both a source of power for females and the "locus of oppression." Many of these mothers struggled to pay for day care and housing while working for indecent wages, barely able to support their children. Polatnick tells how some grown women of color in Mt. Vernon began "to knock on doors in poor Black neighborhoods . . . to make birth control available to teenage girls." These women were coming to the conclusion that the lack of birth control could hurt a woman's life as much as a bad landlord, poor schools and hospitals, and the welfare system. One by one, and then in groups, mothers, domestic workers, factory workers, and welfare recipients were "drawing connections between their daily problems" such as unintended pregnancies "and the larger system of social and economic relations."[26]

In white communities, too, women were defining female fertility and motherhood as a mixed blessing, and not necessarily the route to adulthood. As feminist Betty Friedan famously *regretted* in *The Feminine Mystique*—illustrating the difference between a middle-class white woman's perspective and a Black teenager's—"Having a baby is the only way to become a heroine."[27] In this context, the birth control pill was not a simple gift.

From many standpoints, American women claimed the birth control pill in the 1960s at a complicated and contradictory historical moment. Powerful resistance to female reproductive autonomy clashed with women's claims for control over their own bodies. The Catholic Church insisted that women reject contraception. Outspoken politicians demanded that poor women use birth control for the good of the country. Together, these were two of the most powerful centers of resistance to women's reproductive autonomy. But perhaps the most powerful force eclipsing the interests of women themselves was the alliance between the companies manufacturing and selling the birth control pill, the doctors writing prescriptions for it, and the media reporting on the impacts of the pill. This dangerous alliance put profits ahead of women's health and safety.

As soon as the pill went on the market, obstetrician-gynecologists found themselves pressed by their middle-class private patients to write prescriptions for the new contraceptive. One poll of 2,515 of these doctors in 1967 showed that "89% of respondents said that women *expected* them to prescribe the Pill."[28] Doctors understood that when millions of women adopted a medicalized form of birth control, physicians might find their authority compromised. After all, now their practices had to respond to—not dictate—women's behavior. In addition, many physicians found themselves in the position of also having to respond to the aggressive marketing tactics of pharmaceutical companies.

Historian Elizabeth Watkins found a pharmaceutical company's in-house newsletter from that time that instructed its fifteen thousand salesmen in how to sell the birth control pill Enovid. Salesmen were instructed "to weed out all the negative points." That meant when selling the doctor on pills, the salesman should minimize discussion about cancer, religion, and all other problems the pill might raise. Salesmen should "convince doctors that 'Enovid is . . . His drug.'" Salesmen should point out to the customers that if they chose to, they could require each pill-using patient to pay for a doctor's visit every month to renew the prescription.[29]

Salesmen played down medical problems associated with the pill, and for years, so did the media. In 1966, "as the list of adverse reactions grew longer," one high-profile magazine reported that there was "absolutely no evidence" that the pill was linked to any forms of cancer and presented one authority's "well-founded opinion" that the contraceptive might prevent uterine cancer. Watkins found that journalists were quick to associate the pill with the "sexual revolution" and very slow to investigate any association between the pill and disease.[30]

All of the parties that stood to benefit from the birth control pill faced some facet of the same complicated opportunity: passion and rationality neatly arranged in one small package for sale. Both personal and financial benefits were potentially huge. According to Watkins and others, the commercial profits were so enormous that purveyors became greedy. Pharmaceutical companies permitted incomplete testing and hard-sell tactics. They resisted full disclosure of information and looked to the federal FDA for protection. Unfortunately, this willingness to put profits first continued across the 1960s and 1970s and involved manufacturers of the pill, then manufacturers of the new IUD, and then manufacturers of Depo-Provera, a long-acting contraceptive injection. Both the IUD and Depo-Provera were disseminated or widely tested on women before they were determined safe for use. Women came to expect to visit a doctor to obtain what they now frankly needed or wanted. But these new prescription contraceptions created unpredictable and sometimes dangerous birth control experiences for women.

In 1968, for example, the FDA's committee on the IUD gave this contraceptive high marks for effectiveness and safety and, echoing Planned Parenthood's Dr. Guttmacher, especially recommended it for use by "underprivileged women" because it required no further "motivation" once inserted.[31] Scientists and doctors issued reports that the devices functioned safely, but they neglected to disclose their financial interests in these products. IUD manufacturers ensured that the FDA did not classify the device as a drug, thus reducing the amount of testing required. The FDA also ignored calls for further research and "fudged" data about the effectiveness of IUDs. When the device failed or harmed users, manufacturers ignored problems with the IUD itself and blamed the "promiscuity" of users for causing serious problems such as pelvic inflammatory disease.[32]

Throughout the 1970s the public received ongoing reports that the IUD caused "chronic and acute infection, perforations, infertility, complicated pregnancies, injury to and loss of vital body parts and functions," and even death. By the late 1970s the product was no longer manufactured. But before production was halted, though many experts were aware of the dangers and damage associated with the Dalkon Shield (the brand name of the IUD manufactured by the A. H. Robbins Company), two million of those IUDs had been shipped to seventy-five countries. Many were shipped unsterilized, and packages included only one inserter for every one thousand devices. According to Andrea Tone, altogether about seven and a half million women in "developing countries" were fitted with IUDs by 1974, an accomplishment that grew out of a "collaboration of the federal government, the Population Council, and other organizations such as International Planned Parenthood and the Pathfinders Fund."[33]

The testing and introduction of Depo-Provera in the 1970s was similarly shoddy and opportunistic. Congressional hearings in 1978 on this contraceptive revealed that the injection had been administered to women in Third World countries for more than ten years, and that for eleven years, poor Black women in Atlanta, Georgia, hospitals had been given Depo-Provera shots, even though the FDA had not approved this fertility blocker. In fact, experts were aware that Depo-Provera was linked to serious problems such as stroke, permanent infertility, and fetal anomalies. Questions about the association of Depo-Provera and breast cancer had not been resolved. Throughout the 1960s and 1970s many women were profoundly disconcerted to find out that experts typically evaluated the IUD and Depo-Provera not according to the standard of safety first but according to the relationship between risk and benefit to the corporation.[34]

Many women in this era reported that when they told their doctors that they were experiencing side effects from using one of the new birth control methods, physicians typically offered soothing words and "reassurances in lieu of diagnoses and treatment." As birth control scholar Cynthia Grant put it, "[P]hysicians told their patients that the pain was emotional not physical in origin." Grant shows how, in the period when birth control dangers were becoming public matters, some powerful politicians stood behind doctors and not behind women attempting to control their fertility safely. Senator Robert Dole, a Republican from Kansas, for example, dangerously patronized women as he spoke in Congress on behalf of doctors in 1969: "We must not frighten millions of women into disregarding the considered judgment of their physicians. . . . Let us show some sympathy for the beleaguered physicians who must weigh not only the safety and efficiency of alternative methods for a particular woman, but the emotional reactions of that woman which have been generated by sensational publicity [of contraceptive damage]. . . . It would be unfortunate if efforts to assist American women only served to confuse them."[35]

Many women suffered adverse physical reactions and physical harm when they used insufficiently tested new methods of contraception. And many became feminists and seasoned activists in the process of demanding good information from their doctors and from the government. Elizabeth Watkins describes how the Washington, D.C., women's liberation group—already feminist-activists but new to the halls of Congress—showed up at the 1969 hearings on pill safety with "questions to interrupt the hearings and with bail money tucked inside their boots." According to one of the women, all of whom took the birth control pill, they were "appalled by the fact that all of the senators were men [and] all of the people testifying were men. They [had not invited to testify] a single woman who had taken the pill and no women scientists. . . . So we were there as activists but also as concerned women."

These activist women and others pushed for and won rules requiring birth control pill manufacturers to include information inserts in every package of pills. Catalyzed by the promise and the dangers of the pill, they pushed for women's right to "informed consent" and began building the women's health movement.[36] Two books—Barbara Seaman's *The Doctor's Case against the Pill* (1969) and *Our Bodies Ourselves*, the woman-centered health manual (1970)—reflected the activist energy galvanized by women's determination to have access to safe, effective birth control and to have enough information themselves to insist that physicians and other health professionals deal with them as thinking, mature adults. These two books stimulated the feminist/women's health movement, as well as the consumer rights movement, and inspired feminist activism in these domains.[37]

Throughout the 1970s, though, mainstream experts continued to argue that even if the available methods were sometimes dangerous, women should take the risk "for the good of mankind." But more and more women like "Megan" refused this argument: "It was really my experience with the Dalkon Shield," she recalled in the 1990s, "that pissed me off enough, you know, to really start getting involved in women's organizations and to know more and to become more active. . . . Thanks to A. H. Robbins, I became a feminist."[38]

The birth control pill played an important role in defining 1960s and 1970s feminisms and their agendas. It also had other swift political and policy impacts. Most dramatic, once the pill was on the market, the old Comstock Law was finally doomed.

In 1965, the Supreme Court finally struck down Connecticut's nineteenth-century Comstock Law against dispensing contraception information and materials, even to married couples. (This New England state, with a large Catholic population, was the last state to maintain such a law.) In the court's decision, *Griswold v. Connecticut,* Justice William O. Douglas defined a married couple's right to birth control as a matter "within the zone of privacy created by several fundamental [constitutional] guarantees." Drawing on the idea of family privacy, Douglas argued, in effect, that one ingredient of state-sanctioned marriage was a right to privacy that included the right to use contraception. That is, a woman's legal relation to a man rendered her a bona fide contraceptor. It took another seven years for a Supreme Court decision to finally kill the old Comstock claim that birth control was a crime against chastity: in 1972 Justice William Brennan, writing for the majority and still relying on the concept of privacy in the decision, *Eisenstadt v. Baird,* proclaimed, "If the right of privacy means anything, it is the right of the individual, married or single, to be free from unwarranted governmental intrusion into matters so fundamentally affecting a person as the decision whether to bear or beget a child."[39]

Ultimately, in the era of human rights—and the era of women's visible bodies—the pill became a catalyst for those claiming individual rights of many kinds. Young Gloria Steinem, writing in *Esquire* magazine in 1962, suggested the pill would increase women's sex drive and that it would encourage women to insist that "their sex practices are none of society's business." But still, she claimed, the pill was no "opening bombshell" for a "sexual or contraceptive revolution."[40] (A few years later, as a teenager, I probably would have gotten a kick out of Ms. Steinem's—or her editors'—attempt to comfort folks concerned about unmarried sex, as I slunk into the neighborhood pharmacy to pick up my monthly packet of birth control pills, using the name of my older sister, who had gone off to college, leaving her prescription behind.)

In the 1960s the birth control pill allowed a great many women—though not all users—to choose sex without consequences. But many more girls and women than ever before were having sex *with* consequences. Many more unmarried girls and women were beginning to define the meaning of those consequences in new ways. Between 1960 and 1970, the proportion of births to single women doubled, from 15 percent to 31 percent. And across the 1970s—after the legalization of abortion—these rates grew much more quickly for white women than for Black.[41] During these decades, thousands of unmarried white mothers were still pressed hard to give their babies away to properly married couples. But now thousands resisted the pressure.

Sociologist Joyce Ladner pointed out at the time that "Black women are now beginning to serve as 'role models' for many white women . . . who have decided to have children outside marriage." By the late 1960s many single mothers of color and single white mothers were making claims for the legitimacy of their motherhood no matter how loudly politicians, policymakers, parents, and other community authorities protested. Welfare rights advocates, as we shall see later in this chapter, built their movement partly on the claim that unmarried women, even poor ones, had the right to be mothers. And a swelling number of white women resisted the adoption mandate when they opted to keep and raise their "illegitimate" children and to claim legitimacy for their families. Presciently, Ladner imagined a new world order that could arrive, she thought, sometime in the 1980s, when "illegitimate" children and "promiscuous" women would die out as social categories. The catalyst, wrote Ladner, would be a critical mass of "middle-class white women who decide that they are going to disavow the societal canons regarding childbirth and premarital behavior. But," she added, "this has to occur before the stigmatizing labels that are now attached to Blacks are destroyed."[42]

THE END OF THE LINE FOR CRIMINAL ABORTION

Ladner and others were beginning to imagine and speak publicly about a world in which women could legitimately and legally make a great many fertility-related decisions as individuals on their own behalf. Two

related, very public events in the early 1960s made the idea of female reproductive self-determination—including access to legal abortion—
more visible to Americans, more attractive, and more understandable
than before. One was the terrible rubella, or German measles, epidemic
of the early 1960s, a public health event that put many pregnant women
at risk of delivering damaged babies. The other was the so-called Sherri
Finkbine, or thalidomide, episode in 1962 that helped many Americans
understand why any woman might need to manage her own fertility.

In this case, Sherri Finkbine, a married woman and a mother of
four, living with her husband and kids in a suburb of Phoenix, Arizona,
took some antinausea medication that she thought was harmless. Soon,
though, she realized the pills she had taken to relieve the morning sick-
ness that had come with her fifth pregnancy contained thalidomide.
This compound had recently been identified as causing dramatic fetal
anomalies, such as babies born without arms and legs or with fatal car-
diac flaws. Sherri's doctor advised her to have an abortion. At first her
hometown hospital agreed to allow a doctor on staff to perform the operation, but a few days later, fearing a legal situation that might harm
the hospital, the facility's administrators decided not to permit the
abortion.

By this time, though, Sherri was determined to end her pregnancy.
By this time, also, Sherri Finkbine's case had become public. Mrs.
Finkbine had made a public statement thanking the Phoenix newspaper
for running the news article that had alerted her to the content of the
drug she had taken by mistake. Reporters gathered around the Finkbine
house, waiting to hear the hospital's next move and report on Sherri's
reaction.

When Sherri and her husband, Bob, investigated their options, they
found that their best chance for a legal abortion was to go to Stockholm,
Sweden. There the Royal Medical Board of Sweden had approved two
thousand out of four thousand requests for abortions the previous year,
a rate much higher than any U.S. hospital abortion board. Ultimately,
the board approved Finkbine's abortion, and the Swedish doctors
found that the fetus she was carrying was in fact deeply damaged.

Sherri Finkbine's case captured the attention of America partly because she talked out loud and in public about a subject that women of
that day only whispered about to their best friends, their husbands, or
their boyfriends. Also, Sherri spoke only in terms of a mother's duty to
spare a damaged fetus from a painful life. She did not raise thoughts of

sex-gone-wrong or even of women's rights. Even though she didn't say it, she implied that a woman—especially a well-dressed, attractive, middle-class, married woman, a mother of four, like herself—could justifiably make a choice about a pregnancy that had already taken hold. In 1962, no American had heard a nice woman suggest such a thing in public.

In an entirely new way, Sherri Finkbine's statements and actions throughout her ordeal suggested the complicated proposition that middle-class American women, the world's most careful consumers, had the right to give birth to perfect babies. In the end, many Americans understood and approved of Sherri's actions because, with the rise of the adoption market and other postwar developments, even newborns and children had become commodities of sorts. As a white woman with enough money to be a legitimate choice maker, Sherri Finkbine could make a winning case that, as such, she deserved a "high-quality" child. At the same time, many Americans following this situation supported Mrs. Finkbine because they shared her belief that children deserved a decent quality of life.

Sherri Finkbine opened the door to public discussions of abortion and to the idea that a woman's life need not be in mortal danger for that woman to decide that she could not manage a particular pregnancy. The more than one million women a year who were getting illegal and hospital-approved abortions in the United States surely felt vindicated or at least represented honorably by Sherri Finkbine. The girls and women who arranged for illegal abortions over the next decade may have felt more justified and determined because for a moment in 1962, a "respectable," well-dressed wife and mother had told everybody that she was going to get an abortion, and afterward, her life went on.[43]

While *Roe v. Wade* was still a decade away, though, millions of women—young mothers in the workforce, single women, women carrying damaged fetuses, emerging feminists—were beginning to develop multiple, overlapping versions of what came to be called reproductive politics. This politics was popping up in unexpected places in addition to Phoenix, including on network television. In April 1962, for example, CBS aired an episode of its popular drama *The Defenders*, featuring a dedicated physician who is arrested for his abortion work. Because of the content, all of the show's sponsors (Brown and Williamson, the tobacco company, Lever Brothers, and Kimberly Clark) canceled their ads. In this episode, entitled "The Benefactor," the abortion-performing doctor spoke clearly about what he was doing. He explained that he did not perform the operation for money but because he thought it was the right thing to do. The drama dismissed adoption as a solution for unmarried and unwillingly pregnant women—a feature of the TV play that the television critic for the *New York Times* called "wanton extremism." And CBS affiliates in Boston, Providence, Buffalo, Rochester, Binghamton, New Orleans, Milwaukee, and other cities refused to air the episode.

But CBS stood behind the show that shredded "the national curtain of embarrassed silence." The network was willing to risk shocking many viewers as it "created sympathy for criminal conduct condemned by the laws of all states and the Federal Government."[44] By airing the show, CBS also extended at least temporarily a mainstream imprimatur of legitimacy to the issue of abortion as a personal matter, even as a human right. One wonders whether Sherri Finkbine had managed to tuck all her kids into bed in time to sit down in front of the family's television that early spring evening when CBS aired "The Benefactor."

Like Mrs. Finkbine, more women than ever were treating abortion as a personal matter, no matter what the law decreed. Public health expert Christopher Tietze estimated that in New York City alone, about fifty thousand women each year were having abortions in the 1960s. By the end of the decade, Tietze and many others acknowledged that now an unwed pregnancy seemed more like an accident than a crime. More people admitted that antiabortion laws were unenforceable and utterly incompatible with a society in which women were claiming rights to equal educational and employment opportunities, and were spending longer periods of their young womanhood unmarried.[45] Lucinda Cisler, a white feminist leader, articulated the heart of the matter at this time: "All the excellent supporting reasons [for legalizing abortion]—improved health, lower birth and death rates, freer medical practice, the separation of church and state, happier families, sexual privacy, lower welfare expenditures—are only embroidery on the basic fabric: women's right to limit her own reproduction." Cisler argued that society was more afraid of feminism than abortion. Perhaps she was correct. Only the latter could be outlawed, even if ineffectively, while the former gathered strength and focus across the 1960s.[46]

THE ABORTION RIGHTS CAMPAIGNS

Historian Jennifer Nelson and human rights activist Loretta Ross and others have shown how in the late 1960s and early 1970s, millions of American women associated themselves with campaigns for reproductive rights—campaigns that were in many ways racially defined. For the most part, white women spoke out in terms of personal autonomy. They spoke about how owning and controlling one's own body was a basic ingredient of women's liberation from the bondage of patriarchy.

For the first time in the United States, a California women's organization, the Society for Humane Abortion, explained abortion as a matter of women's right to control their reproductive lives and health. Some white feminists like journalist Ellen Willis argued that owning and controlling one's own body was necessary but not sufficient for establishing women as full citizens in the United States. Willis asserted in 1969, "The 'liberated woman,' like the 'free world,' is a fiction that obscures real power relations and defuses revolution." She asked, "How can women, subordinate in every other sphere, be free and equal in bed?" In other words, Willis argued, sexual freedom and reproductive rights were simply not achievable as long as women were paid lower wages than men for comparable work and shut out of many good employment opportunities. For women to become the equals of men would require work on many fronts.[47]

Campaigns led by white women and by women of color shared a number of ideas: that forced pregnancy was inconsistent with citizenship and constitutional rights for women; that the right to manage pregnancy was a woman's business, not the province of boyfriends, husbands, doctors, the state, or others. But many women of color brought a sharp sense of *community needs* to the task of defining this new human rights terrain. Women-of-color organizations expressed the need for reproductive rights against a history of reproductive exploitation of an entire people. Speaking out against the condemnation of poor women who reproduced, feminist leaders defined reproductive rights as the right to have children, as well as the right not to. They self-consciously spoke out as rights advocates in an era when men and women of color were often cast as agents of social destruction—or as the victims of degradation. Some government-sponsored "public education" campaigns illustrate this context. In 1968, one well-funded ad campaign linking "the population problem" with "urban decay, crime, and pollution" featured posters with tag lines such as "Have you been mugged today?" The poster showed a young Black man as the mugger and suggested that, along with Black women, he was responsible for the "population explosion," violent crime, air and water pollution, and the deterioration of the quality of life." The poster suggested, for one thing, that the world would be a better place if that man had not been born.[48]

Historian Jennifer Nelson shows how between 1969 and 1974 "a very few outspoken and powerful women" within the progressive, nationalist, and male-dominated New York–based Puerto Rican organization the Young Lords "radically altered" the political ideology of the group through their struggle for reproductive rights. These women called for access to birth control on a *voluntary* basis. They called for a high-quality public health system, for free day care, for "the absolute right of all women to have as many children as they wanted." And these women, using nationalist and feminist and community-based arguments, called for safe, legal abortion as an important component of a broad, complex, and inclusive set of reproductive rights. These arguments were rooted in a vision of community welfare and collective needs as much as—or more than—they were a call for individual freedom.[49]

From all communities, though, feminist women entered the struggle for reproductive rights acting as what political scientist Rosalind Petchesky has called "shock troops," doing underground abortion referrals and counseling and other forms of public and private activism at this time.[50] Feminist leadership and the "shock troops" met resistance early and often as they publicly called for reproductive freedom. But before 1973, there was almost no religious objection to abortion in the public square, despite the huge number of illegal abortions performed every day across the country.

This is not to say that religious leaders were silent everywhere before 1973. Historian James Mohr quotes an Iowa woman, an activist member of the Iowa Association for the Medical Control of Abortion, who wrote to a pro-rights Iowa state legislator in 1971: "It seems that no matter what the political parties, the Medical Society, the AAUW, the YWCA, the Council on Churches, or the people of Iowa want, the Catholic Church has the money and the muscle to impose its will on the rest of society."[51]

Resistance did continue to come occasionally from district attorneys and police, still trying to enforce antiabortion statutes with inter-

mittent and sensational raids, still assisting in the project of using state
power to force women to bear children. Resistance also came from doctors. Many physicians continued to use medical authority to force childbearing by channeling abortion decisions through hospital boards. Sociologist Carole Joffe has shown, though, that a number of doctors defied the law by secretly performing illegal abortions in their offices for
private patients.[52]

Resistance from Drs. (margin note)

After 1960 support for legal abortion began to come from a variety
of sources. For example, in early 1960s the American Law Institute issued guidelines for new abortion statues. The American Medical Association acknowledged that criminal abortion laws simply could not be
enforced in the United States. These organizations stressed the rights of
legal and medical professionals in the domain of abortion. While calling for abortion reform, they did not call for reproductive autonomy for
women.

Pros wanted reform—not women's autonomy (margin note)

Other groups promoted the idea of legalizing abortion in this era
simply by focusing public attention sharply on the dangers of "overpopulation." The organization Zero Population Growth (ZPG), for example, considered many ideas to reduce the expanding population,
such as putting antifertility agents in the water supply, issuing licenses
for potential parents, and sterilizing women who were dependent on
welfare. President Richard Nixon, worrying that the time for fixing the
population problem was "dangerously short," signed into law the first
explicit federal legislation to fund contraception in 1970.[53] In these ways
ZPG, Nixon, and others helped clarify the arguments of many public
figures who came (tacitly or explicitly) to include legal abortion in the
approved arsenal of population control strategies. As we will see, many
of these public figures were staunch members of the Republican Party.
And many of these Republicans quite fervently supported legal abortion on a variety of grounds, from population control to women's
rights. Unquestionably, the population controllers helped cultivate the
ground for *Roe v. Wade*.

Over the late 1960s, in the context of flourishing human rights
movements and liberation culture, support for legalized abortion kept
growing. Grassroots groups such as the Clergy Consultation Service on
Abortion, begun in New York in 1967, and Jane, an underground abortion services network in Chicago started in 1969, made safe, clandes-
tine, illegal abortion available for thousands of women. Colorado, California, North Carolina, New York, Hawaii, and Washington all soft-

ened, though they did not abolish, their abortion statutes in the late 1960s. By 1971, over half of Americans favored legalizing abortion.

Feminists organized "speak-outs," claiming expertise for themselves on the matter of abortion. Historian Rosalyn Baxandall described how these events worked, and their power: "We stood up before an overflowing crowd and remembered the details of our illegal abortions and made what had been private and personal, political and public. Keeping sexual secrets imprisons and isolates women. Sharing confidences empowers. We talked about abortion as a lived experience."[54] Feminists also mounted lawsuits as public education and political pressure campaigns. Historian Amy Kesselman described the accomplishments of one such lawsuit, *Abele v. Markle*, brought by women in Connecticut in the pre-*Roe* era: "For three years a handful of women's liberation activists brought the subject of abortion into households throughout the state, forced the conservative politics of state government into the public spotlight, and involved thousands of women in political action on behalf of reproductive freedom."[55]

A complicated group of developments—demographic trends, including the ongoing movement of women into the workforce; the rise of the population control and antiwelfare movements; the persistence of illegal abortion; the emergence of feminism and grassroots support of abortion reform; the actions of a few state legislatures; and the climate of the era that supported "rights" claims—pushed the medical and legal communities to support formal legalization. *Roe v. Wade* was, in part, a pragmatic response to this complex range of developments.

When the Supreme Court decriminalized abortion in 1973, the Court's majority based legalization on four constitutional principles: (1) women have a fundamental, constitutional right to reproductive privacy, and governmental restrictions of that right must be subjected to "strict scrutiny"; (2) the government must remain neutral regarding a woman's decision whether or not to have an abortion; (3) in the period before "viability" (the point at which the fetus is sufficiently developed to live outside of the woman's body), the government may restrict abortion only in the interests of protecting the woman's health; and (4) after "viability," the government may prohibit abortion, but laws must make exceptions that permit abortion when necessary to protect a woman's health or life. *Roe* established a "trimester" concept of pregnancy: during the first third of pregnancy, women have an unimpeded right to abortion; during the following two trimesters, a schedule of increasing restrictions apply, based on women's health and fetal viability.

The Supreme Court fully associated the right to abortion with the (marital) privacy right named eight years earlier in the *Griswold* decision. Now the Court inserted the physician, "his good judgment, his compassion, and . . . his objectivity," into the private space in which women could decide.[56] The woman's dependence on her personal, private physician in the abortion matter (and for other health concerns) did describe the realities of life for many middle-class women. "Privacy" also described middle-class women's determination to act individually and with self-determination, in their own reproductive interests. But the concept of privacy did not account for what legal scholar Reva Siegel calls "the social organization of reproductive relations." These "relations" could refer to a woman whose doctor, likely a man with more social power than his patient, might have his own beliefs and feelings about abortion or about the woman's suitability or unsuitability for motherhood. "Reproductive relations" might refer to the consequences of poverty or racism or male "privileges," including rape. "Privacy" could become, in reality, the right to ask a doctor for permission, not a guarantee of access or a right to decide these matters for oneself.[57]

Many advocates of reproductive rights were disappointed and concerned in 1973 that the majority opinion in *Roe* had relied on privacy instead of on the constitutional principle of equal protection. In retrospect, it seems paradoxical that the seven justices in the majority could have, at that historical moment, imagined a woman's reproductive decisions as private at all. On the one hand, in the waning years of the civil rights movement, granting women reproductive privacy was a way of acknowledging the human dignity of women and of defining their self-ownership. But on the other hand, women's fertile, reproducing bodies had never been so visible or publicly consequential in American society as in this era: the reproducing body had become everybody's business.

THE CIVIL RIGHTS MOVEMENT
AND REPRODUCTIVE RIGHTS

We can revisit the civil rights movement here—its claims and the various forms of resistance to those claims—to clarify how central and visible the fertile female body was in the era of human rights campaigns. During the civil rights movement, the fertile body of women of color was used over and over as a target for punishment and resistance against the movement's achievements toward racial equality. For example, in 1960, immediately after Louisiana was ordered to desegregate public schools in New Orleans, the state legislature prepared a "segregation package"—what an Urban League memo called "an act of reprisal"—that included a law defining the birth of a second illegitimate child as a crime punishable by imprisonment. The legislature also voted to remove more than twenty-two thousand children of approximately six thousand unwed mothers from the welfare rolls. Ninety-five percent of the children were African American.[58]

In 1961, a year of explosive civil rights demonstrations across the South, the city manager of Newburgh, New York, citing the arrival of southern Blacks, announced thirteen new rules to govern who could collect welfare and who could not. Welfare investigators were trained to interrogate mothers about their sex lives, especially pressing them to admit giving birth to "illegitimate children," a fact that the city manager defined as disqualifying women and children from assistance programs. The Newburgh codes included a "suitable home" provision that many welfare departments employed at this time to purge African American women from the rolls. Here the rule stated, "[P]rior to certifying any Aid to Dependent Children cases a determination shall be made as to the home environment. If it is not satisfactory the city shall take such children and place them in foster homes in place of welfare aid to family adults." The chief marker of "unsuitability" in Newburgh and elsewhere centered on the sexual and reproductive behavior of poor women.

The Newburgh case gained national attention. At the time, local and national African American analysts said that the new rules reflected the reaction of whites to the new power in numbers of Democratic Black voters in this Republican-dominated city. They pointed to the desire of the city council and real estate interests to push "Negroes" out of lucrative redevelopment areas in the city's Hudson River waterfront district. Presidential candidate Barry Goldwater had called the city manager's new welfare rules a "breath of fresh air." Others called them "Black codes," reminiscent of the laws restricting the movements —and the freedom, generally—of formerly enslaved people in the South after the Civil War. The infamous Newburgh case clarified once

again that for people interested in preserving traditional power relations—in this era of ferment and shifting power—the sexualized bodies and sexual behavior of vulnerable women made effective targets.
Images of these bodies became totems that racist whites could rally
around.

One Newburgh politician announced, "The colored people of this
city are our biggest police problem, our biggest sanitation problem, and
our biggest health problem. We cannot put up with their behavior any
longer. We have been too lenient with them." Racist talk like this over-
shadowed the fact that most welfare recipients in Newburgh, a city suffering the serious economic consequences of deindustrialization, were
white. Many people in Newburgh and around the country lost sight of
the fact that the city's welfare expenditures had not exceeded the city's
welfare budget, had not even come close. But the city manager understood the politics of backlash, and what it took to achieve a national pro-
file for himself.

The city manager did not stand alone. Drawing on what they read
about Newburgh and the welfare problems in other cities, many white
Americans came to believe in the late 1960s and early 1970s that the
chief "accomplishment" of the civil rights movement and its partner,
the federal government, was the creation (and protection) of the reproductively misbehaving and financially scamming woman: the welfare
queen. The media were instrumental in coloring this woman Black. In
earlier times, say between 1950 and 1964, when newspapers and magazines ran stories about poverty, illustrations typically showed white
people. But, as sociologist Martin Gilens has discovered, "[S]tarting in
1965, the complexion of the poor turned decidedly darker. From only
27% in 1964, the proportion of African Americans in pictures of the poor
increased to 49% and 53% in 1965 and 1966, and then to 72% in 1967."
During this period about 30 percent of poor people were African American.

These media images showed "the most negative aspects of poverty
and the least sympathetic subgroups of the poor." The images especially focused on the iconic poor woman of color, a "person" many
Americans had come to associate with the figure of the prostitute: she
had sex for money—the money she got from the government for having children.[59]

By the mid-1960s the growing belief in the welfare queen was reinforced by an overlapping belief that poor Black mothers were illegiti-

mate mothers of illegitimate children, were illegitimate caretakers, and were out to get illegitimate money.[60] Few Americans noticed that the typical welfare mother at this time was white or that during the great expansionary period of Aid to Families with Dependent Children (AFDC), 1965–1970, the nonwhite birthrate for unmarried women was declining for those twenty and older. (The teenage rates for both Blacks and whites had been rising since 1940.)[61]

My study of welfare provision and public rhetoric about welfare across the 1960s and 1970s convinces me that as grassroots activism and federal law made traditional and daily acts of racial supremacy unacceptable, local officials—and then national leaders—turned ever more often to the welfare system as a citadel of states' rights and local power. Across this period, welfare officials remained empowered—using suitable home rules and man-in-the-house rules—to target and "investigate" and degrade poor mothers of color and their families. This power was often invoked in locations where the civil rights movement was especially successful.

Campaigns against poor, reproducing women harmed individual women while keeping alive opposition to human rights struggles. These campaigns also aimed in the midst of the civil rights movement to define reproducing poor women of color as a class as lacking the fundamental attribute of modern, adult women: the ability to make a rational choice.

In Louisiana, the state constitution explicitly tied the poor choice making of "illegitimate mothers" to the denial of citizenship rights. The law said that women with out-of-wedlock babies could not vote—a bald effort to deny the citizenship right that was the central focus of the civil rights movement. From around the country came a related sentiment: mothers of color who did not benefit from the "guarantees" of the civil rights movement and remained poor had only themselves—and their own bad choices—to blame. Many Americans pointed to the unrealized goals of this liberation movement to show that bad women perpetually making bad choices were not living up to their new rights.

In the era of "women's liberation," these poor, reproducing women were also accused of deepening their status as poor choice makers because they became mothers without being able to afford children, economically. Giving birth while poor became a sign of failure to benefit from women's new economic opportunities. Middle-class women were supposed to achieve personal liberation by achieving economic self-sufficiency. Any woman who didn't achieve economic self-sufficiency had only herself (and her contraceptive ineptitude) to blame.

In this way, the escalating rates of women's workforce participation became a reason to disqualify poor women from proper status as mothers. Women who earned enough at work (or who had husbands who did) were the ones who *earned the right to choose motherhood.* Even though women of color as a group had always had higher rates of workforce participation than white women, those who didn't work—or who didn't earn "enough"—did not merit the right to choose motherhood. By the end of the 1970s, many Americans had redefined the right to reproduce as an economic right.

In a society especially worried in the 1960s and 1970s about the relationship between rights, individuality, selfishness, and depravity, poor mothers became the emblem of what could happen when the wrong people got rights. White people upset about laws and policies that "gave rights" to poor, reproducing women of color retaliated by calling these women welfare queens and also by proposing to take poor children from "lazy, improvident" mothers and give them to foster parents or to "adoptive parents who are not lower class" or put them "in an orphanage."[62]

The 1970s was a decade when populations were separated and distinguished from each other by their association with "choice" or "rights." By the end of the 1970s, fathers were recognized as having "rights." Fetuses had been granted "rights." And children now had "rights," too. Women, on the other hand, had only been given "choice" —or what I call "rights lite"—by the end of the decade.

But women of color and poor people were acutely aware that neither the "choice" nor the "right" to manage female fertility would end poverty in their communities. Communities of color particularly felt the impact of deindustrialization and inflation in the 1970s.[63] Equally challenging, these communities were struggling for access to newly codified rights at the same time that the civil rights movement, as a movement, was under virulent attack and disintegrating across the country. One sign of the vulnerability of communities of color was the call, issued by numerous white politicians, for mandatory use of birth control and sterilization to end illegitimacy in "inner cities."

In 1972 minority communities, and the entire nation, learned the hideous news of an ongoing set of assaults on the bodies of African Americans—the so-called Tuskegee experiments carried out on men in

Alabama since 1932. In this so-called study, 600 poor, uneducated men, 399 of whom had syphilis, were offered certain health care and other benefits. But the men with syphilis were never given any information about what ailed them. They were never given any treatment for the disease either before or after penicillin was identified as a cure. Doctors had mounted this project in order, it was reported in 1972, to study the corpses of the afflicted men, to learn the impact of syphilis on the human body.

When the forty-year experiment was fully exposed in 1972, many Americans were horrified by the willingness of medical scientists to treat human beings as guinea pigs. Many people of color received the Tuskegee news as further proof that white authorities had bad designs on the bodies of people of color.

In this charged context, a number of male Black nationalists spoke out against federal and local birth control programs to reduce population growth in communities of color. Often these spokesmen drew on language from the Student Nonviolent Coordinating Committee (SNCC) of the mid-1960s: "Birth control is a plot just as segregation was a plot to keep blacks down. It is a plot rather than a solution. Instead of working for us and giving us rights—you reduce us in numbers and do not have to give us anything."[64] Capturing a long view of race politics and reproductive politics in the United States, comedian and activist Dick Gregory expressed the problem this way: "For years they told us where to sit, where to eat, and where to live. Now they want to dictate our bedroom habits. First the white man tells me to sit in the back of the bus. Now it looks like he wants me to sleep under the bed. Back in the days of slavery, black folks couldn't grow kids fast enough for white folks to harvest. Now that we've got a little taste of power, white folks want us to call a moratorium on having children."[65]

Women of color, naturally, did not always agree with the birth-control-is-genocide argument. Black writer Toni Cade, for example, expressed her frustration with the movement brothers who might not take their fair share of responsibility in either managing fertility or child rearing. She chastised the men who hadn't really thought about these matters but who burned "the little packet of pills, telling me in breathless ecstasy that it's very revolutionary having babies and raising warriors, conjuring up this Hollywood image of guerilla fighter in the wilds of Bear Mountain with rifle in hand and baby strapped on back under the Pancho Villa bullet belt."[66] By the same token, many Blacks in the

1970s, along with Toni Cade, felt that "[i]t is a sinister thing for the state to tell anyone *not* to have a child."

By 1970, the NAACP, the Congress of Racial Equality (CORE), and Martin Luther King Jr. had all come to support family planning.[67] These and other groups and individuals disassociated themselves from the genocide argument and focused on women's reproductive health and self-determination. And many women of color turned the genocide debates into a forum for constructing and communicating a feminist, women-of-color reproductive politics. In the late 1960s in particular, some women, like the members of the Black women's liberation group in Mt. Vernon, New York, put the issue of female fertility and its control squarely at the heart of race and gender liberation. "Like the Vietnamese have decided to fight genocide, and the South American poor are beginning to fight back, and the African poor will fight back, too. Poor black women in the United States have to fight back, too . . . out of our own experience of oppression. Having too many babies stops us from supporting our children, teaching them the truth . . . and from fighting black men who still want to use and exploit us."[68] Poet Kay Lindsey also analyzed this issue in a way that insisted on the relationship between Black liberation and women's liberation:

> *Anyway I gave birth twice*
> *And my body deserves a medal for that*
> *But I never got one.*
>
> *Mainly because they thought*
> *I was just answering the call of nature.*
>
> *But now that the revolution needs numbers*
> *Motherhood got a new position*
> *Five steps behind manhood.*[69]

Other activist women also cast procreation as a political activity, on their own terms. Mary Crow Dog, a Lakota member of the liberationist American Indian Movement, recalled, "Like many other Native American women . . . I had an urge to procreate, as if driven by a feeling that I, personally, had to make up for the genocide suffered by our people in the past." Angela Davis underscored the importance of the right to reproduce for females living in a society that degraded them: "I would venture to say that many young women make conscious decisions to bear children in order to convince themselves that they are alive and creative human beings."[70]

As the debate about the meaning and use of birth control inspired women of color to define a reproductive politics in their own interests, so the national backlash against welfare in the 1970s stimulated women of color to expand and deepen this politics. In the voice of the National Welfare Rights Organization, poor women spoke loudly about their right to have children and to be mothers. Poor women told politicians and ordinary Americans that they were good mothers dedicated to the well-being of their children. They spoke eloquently against the charge that poor women had children in order to collect welfare benefits, a charge that welfare rights activist Johnnie Tillmon famously called "a lie that only men could make up and only men could believe."[71] Welfare rights organizations in this era became advocates for family planning. They also became advocates for protecting the custody rights of poor mothers against welfare officials who threatened to take children away from their low-income mothers and place them in foster care. Welfare rights organizations clarified again and again the relationship between welfare rights and reproductive rights in the United States. As Tillmon put it, "Nobody realized more than poor women that all women should have the right to control their own reproduction. But we also know how easily the lobby for birth control can be perverted into a weapon against poor women. . . . Birth control . . . is a personal decision, not the condition of a welfare check."[72]

Feminist women of color, like U.S. Congress member Shirley Chisholm, took up the responsibility of educating the public about the terrible health and other impacts on poor women who did not have the resources to control their fertility. Chisholm spoke about these women who experienced what amounted to compulsory pregnancies. She pointed out that among poor women, 42 percent had children they did not intend to have; among all women, only 25 percent reported this experience. Before *Roe v. Wade,* Chisholm took a strong position in favor of legalizing abortion. She based her support in part on the fact that Black women died twice as often from illegal abortion—mostly self-induced—as did white women, and that the rates for Puerto Rican women were higher still.[73]

After *Roe v. Wade,* women-of-color groups such as the National Black Feminist Organization intensified the call to end coercive sterilization of poor women of color in the United States. Without protections against sterilization abuse, and without adequate access to other methods of fertility control, they demanded, what did "choice" mean to a vulnerable woman of color? One woman who defined sterilization as her only "feasible choice" recalled, "The pill made me swell up. After three years I had an IUD inserted. It made me bleed a lot so I had it removed. I was sterilized at the age of twenty-five because I couldn't use the pill or the IUD."[74]

What did "choice" mean when having another child could threaten the family's economic viability? Anthropologist Iris Lopez found that many women who had been sterilized felt that because of their financial situations, they had had *no choice.* Almost half of the women Lopez interviewed reported that if they had had more money, they would not have had the surgery. One woman explained, "If I had the necessary money to raise more children, I would not have been sterilized. When you can't afford it, you just can't afford it. . . . I wish that I could have lived in a house where each of them had their own room, nice clothing, enough food, and everything else that they needed. But what's the sense of having a whole bunch of kids if when dinnertime rolls around all you can serve them is soup made of milk or codfish because there is nothing else. Or when you are going to take them out, one wears a new pair of shoes while the other one has to wear hand-me-downs because you could only afford one pair of shoes. That's depressing. If I had another child, we would not have been able to survive."[75]

Many women at the time posed this question: When the government pays for a poor woman's sterilization but not for her abortion, what does "choice" mean? And many confronted how this question—and these government policies—shaped their reproductive lives in the early 1970s just before and after national legalization of abortion, and following the release of federal funds to pay for sterilizations in 1971 (Medicaid covered 90 percent of the cost of the procedure).[76] Indeed, a Washington, D.C., district court judge determined that the government was paying for between 100,000 and 150,000 sterilizations of poor, minority women annually in these years.[77] Typically, he found, a pregnant woman on welfare was informed that if she didn't have the operation, she would lose her welfare benefits. What was the meaning of "choice" for a woman in this predicament?

Women-of-color organizations were catalyzed by these revelations and by testimonies before Congress that made the impact of these policies plain. Niel Ruth Cox, one sterilized woman, described her experience: "I was living with my mother and eight sisters. My father . . . is dead. My family was on welfare, but payments had stopped for me because I was eighteen. We had no hot or cold running water, only pump water. No stove. No refrigerator, no electric lights. It got cold down there in the winter. I got pregnant when I was seventeen. I didn't know anything about birth control or abortion. When the welfare caseworker found out I was pregnant, she told my mother that if we wanted to keep getting welfare, I'd have to have my tubes tied—temporarily. Nobody explained anything to me before the operation. Later on, after the operation, I saw the doctor and I asked him if I could have another baby. He said that I had nothing to worry about. That, of course, I could have more kids. [Now I know that was a lie and] I know now that I was sterilized because I was from a welfare family."[78]

Mexican-origin women in Los Angeles at this time also encountered obstetricians and gynecologists who misled them. Historical sociologist Elena Gutiérrez has uncovered events that led to a lawsuit, *Madrigal v. Quilligan*, in which Mexican-origin women accused a group of doctors at Los Angeles County Medical Center of sterilizing them in the early 1970s without their full understanding or consent.

Gutiérrez shows how the sterilization of these economically and ethnically vulnerable women was consistent with the willingness of doctors and others to define them as undeserving reproducers, as inappropriate for "membership in the national community," and as potential mothers of "future 'undesirable' citizens."[79] Gutiérrez also shows how grassroots Chicana activists mobilized to resist these assumptions and the actions they justified.

Gutiérrez stresses an aspect of this history that is often clouded over in accounts of this kind of nativism in the United States. That is, in order for poor, vulnerable women to be sterilized against their own desires, members of the medical profession had to be willing to commit these outrages.

The events at the Los Angeles County Medical Center show how physicians reflected, responded to, and reproduced the cultural and political context in which they lived and worked—and, in the process, harmed Mexican-origin women. The fact is, physicians at the medical center were among the millions of Californians who picked up their morning newspapers in those years and read headlines such as these:

"Births to Illegal Immigrants on the Rise: California Taxpayers Finance Soaring Numbers of Foreigners' Babies" and "Blockade at Border Hasn't Cut Births."[80]

The doctors at the Los Angeles County Medical Center who were accused of sterilization abuse seem to have had attitudes toward the reproductive behavior of poor women that matched the attitudes of doctors around the country in the early 1970s. Many obstetricians and gynecologists in the United States in these years supported a variety of interventions to curb the reproduction of poor women. A study of doctors' attitudes, published in the January 1972 issue of *Family Planning Digest*, showed that among ob-gyn physicians, 94 percent "favoured compulsory sterilization or the withholding of welfare support for unwed mothers who already had three children." Doctors at the medical center added "deportation" to the list of appropriate responses to irresponsible reproduction among women of Mexican origin.[81]

Reports from the Los Angeles County Medical Center also revealed that physicians at that hospital were eager to provide certain surgical training experiences for residents and interns. One resident urged young doctors to ask every "girl" if she wanted to be sterilized, no matter how young she was. He said, "Remember everyone you get to get her tubes tied means two tubes [that is, an operation] for some resident or intern."[82]

According to testimony at the trial, women in the process of delivering babies were confronted with threats, demands, strong suggestions, and bribes to allow themselves to be sterilized. One medical student present during sterilizations described the setting: "The general picture . . . was of crowding, screams of pain, bright lights, lack of sleep by patients and staff, and an 'assembly-line' approach so that many women were literally terrified." The medical student also described the behavior of physicians: "On almost a daily basis I saw the following types of coercion being used: the doctor would hold a syringe in front of the mother who was in labor pain and ask her if she wanted a pain killer; while the woman was in the throes of a contraction the doctor would say, 'Do you want the pain killer? Then sign the papers. Do you want the pain to stop? Do you want to have to go through this again? Sign the papers.'"[83]

Elena Orozco, a woman who had given birth at Los Angeles County Medical Center, had heard this demand from doctors a number of times. She had always resisted the pressure. Here she describes the moment of her capitulation: "I just wanted them to leave me alone, sign the papers and get it over with. . . . I was in pain on the table when they were asking me all those questions, and they were poking around my stomach, and pushing with their fingers up there. I just wanted to be left alone."[84]

Gutiérrez argues that Elena Orozco's doctor and the others at the Los Angeles County Medical Center accused of participating in the sterilization campaign were convinced that they were doing the right thing for the United States. They believed that Mexican-origin women were contributing to dangerous overpopulation and were scamming the welfare system. More broadly, Gutiérrez maintains, these doctors practiced medicine that reflected a widespread belief that Mexican-origin women were not "rightfully deserving of social benefits" such as the right to reproduce or the right to receive medical care. Sterilization could rectify all these violations at once.[85]

At the same time that news stories implicitly justified the termination of some women's fertility and a cadre of doctors appeared to agree, a powerful force in the California Mexican-origin community organized itself to object to this kind of medical mistreatment of women. In 1975, a number of Chicanas—lawyers and grassroots activists—mobilized to bring suit against ten doctors who were alleged to have been involved in coerced sterilization procedures at the Los Angeles County Medical Center. Ultimately, the judge in this case, *Madrigal v. Quilligan*, cleared the physicians, citing "communication breakdown" as the source of the women's violation.

None of the sterilized women who participated as plaintiffs in *Madrigal* was "compensated" for her loss of fertility. But the Chicana activists who constructed the case pressed on, racking up a number of accomplishments that protected other women from suffering the same indignity and violation. For example, after *Madrigal*, the Los Angeles County Medical Center began for the first time to enforce compliance with state regulations requiring that women understand that sterilization would permanently terminate their fertility and requiring that women give their formal consent before physicians go ahead with the operation. After *Madrigal*, the state of California accepted "guidelines that required that consent forms be written in the woman's native language and at a sixth grade reading level." Also after *Madrigal*, the federal Department of Health, Education, and Welfare (HEW) established further standards providing that women receive "sufficient information for giving legally effective informed consent," that women could have a seventy-two-hour waiting period between receiving information and having the operation, and that girls under the age of eighteen were ineligible for sterilization.

All of these provisions have been crucial to protecting the reproductive capacity and dignity of women. All of these provisions were won as a result of the activism of Chicana women working to protect the reproductive dignity—and the basic right to be full citizens—of poor women of color.[86]

In response to events like these, women in the Young Lord's Party in New York pioneered a concept of reproductive rights that linked demands for safe, legal abortion "under community control" to the end of coerced sterilization. Later in the 1970s, a feminist organization, the Committee to End Sterilization Abuse (CESA), enriched the notion of reproductive rights when it issued sterilization guidelines that recognized that the needs of minority-group women went beyond what *Roe* promised. CESA demanded that women sign informed consent forms written in the patient's language before the operation, that hospitals honor a thirty-day waiting period between the signing and the operation, and that no woman should be coerced into signing a consent form while she was in labor. CESA demanded that no woman should be threatened with loss of welfare benefits when she was handed the consent form. These demands, some of which were opposed by Planned Parenthood and other organizations as undermining women's "choice," surely expressed and illuminated legal scholar Reva Siegel's notion of the "social organization of reproductive relations."

Women-of-color organizations and their allies pulled strands from the civil rights movement, the welfare rights movement, and the abortion rights movement to construct a unique and powerful set of skills and arguments. These organizations began to claim rights to motherhood, to reproductive health care, and to the right to control one's own fertility in one's own interests. And their work was having an impact on the courts and other seats of power.

In August 1973, HEW called for a moratorium on sterilizations when the patient was vulnerable because of her youth, for example, or her limited intellectual competence, or her poverty. The department was responding to mounting evidence that poor women and women of color had undergone publicly funded sterilizations without having given their informed consent. The next spring, Washington, D.C., district court judge Gerhart Gesell found the new rules insufficient to protect poor women from reproductive coercion. He was explicit: "[F]ederally assisted family planning sterilizations are permissible only with the voluntary, knowing, and uncoerced consent of individuals competent to give such consent." Gesell also insisted that federal regulations should be clearly written so that any woman undergoing sterilization understood that going through the operation—or not—would have no impact on her eligibility to collect welfare benefits.

But even after the government adopted new sterilization regulations, a government study revealed that the Indian Health Service (IHS) and other providers of reproductive services for indigent women of color were not following the new rules. The IHS records in particular showed sterilizations of underage women and violations of the new seventy-two-hour waiting period. Scholar Jane Lawrence noted medical records containing consent forms "dated the day the woman had given birth, usually by Cesarean section, while she was under the influence of a sedative and in an unfamiliar environment." Some forms (evaluated by Native Americans as inappropriately written in English at a twelfth-grade reading level) had been signed the day of the operation.

No one knows for certain how many Native American and other women of color were sterilized in this era. In the mid-1970s, Native American women, some of whom were physicians, spoke out as experts on this matter. Jane Lawrence collected estimates of the percentage of sterilized native women provided by Native American physician Connie Pinkerton-Uri (25–50 percent), Cheyenne tribal judge Marie Sanchez (25–50 percent), and Northern Cheyenne Mary Ann Bear Comes Out, whose study showed 56 out of 165 women, thirty to forty-four years old, had been sterilized in a three-year period in the 1970s. Lawrence observed that these sterilizations had terrible impacts on native women: "The women had to deal with higher rates of marital problems, alcoholism, drug abuse, psychological difficulties, shame, and guilt. Sterilization abuse," she found, "affected the entire Indian community."

Doctors who repeatedly performed sterilizations on poor women of color in this era typically justified their work as the best way to limit the growth of poor families. Many argued that sterilization was an efficient way to reduce the tax burden of the middle class. Many argued that sterilization was the best way to provide poor women who could not manage the responsibility of other birth control methods with permanent, effective contraception. Some even argued that sterilization was a good way to undermine the political radicalism of people-of-color organizations such as the American Indian Movement.

Lawrence also cited other reasons physicians sterilized so many poor women: that the operation was a good source of income and provided an opportunity for gynecological training. At best, some doctors believed "they were helping women because limiting the number of children they could have would help minority families to become more financially secure in their own right while lessening the welfare burden."[87]

THE HYDE AMENDMENT AND THE LIMITS OF "CHOICE"

Almost immediately after *Roe v. Wade,* as women of color were working to extend the meaning of the Court's decision, local policymakers began to limit the impact of the landmark abortion ruling. The first set of efforts to limit *Roe* aimed to deny public funding for the abortions of poor women on Medicaid. When state departments of social services tried to adopt these kinds of rules in the 1970s, most federal courts agreed it would be unconstitutional for a state to refuse to pay for a poor woman's elective abortion while agreeing to pay for other pregnancy-related medical treatment through its Medicaid program.

Senator Edward Brooke of Massachusetts, one of a number of Republican senators who vigorously championed abortion rights in the 1970s, spoke on the Senate floor in 1975 about the reproductive needs of poor women. Brooke, the only African American in the Senate, said that federal courts had repeatedly ruled that "under the Fourteenth Amendment, once a state makes medical services available to poor women, it cannot discriminate against those women who choose to terminate their pregnancies during the first trimester." He warned that funding restrictions could "put an economic test on the question of abortion." Senator Jacob Javits, Republican of New York, told his colleagues that without proper funding, "The poor [will] use coat hangers and the wealthy go to clinics."[88]

Roe v. Wade had seemed to protect women's access to abortion against both religious objections and financial tests. But in 1977 Congress passed the Hyde Amendment, which denied this kind of protection to poor women and only poor women. Henry Hyde, Republican representative from Illinois, explained his strategy: "I certainly would like to prevent, if I could legally, anybody having an abortion, a rich woman, a middle-class woman, or a poor woman. Unfortunately, the only vehicle available is the HEW Medicaid bill."[89] Hyde was probably aware that restricting the access of poor women could eventually impact the access of all women. As one physician presciently observed in 1978: "Denial of abortion to low-income women jeopardizes their availability to all women. Private insurers may now decide to not reimburse for abortions. Anti-abortion forces will be encouraged to pursue further means of undermining the Supreme Court rulings of 1973, now that Congress has led the way."[90]

Hyde's effort to restrict government support for poor women's abortions was so successful because by 1976, the new anti-abortion-rights movement had worked hard to elect a large number of like-minded men to Congress. Also, as we've seen, many Americans did not approve of associating the sexual behavior of poor women, particularly minorities, with "choice." Many, taking cues from the media treatment of poor women, questioned why their tax dollars should go for "cleaning up the mistakes" of careless, oversexed women. Senator Javits pointed out at the time that the effort to deny federal funds for poor women's abortions "eliminates all decision-making and exercise of choice on the part of women who are poor, thereby infringing upon their civil rights and personal freedom."

In 1980, in *Harris v. McRae*, the Supreme Court upheld the Hyde Amendment. The Court justified denying federal funds for the *medically necessary* abortions of poor women. Justice Potter Stewart explained that he supported the Hyde Amendment because the government is not responsible for a person's poverty or for alleviating it. The government's responsibilities, Stewart wrote, must be narrowly drawn: "[A]lthough government may not place obstacles in the path of a woman's exercise of her freedom of choice, it need not remove those not of its own creation: Indigency falls in the latter category."

In the abortion funding cases that were argued before the Supreme Court between 1976 and 1980, the Court backed the government away from responsibility for causing poverty, for alleviating poverty, and for paying the bill for poor women to get abortions—a medical service that many believed *Roe v. Wade* had established as a right of all women. In Congress, abortion often became just another service that a consumer could or could not purchase, depending on how much money she had. Representative Charles Grassley of Iowa made the case for treating abortion more like other "goods and services": "Some argue that the Hyde Amendment deprives poor women of something that more afflu- ent women can pay for." Nothing, he suggested, is the matter with that, since in all other matters that is the natural course of things.[91]

While Grassley tried to make abortion just like any other consumer service, Senator Orrin Hatch of Utah tried to make poor women seek- ing abortions into consumers, just like other women. Imagine the abor- tion-seeking woman as a potential spender who could, if careful, stash away a "five" or a "ten" every couple of days, Hatch said. "[T]here is nothing to prevent [a poor woman] . . . from either exercising increased self-restraint, or from sacrificing on some item or other for a month or two to afford [her] own abortion."[92]

The fact was, though, that when a poor woman went looking for an abortion, she typically had neither the time nor the money to save. Pub- lic health officials were clear about the importance of the time element; studies showed that when abortion was delayed, the risk factor for complications increased by 20 percent every week after the eighth week of pregnancy. Also, when the Hyde Amendment became law, the aver- age cost of an abortion in the United States was $280, or $42 more than the average AFDC, or welfare, check for an entire family for a whole month. Researchers at the time found that poor women could pay for their own abortions only by sacrificing the basics—"food and shelter for themselves or their families."[93]

The Supreme Court ruled in *Harris v. McRae* that *Roe v. Wade* had not established a constitutional right to abortion. It had merely prom- ised women protection from "unduly burdensome interference with [their] freedom to decide" to terminate a pregnancy.[94] In other words, the government would not criminalize abortion, but neither would the government pay for it, no matter where that left a poor woman. The Court and the Congress made access to reproductive options a market matter, not a matter of gender, racial or economic equality, or human rights. The abortion funding cases became a platform from which vari- ous constituencies could express "their growing annoyance with abor- tion rights."[95] The cases also became an opportunity for the government to speak out against the sexual and reproductive behavior of poor, mi- nority females—and to use this subject as an argument for restricting the size and scope of government.

After the Congress and the Court validated the Hyde Amendment, these institutions did not investigate its impact on the lives of poor women. But others did investigate. A federal district court judge found evidence that "many indigent women who were able to raise the money for their abortions [did] so only by not paying rent or utility bills, pawning household goods, diverting food and clothes money, or journeying to another state to obtain lower rates or fraudulently using a relative's insurance policy."[96] The Alan Guttmacher Institute found that just before the Hyde Amendment went into effect, 295,000 poor women a year had abortions paid for by Medicaid. Just following the enforcement of the amendment, the number declined to about 2,000 yearly.[97]

Horror stories began to crop up in the late 1970s, stories that attached faces and other details to these statistics. One story from Ohio, a state where the impact of the abortion-funding decisions was harsh, captured the full tragedy of transforming abortion from a woman's right into a consumer's privilege in the years immediately following *Roe v. Wade.* A teenage mother, eligible for Medicaid but ineligible for abortion coverage, by no definition in the world an empowered consumer, shot herself in the stomach after having been told by a public hospital "that she could not have an abortion unless she paid $600 in cash."[98]

To many ordinary Americans and government officials, this poor teenager was a representative girl, one of many who needed a strong dose of discipline. She needed a regimen of punishment convincing enough to turn her and other females like her away from engaging in sex and reproduction outside the bounds of the traditional family.

THE RISE OF THE MOVEMENT AGAINST ABORTION RIGHTS

Public health experts tried to figure out after *Roe v. Wade* whether rates of abortion were actually higher following legalization than they had been before. After all, by the end of the criminal era, hundreds of thousands, even millions, of girls and women a year decided they had to manage their own fertility despite the law. But after *Roe,* one thing is clear: most women reported that getting a legal abortion was an enormous relief and surprisingly routine, like any non-life-threatening medical procedure. One set of researchers studying the experiences of women who obtained legal abortions in the early years of legalization reported, "What is most striking to us is the matter-of-factness of these women's accounts of their abortion experiences."[99] Some reported how lucky they believed themselves to be compared with other women who had to give their babies away to strangers. Many women reported what was surely a related response: that they had had very quick recoveries from the procedure, both physically and psychologically. In those early days following *Roe v. Wade*, women walked into abortion facilities unimpeded. They did not face picketers brandishing photographs of fetuses and shouting at them. They were not barraged by claims that abortion inevitably caused trauma. No one had yet constructed this claim. In this immediate post-*Roe* period, getting an abortion was a simple, legal expression of a woman's right to control her body.

In retrospect, 1973 was a fraught year for this profound redefinition of reproductive authority to occur. For one thing, 1973 was the year that the earning power of the ordinary male worker began to decline, a first for the postwar era. The blow to male earning power occurred in the context of general economic dislocation: runaway inflation, cuts to social programs, soaring interest rates, layoffs that hit thousands of workers in the United States.

Americans were also suffering from what might be called political dislocation. National leadership lacked credibility and continuity. The United States had three presidents between 1974, when President Nixon resigned in disgrace, and 1977, when Jimmy Carter (who defeated Gerald Ford after Ford had stepped in to complete Nixon's term) was inaugurated. During this period, much of the nation's political energy was drained by the failed war in Vietnam, the traumas associated with recent assassinations of politically progressive leaders, the deeply stressed economy, and a culture violently rent by ever-stronger resistance to the accomplishments of social justice movements.

The accomplishments of the feminist movement in particular— symbolized by new educational and economic opportunities for women, by new sexual freedoms, and by abortion rights—became key flash points of resistance for those who surveyed the economic and cultural upheaval and longed for the familiar past. When traditionalists of the 1970s assessed the wages of women's rights campaigns, they focused on divorce, single motherhood, welfare queens, unchaste sex, neglected children, and abortion. Traditionalists drew a tight connection between the need to restrain and discipline the economy in the 1970s, the need to restrain and discipline the politics of *excessive equal-*

ity, and the need to restrain and discipline women grabbing social power from husbands, priests, and other traditional authorities.

Many traditionalists in the United States turned to religion at this time of social change and anxiety. Political scientist Petchesky explains the effectiveness of the "religious framework" at such moments, when questions of power—who controls the economy? the state? the family? the church?—are begging for reassuring resolution. "Religion supplies a language and symbolism through which [the traditionalists of the 1970s laid] claim to the righteousness and purity of its vision." "Abortion," writes Petchesky, "became the occasion" for the traditionalists—politically organized as the New Right—to define and organize their "crusade."

The religious crusade of the 1970s had two main centers, both of which combined religion and politics. Immediately after *Roe v. Wade,* the National Conference of Catholic Bishops created the Pro-Life Legal Affairs Committee, a political action group meant to influence elections. The committee was also the steward of efforts to implement a "pro-life" constitutional amendment defining life as beginning at the moment of fertilization and defining abortion as murder.

The other center of religious and political work against legal abortion was the National Right to Life Committee, founded the year after the *Roe* decision. By the mid-1970s, these religious groups and their allies—a rapidly growing, resourceful, and innovative force in the United States—were "devoted to preservation of the traditional social roles of the family, the churches, and the schools."

Petchesky and others have clarified the ways that members of the New Right, in its various forms, were responding as pro-family advocates to real changes: "New Right organizers understood all too well that the main threats to maintaining a traditional family structure in which men dominated women and children and women seek their identity in motherhood" were women's growing economic independence from their husbands; teenagers' growing cultural independence from their parents; and the strength of the feminist movement.[100]

In response to these challenges, New Right leaders and foot soldiers defined a "value-crisis more sever [*sic*] than any other crisis our nation has ever known."[101] At the heart of the crisis was a failure of the courts and of too many people to see that "the right to live . . . is the substance upon which all other human rights are based." One physician, speaking before Congress in behalf of the Human Life Amendment in 1974, offered his analysis of the abortion-rights position in a "humanistic" society: "It is ironic [that Americans] have shown such an abhorrence of the willful taking of life that they are gradually eliminating capital punishment; mounting prodigious and laudable campaigns to save plants and animals; seeking limitations on the arms race; speaking out against private and public weaponry; condemning and adjudicating mass executions in the past; demanding a cutback in military involvement and in defense expenditures. . . . How ironic that in these fifty states you can and are encouraged by the Supreme Court's ruling . . . to dial your friendly abortionist death-dealer who will kill your baby for a modest fee."[102]

This physician joined 350 of his colleagues who sent an open letter to the Supreme Court in 1974, asking the justices to reverse *Roe*. The doctors did not explicitly consider women's needs when they deplored the legalization of abortion as a way to "solve problems of poverty, ignorance, and disease." Opponents of *Roe* often effaced women's needs and women's voices, a frustrating situation for supporters of reproductive rights. One woman who attended the congressional hearings on the proposed Human Life Amendment complained, "We went to the hearings and heard anti-abortionists claim that a zygote is a human life, that a fertilized egg is a citizen; and we grew angrier and angrier. No one ever said the word 'abortion' and no one ever mentioned women—our bodies, our decisions, our lives."[103]

Even many who opposed abortion and believed it was tantamount to murder nevertheless tried to find grounds for compromise in the wake of the Supreme Court's decision. The Pekin, Illinois, Right to Life Organization, for example, did aim to weave together a social justice perspective and a "pro-life" perspective with an empathetic outlook on women's needs. The group expressed its mission this way: "Most women seek abortions because they are in social or economic difficulties. To merely oppose abortion and do no more is not only useless, but frankly immoral. Anyone active in the pro-life movement should be equally as active in a wide variety of social actions. Correcting social injustice is a most important aspect of the entire abortion problem." This right-to-life group suggested that its members work to promote marriage; family planning; psychological, legal, and religious counseling; maternity homes; adoption; child care; and employment policies that would assist women's mothering work.[104]

Some anti-abortion-rights groups attempted compromise by promoting laws and policies permitting abortion in the case of rape and incest but not in cases where a woman willingly engaged in sex. Reva Siegel describes such provisions as state distinctions between "good abortions and bad abortions," which translates into good women and bad women. If a woman appeared to participate voluntarily in an act of sexual intercourse, she would forfeit any claim to abortion. Put another way, if the woman engaged in sex without coercion, the state had the right to compel her to bear any child that resulted.[105]

Throughout the 1970s, anti-abortion-rights forces spoke out against *Roe v. Wade.* Some attempted to modify abortion rights with compromises or by calling for social justice for vulnerable women and their fetuses and children. Many legislators tried to reduce access by passing laws blocking public funding or requiring consent of a third party (husband, parent, judge) before she could secure an abortion. By 1977, 80 percent of all public hospitals and 70 percent of private hospitals in the United States did not permit abortions. The same year, a number of anti-abortion-rights individuals and small groups began to make clear that they were not interested in these various institutional or procedural forms of objection to legal abortion. These forces wanted to express their opposition to abortion in the most powerful way that a small number of people could: by attacking the source and the symbol of women's reproductive autonomy.

In 1977, the Planned Parenthood clinic in St. Paul, Minnesota, became the first such facility to report an arson attack. (This attack followed a campaign waged in the city's diocesan newspaper labeling the clinic "Little Dachau.") The next year the Women for Women clinic in Cincinnati was the first abortion clinic to be bombed.[106] The era of violence had arrived.

By the end of the 1970s, a visible and frightening cadre of antiabortion extremists had eclipsed the religious-based "right to life" as the movement's most visible segment. Scholar Carole Mason identifies these extremists as "nurtured by the paramilitary culture that flourished in the United States after the Vietnam War, by the apocalyptic rhetoric of New Right politicians who inspired Christian voters, and by the revitalization of white supremacist" groups. In this mix, "a new type of abortion warrior emerged," devoted to waging battle "in the courts, at the clinics, in the womb."[107]

Just a few years after the legalization of abortion, human rights groups and feminist organizations that supported reproductive freedom were reeling and on the defensive. The Hyde Amendment and *Harris v. McCrae* demonstrated the government's willingness to turn reproductive freedom into a service-for-purchase. When communities and law enforcement agencies around the country passively tolerated clinic violence, women's reproductive "choice" was weakened further.

Now *Roe v. Wade* joined *Brown v. Board of Education* as a landmark Supreme Court decision written to empower an oppressed group to act in its own interest. The implementation of the decision in both cases unleashed a violent backlash against the rights of the population in question. This backlash pushed activist-advocates for reproductive rights—often led by women-of-color organizations and ignored by middle-class women who quickly adapted to "the right to choose"—to craft an ambitious agenda for the rest of the century and beyond. Activists insisted on the importance of making women, not fetuses, the center of pregnancy. They also focused on making access to reproductive health services, regardless of ability to pay, a centerpiece of the reproductive rights struggle.

6

Revitalizing Hierarchies

How the Aftermath of Roe v. Wade *Affected Fetuses, Teenage Girls, Prisoners, and Ordinary Women, 1980 to the Present*

AFTER 1973, all over the country women spoke out about how the *Roe v. Wade* decision changed their lives. One woman explained how having the legal right to manage her own fertility helped her be a responsible mother: "My job on the assembly line at the plant was going well and I needed that job desperately to support the kids. Also I had started night school to improve my chances to get a better job. I just couldn't have another baby—five kids were enough for me to support."[1]

A Native American woman put it this way: "Personally, legal abortion allowed me the choice as a teenager living on a very poor Indian Reservation to finish growing up and make something of my life."[2]

As soon as public health officials and demographers were able to collect statistics on the impact of *Roe v. Wade,* the evidence was overwhelming: when women gained the legal right to manage their fertility, their lives changed dramatically. In the first section of this chapter, I will summarize a number of these dramatic changes. Then the chapter moves to a discussion of the decades of resistance to *Roe* and to the changing status of women.

The third section of this chapter looks at the ways that what I'll call "emblems of life" have become particularly important in the struggle over reproductive rights in the United States. In "Enlarging the Fetus," I consider newly assigned meanings of the fetus in reproductive politics and some of the impacts of fetal politics. Next I look at how the teenage girl has been used in the debate about abortion and other reproductive matters. And then I look at the emergence of the female prisoner as "the ideal pregnant woman," a surprising development, indeed.

Each of these "emblems of life" demonstrates that ideas about how "proper women" should behave—sexually and maternally—still shape reproductive politics in the United States. These examples also illustrate how the law continues to constrain some women from acting in what they believe is their own reproductive interests. The examples demonstrate very clearly how, a generation after the Supreme Court legalized abortion with *Roe v. Wade*, a woman's race and her class position—her access to financial and other resources—profoundly shape her access to reproductive self-determination.

The conclusion of *Pregnancy and Power* shows how the very idea of "reproductive rights" has evolved since 1973, particularly after women-of-color organizations began to define this concept as a much more complex matter than abortion rights alone. Finally, the chapter—and the book—ends with the presentation of three overarching principles that emerge most vividly from the history presented in all the previous chapters. I hope these concluding principles help readers rethink once again the meaning of reproductive politics. I hope they help clarify the ways that reproductive politics—the struggle over who has power over women's fertility—shapes women's lives, and also shapes a host of other aspects of American society.

HOW *ROE V. WADE* CHANGED THE LIVES OF ORDINARY WOMEN

Two years after New York State legalized abortion in 1970, the country's leading public health expert on this subject looked at the number of abortions performed in New York City. He found that 70 percent of the legal procedures in that city simply replaced "abortions previously obtained clandestinely and illegally" in the recent past. Other experts found an even closer match between the number of legal abortions after 1973 and the number of pre-*Roe* illegal ones.[3] This may be surprising to people who instinctively believe that, for the most part, women started having abortions in 1973. But as we've seen throughout this book, whenever physicians or others have tried to count how many pregnant women terminate their pregnancies, no matter what the law has said at any given time, the percentage has remained amazingly similar: for generations in this country about one-third of pregnancies have been aborted.

This historical fact reflects many things about the lives of fertile women over time in the United States. Most basically, it reflects the fact that girls and women have always felt the need to manage their fertility. It also reflects the fact that most women throughout American history have experienced at least one unintended pregnancy, before and after effective contraception was legal and more or less accessible.

Indeed, rates of unintended pregnancy remain high today. Demographer Stanley Henshaw has discovered that one-half of all pregnancies in the United States are unintended. And more than six out of ten women in their thirties have experienced either an unintended pregnancy or an abortion or both.[4]

While the percentage of terminated pregnancies appears to have remained fairly steady before and after *Roe v. Wade,* the legal environment that *Roe* created has brought many positive changes to the lives of women. To begin with, before legalization of abortion, most women who died from botched procedures—usually self-induced—were women of color.[5] Most women able to get "therapeutic abortions" in hospitals were white and possessed financial and social resources. After legalization, death from abortion became very rare. In fact, contemporary studies show that childbirth itself causes eleven times more deaths than abortion.[6]

We also know that since *Roe,* birthrates have declined for categories of women who might have the strongest motivation for controlling their fertility, including teenagers, women over thirty-five, and unmarried women. Overall, since *Roe v. Wade,* the birthrate has declined between 5 and 8 percent.[7] Teenagers, who accounted for half of all births outside of marriage before *Roe,* now account for 29 percent.[8]

Since 1973, pregnancy rates have declined, and so have rates of marriage.[9] For many Americans, this has been a sign of moral decay, a sign that too many Americans are falling away from "family values." Others argue that historically, the relationship between pregnancy and marriage has often been coercive.[10] Many pregnant girls and women in our recent past *had to get married,* even when they did not want to marry the man who impregnated them. As we saw in chapter 3, many for whom marriage was not an option were punished by family and community authorities who made sure that these deeply shamed unwed mothers surrendered their babies for adoption. Now that pregnancy outside of marriage is generally no longer considered a disgrace, many unmarried girls and women who get pregnant are freer to resist coercion and get married or not, be mothers or not, as they decide.

The rise of single motherhood (women between twenty and twenty-four have the highest rates) is, I believe, a direct consequence of *Roe v. Wade.* When women gained the right to end a pregnancy, the evidence suggests that many reasoned: "If I can decide for myself whether or not to stay pregnant, surely I can decide whether or not to be the mother of the child I will give birth to." Immediately following *Roe v. Wade,* most unwed mothers in the United States—that is, the ones who stayed pregnant—ended up keeping their babies. Domestic adoptions plummeted. Many people seeking babies to adopt had to look abroad. These developments—the end of a long era in which fathers could force "shotgun weddings" and pregnant girls could be sent away to maternity homes in shame and forced to give up their babies—represented, for one thing, a dramatic shift regarding reproductive politics within the family. Power shifted from the father (or parents) to the daughter herself. These developments have been unsettling or enraging for some, welcomed by others.

We can look at women's employment patterns and work experiences to find more evidence of the impact of *Roe v. Wade.* First, though, it is important to acknowledge that as we saw in chapter 4, a steadily rising percentage of women have worked for wages since World War II, long before the liberalization of reproductive laws and policies. From the 1950s to the present, women—including the mothers of young children—have swelled the labor force. Women entered the workforce for many reasons. Some had to do with personal fulfillment; many others involved basic economic survival. Over these postwar decades, the workforce required more low-skilled workers and more highly educated workers. Families increasingly required two wage earners to achieve and sustain middle-class status. In the 1970s, the real wages of ordinary male workers began to decline at the same time that divorce rates soared. Rates of child support were dismal. For example, in 1975, a large majority of divorced or separated women with children under eighteen received no child support. Among mothers who had never been married, 96 percent received no support.[11]

More women of all races and classes than ever before had to earn a living as the head of a household in order to sustain their families.

Labor force needs and family needs led many Americans to conclude that laws governing women's reproductive lives had to support women's new roles. Women earners needed protection against having to leave the workforce unexpectedly because they were expecting.

In the 1970s, as women claimed more sexual freedom for themselves *and* were mothers *and* were wage earners, many insisted that the meaning of pregnancy itself had to be legally changed. Women were no longer willing to be condemned by a pregnancy that occurred under the wrong conditions. Women who needed to earn a living every week of the year insisted that pregnancy was a social as well as a biological event. They insisted that pregnancy should be defined legally as a contingent fact of life, one that women needed to agree to in order for it to become a process leading to birth. By the early 1970s, a critical mass of women publicly defined pregnancy in this way.

After *Roe v. Wade* legalized the idea that pregnancy did not represent a woman's destiny or place a woman under coercion, a growing number of Americans came to believe that the country needed new laws that treated a settled pregnancy as the dignified condition of a dignified woman. Responding to this mandate, in 1978 Congress enacted the Pregnancy Discrimination Act (PDA), which decreed that "discrimination [in employment] on the basis of pregnancy, childbirth or related medical conditions constitutes unlawful sex discrimination." This act reflected and protected an enormous status change for women. Until the PDA, employers could and regularly did fire pregnant female employees; they also turned away pregnant job applicants on a regular basis. With the PDA, women who had recently claimed new degrees of sexual independence—and who now legally possessed the right to independent judgment about the course of a given pregnancy—were in a much stronger position to achieve or sustain new degrees of economic independence, even while pregnant.

All of these developments facilitating women's management of their own lives stimulated women's rights activism in the 1970s and into the 1980s. For example, after *Roe*, women who had fought for reproductive rights and invented campaigns for reproductive safety forged new campaigns. Now that the law gave women the right to make profound decisions about childbearing, women's health advocates argued that women should no longer be at the mercy of doctors and other health workers. Activists imagined women receiving reproductive health care in settings where professionals treated them with re-

spect. They imagined a world in which professionals listened and responded to women's health concerns instead of issuing dicta to infan-
tilized patients. Journalist and activist Barbara Seaman, who had
pressed in the 1960s for a safe birth control pill and for women's "informed consent," now issued a sort of four-part "modest proposal,"
that is, a manifesto proposing outrageous solutions in order to call attention to a real-life grievance. Now that women were legally directing
their own reproductive lives, Seaman figured it was time to call for
women-centered reproductive health care:

1 Effective immediately, only women shall be admitted to obstetrics and
   gynecology residencies. Males who are currently in training may remain, as may those who are in practice.
2 Effective immediately, no more foundation monies will be awarded to
   men for any kind of research into the female reproductive system.
3 Effective immediately, the establishment and administration of laws
   concerning female reproduction, abortion, and sterilization shall be removed from the court and legislative systems. An agency modeled
   after the NLRB, FCC, FTC, or Atomic Energy Commission shall handle all such matters.
4 Effective immediately, the United Nations and the United States will
   not sponsor nor participate in any international population activity or
   conference unless women are represented in proportion to their numbers in the population of every participating nation.[12]

Another result of feminist activism after *Roe* was that now many
women could see clearly for the first time that reproductive health and
reproductive rights were *women's issues,* not just problems that afflicted
a scared, lonely woman by herself, trying to figure out what to do.
When abortion had been a secret and a crime, most women had to find
secret, individual solutions. Now they could try to build coalitions and
organizations and speak jointly and publicly about reproductive politics and reproductive rights.[13]

Many Americans in the late 1970s and early 1980s began to fit the
idea of "reproductive rights" into the very idea of democracy. In this era
many leading Republican politicians supported abortion rights as an
appropriate expression of individual rights and hands-off government.
For example, Senator Robert Packwood, Republican of Oregon, often
spoke out in these terms on the Senate floor. In 1981 Packwood re-

sponded to a senator from Iowa who objected to the idea that, without the Hyde Amendment, taxpayers would have to pay for the abortions of poor women. Packwood explained to the senator: "Well, . . . the way a democracy works . . . is by majority vote. . . . [The Senate] frequently votes money for things that a great portion of the public does not agree with. We do not have to go very far in our recent history to remember a good portion of this Republic vehement in their opposition to the Vietnam war[,] absolutely irate that their taxes were being used to further that war. But you do not run a free government on the basis of 'I will take back from the Government that portion of my tax money that they are spending for things I do not like.'"[14]

On the ground, abortion rights became a permanent feature of democratic politics, every related Supreme Court decision becoming an occasion for vibrant public response. For example, hundreds of thousands of people protested in Washington when the court issued the *Webster v. Reproductive Health Services* opinion in 1989 upholding various Missouri restrictions on abortion, including a prohibition on using public facilities to perform the procedure. The National Organization for Women received forty thousand new members, and pro-rights student groups formed on campuses around the country. In April 2004, one million people demonstrated in Washington, D.C., against President George W. Bush's attempts to take reproductive rights away from women in the United States and against his policies crippling contraception programs internationally. Unprecedented numbers of marchers joined the demonstration from all over the country, chanting and waving signs like "My Body Is Not Public Property!" Some analysts have observed that anti-reproductive-rights sentiment was a core element of George W. Bush's reelection in 2004.

Clearly, abortion has come out of the shadows and into the center of American politics. While Presidents Ronald Reagan and George W. Bush have talked of abortion as an issue about unborn children, millions of women believe that abortion politics represent a national debate first and foremost over women's rights to control their own bodies and about the new society that has been emerging since the law gave women that right.

Dr. Mildred Hanson, a longtime physician and abortion provider, reflects on the "soul-searching" a provider has to undergo to keep doing this work. For her, the justifications are clear because of what she knows about how legal abortion has improved women's health in the

United States, ended abortion-related deaths and sterility, ended self-mutilation, and reduced unwanted parenthood. Dr. Hanson explains how she has changed personally since the pre-*Roe* era. Before legalization, she practiced medicine but she was obedient and law-abiding, even though she was aware how desperately women needed to control their fertility. Now she is bold: "If *Roe v. Wade* were repealed," writes Dr. Hanson, "I think I'd go right on doing abortions. . . . And I would frankly just wait for them to come and get me, because . . . our experience since *Roe v. Wade* has convinced us so strongly of the need for safe, legal abortion. I feel more strongly about it now than I did in the days before *Roe v. Wade*. These days, I would go right on doing it. I would wait for the cops to come and take me. Absolutely. Absolutely"[15]

After *Roe,* as many women achieved better health, more predictable work lives, political consciousness about women's rights, and constructed lives as active citizens, the status of women in the United States changed and the country's culture changed as well. After *Roe,* for example, a young woman who became unwillingly pregnant did not have to bear a permanent stain on her life. Substituting personal judgment for permanent stain represented new social power for women.

As I noted earlier, immediately after legalization, young women demonstrated their new social power by deciding against giving up their babies. Between 1970 and 1975, the rate of adoption of babies by unrelated adults fell 63 percent.[16] Babies were simply no longer available within the United States. Americans who still wanted to adopt had to find new groups of women without rights and resources—without the social power—to claim their own children. Karin Evans, an author and the adoptive mother of a Chinese girl, is clear-sighted about the relationship between resourcelessness and adoption. She writes, "Behind all too many goods made in China, I now know for certain, are exploited workers, most of them women, any one of whom could be the mother of a child who winds up lost [adopted]."[17] Today in the United States, less than 1 percent of children born to never-married women are put out for adoption.[18] Most women in this country, even poor women, have more social power than women in other countries, who are pressed hard to give up their children.

Studies show that women who are protected by the combination of legal contraception and abortion view sex differently. They are more willing to have sex even though men are generally less willing than earlier to marry them in the event of an unplanned pregnancy. Undoubtedly, with accessible birth control and legal abortion, men's relationship to pregnancy has changed in more ways than one, though sometimes male attitudes seem contradictory. For example, many men have come to expect women to take responsibility for birth control, but a study after *Roe* of men's attitudes about the abortion decision showed that 90 percent wanted "equal say."[19] As one twenty-seven-year-old said to a journalist exploring the ways that legal abortion affected men, "But what about my choice?"

A culture that has constructed maleness and femaleness as perfectly complementary opposites must pay a high price for improving the status of women. Any gain of autonomy—or power—for women as a group necessarily appears to undermine the power available for men. An abortion clinic worker in the 1980s observed that men accompanying women to their appointments seemed to "feel excluded because the power over their lives now lies with the woman."[20]

As women have gained reproductive rights, they have also gained social status. But ironically, since *Roe*, many women have wanted to associate their new rights and their new status with their own *individual* righteousness. That is, now that pregnancy has become a "choice," many middle-class women, most politicians, and others define the good choice maker as the woman who has *earned the right* to exercise choice properly by having enough money to be a legitimate and proper mother. In the minds of many Americans, legitimate pregnancy now has less to do with having a husband and more to do with having "enough money." In the minds of many people, legitimate pregnancy has now become a class privilege reserved for women with resources. Other women—those without resources—who get pregnant and stay pregnant are often regarded as making bad choices. As middle-class women have claimed reproductive privacy for themselves—defined as the right to use privately purchased contraception, the right to get pregnant, the right to get a privately paid-for abortion, and the right to make private decisions about becoming mothers—they have too frequently allowed the fertile bodies of women without private resources to be assessed and condemned in the public sphere.

These ideas about righteous women earning choice and deserving privacy shaped the ways that many Americans thought about the new reproductive technologies emerging in the years after *Roe*. Which childless women deserved access to fertility treatments, and which ones did not? Was it okay for a poor woman to carry a fetus to term for another, reproductively impaired woman rich enough to pay her to do that labor? What about a college student selling ova to pay for tuition? If a woman has enough money to pay for pregnancy—in the ordinary way, or in any of these new ways—does that always mean she is entitled to pursue motherhood, no matter how? Does having money automatically make a woman a good choice maker? Is it okay for one woman's reproductive choices to depend on the choicelessness of another woman?

Another problem that emerged in the wake of *Roe v. Wade* was this: as women got used to possessing some reproductive rights—and to making what felt like private, individual decisions about when and if to call on these rights—many Americans seemed to forget about the past. The vulnerability and danger that women had faced in all areas of their lives before the laws changed seemed to slip away in what abortion rights leader Kate Michaelman has called a loss of "collective memory."[21] And as Dr. Hanson said in 2003, "When you talk about abortion deaths that occurred in pre–*Roe v. Wade* days, young people today don't believe it. Young doctors today do not believe it."[22] Many people have no memory of the danger, and so they lack an immediate, visceral understanding of these matters. They lack basic information about the ways that women's access to dignity today has depended on their legal ability to manage their bodies.

DECADES OF RESISTANCE TO *ROE V. WADE* AND REPRODUCTIVE FREEDOM

As long as abortion was illegal, Americans did not protest against the vast number of abortion procedures carried out in the United States each year. As long as the law defined women, with regard to pregnancy, as what philosopher Susan Bordo calls "mere bodies," no one picketed the offices of known abortionists, and few spoke out in public against women seeking abortions.[23] This remained true as long as the courts and the culture at large considered pregnancy simply a physical fact and the core of women's fate.[24]

With *Roe v. Wade*, of course, all that changed. *Roe* said that women were not "mere bodies" and that pregnancy may be considered a social as well as a physical phenomenon. *Roe* suggested that women could properly weigh the conditions of their lives to determine the timing of motherhood. *Roe* acknowledged that women needed contraception and sometimes more to be able to do this. *Roe* even suggested sexual equality between men and women in this way: women could legally separate sex and pregnancy. And *Roe*, if inadvertently, suggested that women could legitimately separate motherhood and marriage.

As soon as abortion was legalized, giving women the right to accept the responsibilities and liabilities of pregnancy—or not—antiabortion resistance flourished. Political scientist Rosalind Petchesky has written about the abortion clinic as a symbol that threatens "patriarchal control" over "'their' young women's sexual 'purity'" and their subordinate status. Unwilling to tolerate these changes, bands of activists have made the clinic into "a target of white patriarchal wrath."[25]

Before moving into a discussion of violent resistance to *Roe v. Wade*, I want to look at some of the ways that recent public policy has denied the social dimension of pregnancy and sustained fertile women as "mere bodies." I also want to consider why there was so much resistance to reproductive rights after *Roe*.

Not surprisingly, poor women are most vulnerable to public policy initiatives. They depend more heavily on publicly funded health care programs than do middle-class women. When public funds are cut for family planning services, a poor woman may well lose access to contraception and thus lose considerable control over her fertility. In the late 1990s, public funding for these services fell to 65 percent of the 1980 level.[26] When welfare reform legislation was implemented in the mid-1990s (during the period of the most intense antiabortion activism in U.S. history), the proportion of women of childbearing age covered by Medicaid declined. The proportion of women with no health insurance increased. At the same time, the government did not augment funding for Title X, the largest source of public funding for contraception for women not covered by Medicaid.[27]

What was the result of these policy events? First of all, more poor women got abortions. Between 1994 and 2000, as abortion rates fell 20 percent for white women, they increased among poor, minority women. In 2000, low-income women made up 30 percent of all women of reproductive age but accounted for 57 percent of all women having abortions. Today the poorest women in the United States have the worst access to birth control and the highest abortion rates. In fact, the typical woman having an abortion in the United States today is between twenty and thirty years old. She has never been married. She has had a child. She lives in a city. She is poor, and she is Christian. These facts allow us to see again that pregnancy is more than a physical fact. It occurs in a social context, and when women lack social resources, including contraception and other reproductive health services, they often turn to abortion.[28]

Clearly, recent public policy has become the venue and the vehicle for denying poor women reproductive resources that other women can buy. When politicians and others champion restrictive public policies harmful to poor women, they are resisting and refusing some women's right to reproductive dignity. This is arguably another form of Petchesky's "white patriarchal wrath."

But why has the United States been so receptive to this wrath? If rates of abortion were almost as high before *Roe* as after, why has resistance to abortion and to some women's reproductive autonomy become so fierce after? Why are politicians who cut Title X funding (leading to higher rates of abortion) so often the same politicians who oppose abortion? Why have we seen an upsurge of antiabortion attitudes at the same time that cuts to funding for day care, health care, and housing, and opposition to living wages, for example, have made being a mother in the United States so difficult? What ties together these contemporary beliefs: first, that high school students must not receive any "sex education" other than abstinence-only instruction; second, that poor women should not have access to government-funded birth control; and, third, that almost all abortions should be recriminalized?

These expressions of reproductive politics all reflect, of course, the worldview of Comstock-era lawmakers. In the 1860s, the idea of teaching "sex" or distributing contraceptives in schools and the idea of a woman freely going to town for an abortion were blasphemy. According to many Americans, the loss of our capacity to recognize blasphemy —that is, our contemporary inability to recognize contempt for God— is at the heart of our ruined (or deeply tarnished) culture.

At the heart of the new fundamentalist religious movements in the United States is a belief that revitalizing traditional gender relations and gender roles is key to revitalizing our sense of blasphemy—and hence our sense of religiosity and reverence for God. In order to revitalize women's traditional role, it would be necessary, fundamentalists argue, to resurrect and revere both men's authority and women's natural destiny as mother. Fulfilling this destiny was incompatible with the use of contraception and abortion in the Comstock era. Religious fundamentalists argue that interfering with the outcomes of sex today is still incompatible with women's traditional roles, and still blasphemous. Today's traditionalists—the fundamentalists—call on this view that ties religion into government whether the object is a teenage girl, a poor woman, or any woman who is unwillingly pregnant.

Two other powerful ideas have interacted with the religious urge to revitalize our commitment to "women's destiny." First I'll look at how reproduction and reproducing women have emerged ever more strongly as symbols of insubordination that must be subdued by revitalized state and family authorities. Then I will discuss the rise of violence against abortion providers and clinics as a "valid" form of social protest. Together these developments, among others, have supported powerful and broad resistance to both abortion and *insubordinate reproduction*—that is, pregnancy and childbearing outside of traditional arrangements and against the rules of authority. We will see that this resistance is broad enough to account for the rise of apparently contradictory policies that govern women's reproductive lives in the United States today. I am thinking of policies that oppose abortion but punish childbearing.

In chapter 4 we saw how resistance to the civil rights movement was frequently expressed as resistance to the "excessive" fertility of African American women. Building on this history, by the late twentieth century, many Americans believed that insubordinate reproduction was the engine of social collapse. Social commentator Charles Murray expressed this attitude most famously in 1993 when he defined the harms caused by women who had babies but no husbands: "Illegitimacy is the single most important problem of our time—more important than crime, drugs, poverty, illiteracy, welfare or homelessness—because it drives everything else."[29] Murray made his assertion cleverly. He did not draw word pictures of actual "mothers" or "babies" in his famous pronouncement. He did not refer to "race." He knew that Americans had been well trained by the early 1990s to generate for themselves the implicitly Black images he intended.

Three years later, a group of prominent religious and intellectual elites published a document entitled "The America We Seek: A Statement of Pro-Life Principles and Concerns." This essay located the collapse of American society—measured by childhood poverty, illegitimacy, and child abuse—quite differently. The "abortion license" was the chief cause of collapse because it "gives excuse to women shirking responsibilities and contributes to the marginalization of fatherhood.

Despite the different emphases, Murray and the signatories of "The America We Seek" stood on common ground. They agreed that women's proclivity to sexual and reproductive misbehavior turns female reproductive capacity into the source and the site of the worst problems afflicting the United States.[30] They agreed that the source of the country's problems was not employers who paid women nonliving wages inadequate for supporting a child; nor was it men who preyed sexually on teenage girls or men who behaved violently toward women, or school systems that disallowed birth control education, or politicians who cut allocations for child care, ignoring the needs of working mothers. The problem was women themselves. The problem was women having children under the "wrong" conditions and women having abortions.

Defining the problem this way has led judges and legislators and others to craft solutions that punish women for misusing their reproductive capacity. The solutions aimed to prevent them from further insubordinate reproduction. For example, in the early 1990s, a judge in California began crafting conditional sentences for certain fertile women. If the lawbreaker gave up her reproductive freedom, she would get a more lenient punishment. This judge pressed one woman in his courtroom to agree to a Norplant contraceptive implant as a condition of probation. Realizing that the judge was issuing a legal order and ignoring the woman's right to a physician's determination that she could tolerate this contraceptive medicine, the woman said to the judge, "My health—that's just like saying, 'Take a gun and blow my head off. I don't want to risk my life.'"[31] In Kansas, as in many other states, legislators were enthusiastic about the prospect of paying $500 to any woman on welfare who agreed to use Norplant. A lawyer opposing such proposals said at the time, "We would be delighted if this were part of a package to improve reproductive health care for women, and there were no monetary incentives, but it's a bribe that pushes women into one choice instead of creating more choices. . . . [When a woman is on welfare] it crosses the line into unconstitutional coercion."[32] Yet judges around the country have ordered women to use birth control or otherwise avoid having children, with prison the price for refusing or violating the order.

Judges and legislators defined poor women's reproductive behavior as both insubordinate (resistant to authority) and expensive. The valuable reproduction of middle-class women, whether inside or outside of marriage, whether subordinate or insubordinate, has been subsidized by tax laws that allowed deductions for dependent children, child care, mortgages, and other family expenses. But politicians worked hard in the 1990s to "end welfare as we know it," by which many of them meant to stop "rewarding" poor women for having babies who, to put it crudely, cost society more than they were worth.[33] As legal scholar Dorothy Roberts has pointed out, all of these programs to constrain the reproduction of women on welfare have had a racial dimension "because such a large percentage of Black women rely on public assistance." In addition, media representations long encouraged Americans to believe in "the perception that all welfare women are Black" when in fact the majority have always been white.[34]

Almost all of the schemes offered in this era to stop poor women from insubordinate reproductive behavior had money at their center, either cost-cutting measures or bribes. Some involved cash bonuses to poor women if they agreed to use long-acting contraceptives. Legislatures mandated "family caps"—policies that denied a welfare-check increase to a woman who had an additional child while on welfare. Eventually the Congress mandated a five-year lifetime limit on welfare, or "legitimate" poverty, for any mother collecting benefits. Again, Charles Murray expressed the project clearly. He advocated "restoring a situation in which almost all women either get pregnant after they get married or get married after they get pregnant." Failing that, Murray wanted to bring back domestic adoption, a practice that honored traditional power relations. Murray's explained his goal: to "revitalize the natural mechanisms that used to work so effectively."[35] Murray and the conservative politicians, foundations, and think tanks he worked with on this project now argued that reproductive misbehavior caused a money problem for which there was a money solution.

When politicians broadcast disrespectful attitudes about poor women and their fertility, their attitudes tended to bleed across class lines. Attitudes toward the reproductive behavior of poor women tended to interact with and infect attitudes toward the power of any woman to manage her own fertility. Politicians crafting public policies to punish poor women for having babies drew on Supreme Court opinions justifying constraints on any woman's abortion access. At the same time, these politicians remained silent in the face of clinic bombings and murders—behavior that can most accurately be called a form of violent terrorism.

In all these ways the resistance to reproductive rights shaped the lives of women. When authorities limited women's power to make their own reproductive decisions, they also effaced the personhood of pregnant females and made them "third parties" to their own pregnancies. In Grand Rapids, Michigan, for example, a judge refused permission to a thirteen-year-old girl's request for abortion saying, "I find it impossible not to give regard for this totally innocent and defenseless creature that is within the womb of this lady."[36] A judge who calls a thirteen-year-old girl "a lady" is looking at the young girl standing before him and seeing something else. Politicians such as Newt Gingrich who joined Charles Murray in promoting the placement of babies of poor women in orphanages participated in an even more dramatic erasure. As feminist writer Katha Pollitt put it, they were teaching Americans "to think of children who have living parents as 'orphans' just because those parents are young, female, unmarried and poor. We are also being taught to see these women as having no rights and nothing to contribute—as being, in effect, dead."[37]

Judie Brown, the president of the American Life League, promoted a religious theory of procreation that could touch the life of any woman and even deny her personhood. "The woman who is raped," she wrote, "has a right to resist her attacker. But the preborn child is an innocent non-aggressor who should not be killed because of the crime of the father." Imagining the woman as a powerful participant in the sex act, if nowhere else, she added, "Incest is a voluntary act on the woman's part. . . . And to kill the child because of the identity of his father is no more proper in the case of incest than it is in the case of rape."[38]

In the post-*Roe* decades, many voices articulated the case against reproductive rights without ever confronting the proposition that legal scholar Reva Siegel offers: "that coercing [or punishing] motherhood is an act of violence against women, one that devalues what women give and give up in mothering."[39]

Some people impatient with public policy—feeling its impacts were too slow or too slight—resisted *Roe* with violence and in the name of "life." Many of these resisters spoke and wrote about being nourished by religious fundamentalism. Many were distressed about the loss of traditional gender roles and traditional families in American society. They mourned the loss of effective authority figures. Under the aegis of a wrathful God who directed them to punish sinners, resisters focused on abortion facilities. Frustrated that the Reagan administration did not succeed in overturning *Roe* in the 1980s, frustrated by the rising status of women in the United States and by the spread of "deviant" lifestyles, some resisters believed that only violence could be effective.

Randall Terry, founder of Operation Rescue, a violence-prone group that targeted clinics, spoke for many of the violent resisters: "If you believe abortion is murder, act like it's murder." Between 1977 when the first clinic was attacked, in Cincinnati, and 1988, abortion providers reported 42 arson attacks, 37 attempted bomb and arson attacks, 216 bomb threats, 65 death threats, 162 incidents of hate mail, and 220 incidents of vandalism. Then things got worse.[40]

[handwritten margin note: Pro-life terrorism]

In one year, 1992, with an abortion-rights president in the White House, one hundred acts of violence and harassment against women and health care providers were reported at abortion clinics. That year a number of doctors gave up providing abortions because they were unwilling any longer "to deal with pickets, protests, and bomb threats that came with doing abortions."[41] Then in the next two years, the violent resisters murdered Dr. David Gunn and Dr. John Bayard Britton, abortion providers; James Barrett, a doctor's bodyguard; and Shannon Lowney and Leanne Nichols, abortion clinic workers. In 1998 a violent resister murdered Dr. Bernard Slepian. Other abortion-related shootings and a great deal of clinic-directed violence took place in these years as well.

Resisters also produced tracts and other political and cultural materials, many of which justified or were used to justify the righteousness of violent tactics. The film *The Silent Scream* was released in 1984. The Reverend Michael Bray's "instructional" pamphlet "A Time to Kill" was published in 1994. In between, resisters produced countless materials teaching how to bomb and torch clinics, commit assault and battery, kidnap clinic personnel, and deliver a death threat. In 1997 antiabortion terrorist Neal Horsley created "The Nuremberg Files," a Web site displaying names and pictures of abortion doctors along with personal information about them such as their addresses. The names of three doctors who had been murdered appeared crossed out. Within hours of Dr. Slepian's murder, his name was "crossed off" as well. When the still-living doctors whose names and pictures were on the

Web site sued Horsley, they testified that the site's threat caused them and their families to live in constant fear. A jury found that, indeed, "The Nuremberg Files" represented "true threats to kill." Later, an appeals court found that the site did not exceed "free speech" guarantees and overturned the lower court's ruling against Horsley.

IMPACT OF RESISTANCE

What were the political and cultural consequences of these decades of resistance to *Roe v. Wade*'s claim that women had a legal right to decide whether or not to accept a pregnancy? How has *Roe's* claim stood up to pervasive suspicion that any woman might misbehave reproductively? How has *Roe's* claim been choked by the rise of religious fundamentalism and antiabortion violence?

First of all, the decades of resistance supported a complex variety of high-profile antiabortion institution-building. On the local level, nonviolent resisters created "problem pregnancy centers" in cities and towns around the country. In the mid-1980s, experts estimated that about two thousand of these centers were "counseling" pregnant girls and women to convince them to keep their babies or give them up for adoption, to make any choice but abortion.[42] These groups have since proliferated even further and now seek public funding for their work. New groups, often small but well publicized, assembled and reassembled, aiming to persuade the public, disrupt abortion practices, and change the law. These groups included the Pro-Life Action League (1980), Human Life International (1981), Operation Rescue (1986), Rescue America (the late 1980s), Missionaries to the Preborn (1991), Life Dynamics, Inc. (1992), and the American Coalition of Life Activists (1994), as well as the National Right to Life Committee (1973).

Anti-abortion-rights legislators at every level were energized by the array of organizations and the way that the public spotlight lit up their resistance. In these years legislators themselves mastered the art of resistance, establishing abortion-funding bans and mandatory waiting periods. They championed laws mandating distribution of cautionary information about fetal development, as well as laws mandating birth and death certificates for fetuses. They passed laws that limited abortions to hospitals and laws allowing public hospitals to refuse to perform abortions. They passed TRAP laws—Targeted Regulation of

Abortion Providers—imposing burdensome requirements on abortion practitioners that are not required of doctors who provide comparable outpatient health services.

Federal, state, and local legislators have also passed laws requiring "parental notification" and "spousal consent" and bans on certain methods of abortion as defined by politicians, not physicians. They have banned advertising and other activities informing the public about abortion services. They have generally created a labyrinth of rules and regulations that leave many women across the country confused and uncertain about their rights. Two students in a women's studies course at a campus of the State University of New York may be typical of far too many young women. Recently they mentioned in class that in high school their counselors had told them that New York State has a parental consent law. But this is not the case. Confusion, misinformation, and uncertainty prevail in an arena where clarity and good timing are of the essence.

In 1974, the U.S. Congress prohibited the Legal Services Corporation—lawyers for the poor—from advocating for only one constitutionally protected right: abortion. In 1983, Congress prohibited the U.S. Civil Rights Commission from authorization "to appraise, or to study and collect information about laws and policies of the Federal government or any other governmental authority in the United States, with respect to abortion." For years, Congress has extended the Hyde Amendment to virtually every relevant federal program—from Medicaid and the Indian Health Service, to the military, the Peace Corps, federal employees, and federal prisoners.

Extending the government's bias in other ways, legislative bodies have funded and promoted the dissemination of "bad science," that is, unproven, false, and scary "information" about the relationship between abortion and breast cancer, and the inevitability of postabortion trauma. All this abortion-related legislative activism and even more is based on the proposition that women must not be able to control their own fertility. This activism was not dampened—and was perhaps refueled—by the Supreme Court's recognition in *Planned Parenthood v. Casey* (1992) that "the ability of women to participate equally in the economic and social life of the nation has been facilitated by their ability to control their reproductive lives."

Since 1973, the nation's courts have regularly decided whether or not various activist-generated legislative bans and mandates are constitutional. Since the early 1980s, a majority of the Supreme Court has most often justified the demands of antiabortion activists while stopping short of outlawing abortion. In *Webster v. Reproductive Health Services* (1989), the Court allowed the state of Missouri to base public policy on the theological proposition that "life begins at conception."[43] It allowed the state to prohibit public employees and facilities from performing an abortion unnecessary to save the life of a woman, and imposed other abortion-limiting restrictions. Two years later, with *Rust v. Sullivan*, the Court upheld federal regulations barring physicians at publicly funded family planning clinics from providing their patients with abortion counseling or referrals.[44]

Then in 1992, while still declining to overturn *Roe v. Wade*, the Supreme Court made it much easier for the government's authority to trump a woman's authority over her own fertility.[45] *Roe* had required a "strict scrutiny" standard to test whether abortion restrictions interfered with a woman's ability to decide to end a pregnancy before "fetal viability," unless the restriction in question would actually promote a woman's health. If a restriction did interfere, courts were required to find it unconstitutional. *Planned Parenthood v. Casey* replaced the "strict scrutiny" standard with a lesser test, the test of "undue burden." Now courts have to weigh each restriction, measuring the degree to which it interferes with the woman's ability to decide to have an abortion. *Casey* ensured that judges could find an "undue burden" only under very limited circumstances. *Casey* also affirmed that even when federal government money is not at issue, the government can still enforce its preference against abortion.

All three of these decisions between 1989 and 1992 had the effect of deepening the impact of the Hyde Amendment. Court decisions that allowed public facilities serving mostly low-income women to restrict abortion access naturally mostly hurt poor women. Antiabortion activism in the courthouse, together with antiabortion activism in legislative settings, made two distinct imprints on American political culture in the post-*Roe* decades. First, this activism justified alienating poor women from "choice," broadcasting the message that poor women were bad choice makers and hadn't earned the right. Second, anti-abortion-rights activist judges and legislators showed where the fight against reproductive freedom could begin and could succeed. Standing with legislative activist Henry Hyde, these activists agreed that they would like to see all women prohibited from exercising abortion rights.

Since they couldn't at present accomplish that, they would do what they could, beginning with restricting the rights of poor women.

As we saw in chapter 5, President Eisenhower declared in 1959 that reproductive matters were a highly inappropriate subject for presidential comment. (And of course Eisenhower was referring only to a relatively tame topic like "family planning.") Things have changed. As female fertility became ever more politicized in the United States, presidents have found that this subject absolutely demands both their comment and their activism. Ronald Reagan regularly used his presidential platform to issue statements on the anniversary of *Roe v. Wade*. In 1983, on the ruling's tenth anniversary, Reagan published an essay entitled "Abortion and the Conscience of the Nation" that compared the fight against legal abortion to the fight against slavery. He wrote, "Abraham Lincoln recognized that we could not survive as a free land when some men could decide that others were not fit to be free and should therefore be slaves. Likewise, we cannot survive as a free nation when some men decide that others are not fit to live and should be abandoned to abortion and infanticide. My Administration is dedicated to the preservation of America as a free land, and there is no cause more important for preserving that freedom than affirming the transcendent right to life of all human beings, the right without which no other rights have meaning."[46]

In 1986, President Reagan designated January 19 National Sanctity of Human Life Day. Two years later, he issued the infamous "gag rule," limiting the reproductive health information that a publicly funded health clinic can give to a pregnant client—even if she specifically asks about abortion, even if she has heart disease, for example, or breast cancer.

Both President Reagan and President George H. W. Bush were unabashed anti-abortion-rights activists, employing a "litmus test" for appointees to the federal judiciary. By 1992, together they had appointed 60 percent of the country's sitting federal judges, a group that overwhelmingly upheld the restrictive abortion laws and policies that came before them.[47]

President Bill Clinton, the first president to support abortion rights, was equally activist, lifting several restrictions on abortion, including the "gag rule," as soon as he took office. He supported the Freedom of Access to Clinic Entrances Act (FACE) that prohibited the use of force, threats, or physical obstruction to interfere with a person trying to enter or leave an abortion clinic. Since 2000, George W. Bush has used his office to reinstate restrictions and to elevate the legal status of the fetus over the interests of pregnant women, among other forms of antiabortion activism. For the last generation, every president of the United States has been an abortion activist, pro or con.

Ten years after the *Roe* decision, one abortion rights activist reflected on the impact of antiabortion activism on ordinary women: "If you have to drive five hundred miles to get to a clinic, if you have to go through a picket line when you arrive, if you have to hear a doctor say that what you are about to do is killing someone, and if then you must go home for a 24-hour waiting period . . . they are trying to take out from the back door what they can't get out the front."[48]

Finally, the most lasting impact of antiabortion activism so far has been widespread public support of a severely constrained arena of choice, a kind of *supervised reproductive consumerism*. Constrained choice justifies legal abortion only on narrow grounds that have little or nothing to do with women's rights or women's dignity as adult persons or as citizens. For example, anti-abortion-rights activists have been successful, convincing many Americans that abortion should not be available as a remedy for "sexual carelessness," but may be a legitimate solution as a victim's right in the case of rape.[49]

Constrained choice follows the tradition of the Comstock Law, in which the government has the right to withhold information about reproductive control and to decide what kinds of information are appropriate or inappropriate for fertile females to have. The government may decide what kind of information medical professionals may disseminate. *Rust v. Sullivan* limited the speech and the medical practices of physicians. When laws force women to sit through mandated "counseling" sessions, the women must listen to a script that "scolds" them for considering abortion and discourages them from pursuing this legal option.

The government also constrains choice when it tries to "protect" young people from information about birth control, sexually transmitted diseases, and all other subjects related to heterosexual relations and reproduction. When public funding is available only for "abstinence" education, we aren't preparing young women for reproductive freedom. We are conditioning them to adapt themselves to severely constrained choices.[50] When the National Institutes of Health is barred from funding research into any reproductive-control method that terminates pregnancy, we have constrained choice.

In 1981, state courts in Massachusetts and California decided, based on their state constitutions, that (in the words of the California court) "when the state finances the cost of childbirth, but will not finance the termination of pregnancy, it realistically forces an indigent pregnant woman to choose childbirth even though she has the constitutional right to refuse to do so."[51] The federal government has expressed its bias against women's constitutional right to privacy as defined in *Roe v. Wade* by paying for childbirth but not abortion and by paying for sterilization procedures but not abortion. These laws and policies also construct constrained choice.

Some observers have claimed that the government's response to anti-abortion-rights violence—too often tolerant—is another element of constrained choice. Reproductive health and rights advocate Brenda Joyner has linked clinic violence to other forms of vigilante activity such as lynching and Ku Klux Klan terrorism. Historically, authorities have ignored or treated these forms of terrorism lightly, forcing targeted populations to live without basic protections and dignity.[52] Also, by the end of the 1980s, such a massive portion of abortion-rights groups' resources were allocated to clinic defense work that all other activist initiatives—such as building broad access to reproductive health services for all women—were stunted.

Altogether, these strategies to construct and enforce a very narrow kind of choice (allowing a range of options for middle-class women and very few choices for poor women) have had harsh consequences for women struggling for reproductive rights. Here are three major consequences: First, when public policies enforce distinct reproductive experiences for distinct groups of women, coalition-building becomes very difficult. Since 1973, middle-class women have gotten used to having "the right to choose" and to thinking of themselves as modern, choice-making individuals. Typically, middle-class women lose sight of the fact that all women require reproductive rights and that broad access to these rights is a political, not merely an individual, issue.

Second, the Supreme Court's "undue burden" test of the impact of restrictions, one by one, doesn't measure the accumulated impact of restriction upon restriction—the "constellation" of restrictions. Studies have shown that these restrictions "work." They decrease the number of abortions. Wouldn't the "undue burden" test be fairer if it measured just how constrained choice has become state by state, taking all restrictions into account?

Is it possible for the "undue burden" test to measure "the impact" of restrictions on *all women* when we have seen that restrictions impact different groups of women so very differently?[53]

Finally, all the many efforts to constrain women's reproductive choices have been built on the idea that a woman who decides to end a pregnancy may well be a bad woman: sexually careless or lacking in maternal feeling or both. Legislators and judges continually narrow the meaning of choice on the grounds that women with characteristics like these need supervision. They cannot exercise good judgment on their own. Legislatures and courts can justify forcing women to have children because allowing women to decide whether or not to have a child might lead to a bad decision. Legal scholar Reva Siegel observes, "Basing abortion regulations on deeply biased attitudes toward women makes fetal-saving by compelled pregnancy seem reasonable where otherwise it would not."[54]

ENLARGING THE FETUS

The Supreme Court has never issued a decision that explicitly interprets the Constitution as allowing the government to force women to bear children. Yet legislators, judges, and others pursue laws and policies that value the fetus more highly than the pregnant woman and use this valuation to justify compelling pregnant women to give birth. Fetal-rights politics, like anti-abortion-rights politics, effaces the needs and rights of pregnant women in order to elevate the status of the fetus, to protect men, to shore up traditional social relations, and to control pregnant women.[55]

As we've seen in earlier chapters, abortion opponents (especially those who were not Catholics) did not historically put the fetus first. People who spoke out against abortion in the past worried about physical danger to the woman. They worried about the impact on society of the separation of sex and pregnancy. They drew attention to the "inevitable" relationship between abortion and women's sexual promiscuity and worried about how abortion undermined traditional patriarchal prerogatives over all matters of reproduction.

Across the second half of the twentieth century, however, the concept of fetal personhood gradually emerged. Technology played a role as sonogram imaging allowed us to "see" the fetus while "not seeing" the pregnant woman on the examination table. Imaging technology supports a kind of zero-sum visibility: you can see either the fetus on the screen, or the woman, but not both together. At the same time, some Americans began to regard babies as a kind of commodity, in part the result of the rise of adoption. This practice has typically been pursued as a competition in which many white "families" compete against each other for the valuable prize: a white baby. It is useful, too, to remember Sherri Finkbine's experience in the early 1960s. Finkbine's ordeal moved many Americans to sympathy for a nice woman who only wanted—and deserved—a "perfect child." Today, the whole raft of new genetic tests that can assess the "quality" of the fetus feeds an ever more intense sense of parents' entitlement to this perfect baby.[56] In short, once the fetus/baby became visible, valuable, and potentially perfect (or perfectible), the concept of "fetal personhood" flourished.

And once the fetus could be imagined as a baby "person," some people took the position that it should be endowed with "rights." Others have argued that since the fetus cannot sustain life independent of the pregnant woman's body, and since the fetus cannot be reached except through the woman's body, it can hardly be defined as a "person" with "rights" in the same way that we ordinarily use these terms.[57]

Nevertheless, the emergence of "fetal personhood" and "fetal rights" has been a culturally and politically powerful development. These ideas have reshaped the possibility of women's reproductive rights. To begin with, "fetal rights" language has provided many people with a way to think and talk about pregnancy that eliminates the woman from the picture. Even though those most fiercely focused on the fetus are typically religious persons, "fetal rights" has a secular sound. "Fetal rights" seems to place questions about the fetus in the civil, not the theological, domain. Political scientist Rachel Roth has pointed out how courts have used this association, misconstruing *Roe v. Wade* by turning the state's interest in the potentiality of human life into actual constitutional rights for fetuses. Feminist theorist Susan Bordo describes this new rights-bearing fetus as a "super-subject," with far more civil rights than a two-year-old child.[58]

At the same time, "fetal personhood" allows fundamentalist Christians to condemn abortion as a sin, since it kills the fetal *person*, a creature made in God's image. The enlargement of the fetus allows this emblem of life to incorporate both civic and theological meaning while draining away the personhood—the rights and needs—of the pregnant woman, leaving her at the mercy of the "super-subject" inside of her body.

Now that the "fetal person" has become so powerful, we must think about "who" this person is. What kind of person do "fetal rights" advocates imagine the fetus to be? First of all, photographs and prose capture the fetus as precious, beloved, white, and vulnerable. Scholar Carol Mason shows how anti-abortion-rights zealots aggressively cast fetuses as the victims of a "Jewish-engineered" holocaust, a murdered "next generation."[59]

Susan Bordo points out that the fetus has "come a long way" over the past several hundred years. "From 'biblical seed' to mystical 'homunculus,'" the fetus is now "an individual with medical problems that can be diagnosed and treated, that is, a patient. Although he cannot make an appointment and seldom complains, this patient will at all times need a physician."[60] Others have pointed out that the fetus (typically a "middle-class fetus," since many poor woman cannot afford prenatal screenings) has become more "deserving" of medical care than a child, especially the child of a poor woman. In 2002 President George W. Bush proposed defining fetuses as children for the purpose of using the federal Child Health Insurance Program (CHIP) to support prenatal care for low-income pregnant women. With this plan, President Bush defined the fetus as the primary beneficiary of health care, the pregnant woman as secondary, a mere vessel for the fetus.

The fetus's valuable and beloved personhood is most clearly imagined through the claim that it must be "rescued" from harm, like a princess in a tower or a prisoner of war. When we imagine the fetus in either of these ways or in other kinds of mortal danger, we usually imagine the pregnant woman as incompetent, irresponsible, murderous, or all three. For example, quite often the fetus is portrayed as needing rescue from a misbehaving pregnant woman such as a "drug user." In this scenario, the pregnant woman is a criminal whose wanton hedonism puts the fetus at risk. Or the fetus must be rescued from the murderous woman whose "right to choose" is portrayed as ludicrous next to the fetus's "right to life."

These ways of imagining who the fetus is—and the plight of the fetus—are rarely coupled with visions of the *vulnerable* pregnant woman or the *responsible* pregnant woman. She is rarely the patient who needs medical care herself or a person who resists having a child she cannot manage. Our contemporary ability to visualize the fetus and to test its health and treat it like a patient allows us to imagine the fetus as a more-real person than the pregnant woman. The pregnant woman, drained of reality, increasingly becomes a dehumanized container whose only purpose should be to serve the fetus correctly. This remains true whether or not the woman has the resources to fulfill this purpose. Plus, once she chooses to get pregnant and stay pregnant, the woman-container is held responsible for any less-than-perfect outcome. She is blamed if she gives birth to an imperfect baby.[61] Imagining the fetus as a perfect victim seems to require imagining the pregnant woman as a perfect villain.

We know that *Roe v. Wade* affirms a pregnant woman's rights to privacy, to bodily integrity, and to due process—a package of rights that should protect her from being singled out for unique restrictions and penalties associated with her pregnancy. But given the good fetus/bad woman way of thinking that prevails in many minds, pregnant woman are still frequently degraded by their pregnancies in the name of protecting the fetus. For example, corporations have excluded all fertile women from certain jobs defined as potentially harmful to their fetuses. Corporations have excluded women rather than take the responsibility for providing all workers with environmentally safe working conditions. "Fetal protection" policies in chemical, steel, and auto plants and other manufacturing industries tend to exclude women from high-paying, traditionally male jobs and send them back to low-paying, traditionally female jobs. Often these policies have offered women the false "choice" of getting sterilized—giving up the right to reproduce—if they want a traditionally male job. Rachel Roth points out that traditionally lower-paying female jobs that carry potential dangers for pregnant employees, like nurse or farmworker, have not been subject to fetal protection regulations.[62]

Roth also catalogues other degradations and coercions in the name of the fetus that pregnant women face, especially if they lack the personal and financial resources to protect themselves. Pregnant women have been forced to have Caesarian deliveries, submit to unwanted medical procedures on behalf of the fetus, medicated, forced to stay in the hospital. Even when pregnant women in these situations are demonstrably mentally competent adults, Roth shows that physicians and judges have defined them as "irrational, incompetent, and bad."[63]

Women's reproductive capacity has been used to reduce them to "second-class citizens" in relation to their first-class-citizen fetuses in still other ways, especially when they are poor. This is particularly clear in situations involving poor, pregnant drug-using women. In a number of cases, most egregiously in South Carolina, poor women who became pregnant tried over the course of their pregnancies to get treatment. But no public drug treatment centers in the state admitted pregnant clients. Subsequently, women were arrested, found guilty of "fetal endangerment," and incarcerated for long sentences. Many middle-class people who are substance abusers, including pregnant women, have the resources, such as private health insurance, to arrange for their drug use to be treated as an illness and not a crime.

Legal scholar Dorothy Roberts highlights the racial dimension of these prosecutions. She writes about a study of pregnant women in Florida, a state where hospitals are required to report to police when pregnant women test positive for having used drugs or alcohol. This study and others have shown "little difference" regarding substance abuse behavior among women no matter what their race or class. But "Black women were ten times more likely than whites to be reported to government authorities." Roberts argues the chilling point that "choosing these particular mothers makes the prosecution of pregnant women more palatable to the public." Observing that pregnant drug users could have an abortion to avoid prosecutions—ending the pregnancy altogether—Roberts concludes, "It is the choice of carrying a pregnancy to term that is being penalized."[64] If the state valued these pregnancies and children, wouldn't the government respond to the drug addiction of a poor, pregnant woman of color by making treatment available?

This discussion has shown how the "enlargement of the fetus" depends on the degradation of the pregnant woman. Unfortunately, public policy and public opinion too often grab value from the pregnant woman and grant it to the new "fetal person." People who are concerned about this trend have asked questions about how deeply policymakers or the public really care about the fetus, and especially about the children, once they are born. Perhaps their rhetoric and their willingness to punish and constrain pregnant women in the name of the fetus actually point away from the fetus and toward women. If the state or the public were primarily concerned with the fetus, this concern could take the form of public supports for women who want to become mothers so that all women are more likely to bear and raise healthy children.[65]

TEENAGE PREGNANCY AND
REINSCRIBING THE LINES OF AUTHORITY

In 1966, a doctor concerned about pregnant and childbearing teens drew attention to the ways that authority was arrayed against these girls. He said, "What irony it is that a society which denies sex education, contraception, and abortion, a society which gives less than adequate medical care and almost non-existent counseling, and a society which unilaterally excludes educationally high-risk girls from school because of the non-criminal condition of pregnancy, is the same society which publicly condemns the female who is pregnant out of wedlock."[66]

Not long after the doctor published his lament, laws and policies governing society's response to teenager sex-and-pregnancy began to change dramatically. In 1971, in a decision called *Ordway v. Hargraves,* a Massachusetts court said that schools could not expel unwed pregnant girls, and with the passage of Title IX in 1972, Congress made this a national policy, by denying funds to schools that didn't comply with *Ordway.*[67] Hundreds of programs sprang up around the country in the early 1970s to accommodate the educational needs of girls who just a few years before would have been tossed out of school.

A series of court decisions and congressional acts granted teenagers new rights and services. In 1972 the Supreme Court decision in *Eisenstadt v. Baird* extended the right to use birth control to unmarried people, millions of whom would be teenage girls. In 1973, of course, all fertile women, including teenage girls, were granted rights to end a pregnancy. In 1978 Congress amended Title X to require that family planning clinics serve teenagers confidentially, for free, without parental notification.[68]

But the earliest parental notification law also came soon after *Roe.* The Supreme Court found the first efforts to impose this restriction unconstitutional—for an interesting reason. After *Roe,* Missouri created a raft of restrictions, including one that required girls below eighteen years old to present written permission from their parents when they went for a first-trimester abortion. The Court found that "Constitutional rights do not mature and come into being magically only when one attains the state-defined age of majority."

When the Court considered why parental consent might well be justified, it focused on the issue of parental *authority*. Justice Blackmun, writing for the majority, suggested that parents with the power to veto a girl's decision to get an abortion would probably not "strengthen the family unit" by vetoing their daughter's plans. Blackmun added, "Neither is it likely that such veto power will enhance parental authority or control where the minor and the non-consenting parent are so fundamentally in conflict and the very existence of the pregnancy already has fractured the family structure."[69]

Justice Blackmun understood the fraught role of parental authority here. When sexually active and pregnant teenage girls began to use their new rights—birth control, abortion, school attendance—and when white teens followed Black teens, claiming their right to be mothers, these developments caused crises of authority. Parents were in shock over public evidence of their daughters' sex lives. They were horrified to realize that unmarried daughters were making their own sexual and reproductive decisions. They were mortified to realize that parental rules about sex and its consequences didn't seem to matter anymore.[70]

Shock reverberated beyond the family. Clergy, teachers, policymakers, politicians, and other protectors of adult authority defined this kind of behavior as constituting the ultimate crisis of authority. They described what they saw using metaphors—*epidemic* of teen pregnancy, sexual *revolution*—that summoned up the sense of dangerous forces completely resistant to control. These terms suggested events that overturned existing structures and relationships of authority in which grown-ups controlled young people.

As teenage girls became threatening emblems of sexual and reproductive insubordination, politicians and others devoted national and community resources to reestablishing parental authority. For example, they devised new parental consent laws that gained Supreme Court approval, new welfare rules mandating that poor young mothers live with their parents, and abstinence-only sex education programs that aimed to reestablish stigmas associated with unwed sex and childbearing.

These policy initiatives have been coupled with a general education campaign focused on the old eugenic lessons: poor young women produce poor-quality babies. Poor babies shouldn't be born. If poor babies are born to poor young women, they should be transferred to deserving families headed by middle-class grown-ups.[71] The year that welfare reform was implemented, 1996, a former official of the Reagan administration and a prominent spokesperson for revitalizing parental authority identified adoption—termination of the mother's rights—as "the best alternative we have to protect a child's interest in a postwelfare world."[72]

Recently, rates of teenage pregnancy and teenage abortion have declined significantly. Between 1991 and 1996, the birthrate fell across the board for white, Black, American Indian, Asian, and Hispanic young women fifteen to nineteen years old in every state. The decline was steepest for Black teenagers. Also, the teen abortion rate fell about 30 percent in these years.[73]

Often these developments are interpreted as signs that adults are successfully reinscribing their authority over teens. To a degree, this is probably true. But other factors may contribute as well. For example, many teenagers are using condoms more consistently as protection against HIV/AIDS—and thus, pregnancy. And the strong economy during the 1990s meant that many teenagers had more to lose by having a baby than they would have during leaner economic times.

On closer inspection, though, strong adult authority does not always guarantee health and safety for teenage girls. Sometimes forcing young women to bow to authority can be dangerous. For example, we know that after a parental notification law was put into effect in Minnesota, the birthrate for teens under eighteen rose 38 percent in Minneapolis while it held steady for women over eighteen. Was this a positive development? How do we factor in the results of studies suggesting that teenage childbearing can create huge problems for young mothers? One four-year, federally funded study found that teenage girls who got abortions "did better economically and educationally and had fewer subsequent pregnancies than those who chose to bear children."[74]

How do we compare the value of parental authority and parental wishes with what we know about the risks of pregnancy for young women, including elevated rates of anemia for teenagers and higher rates of complications at birth, preeclampsia, and elevated rates of mortality? How do we assess the value of new welfare policies that make teenage parents live in their parents' homes against the findings of a study that reports 31 percent of welfare-receiving minor parents reported that this rule actually put them in an unsafe situation? Other studies have shown that teenage mothers who live with their own par-

Stunting maturity ✗

ents tend to be more "dependent" than other young parents. Coercing young mothers to live with their parents may, in fact, turn out to stunt their maturity at just the moment when, as mothers of young children, they must develop personal resources.[75]

Efforts to use public policy to restore authority over teenage girls have not been confined to the parental variety. Recent policy initiatives "promoting marriage" are designed to restore this beleaguered institution to its pre–World War II status as a citadel of social, sexual, and reproductive stability—and to its status as a site of male authority. Again, how are we to evaluate such initiatives when numerous studies have shown that when teenage girls marry because they are pregnant, they are much less likely to go back to school after the baby is born than girls who do not marry? Girls who marry are much more likely to have a rapid second birth. Both of these impacts are linked to worse economic and educational outcomes for both the young mother and her child.[76]

Public policies have also been crafted to restore religious authority over the lives of sexually and reproductively insubordinate teens. The Adolescent and Family Life Act of 1981 (AFLA), often referred to as "the chastity bill," handed some major traditional parental and religious duties over to government-funded programs. The AFLA announced that the government and its agents would teach a particular moral or religious stance toward teenage sex (don't do it), toward abortion (don't do it), and toward adoption (the only appropriate outcome of any teenage pregnancy).

Despite the fact that by the end of their teens, 70 percent of American teenagers have had sexual intercourse, the government promotes withholding contraception information on "moral" grounds more vigorously than ever. By the early 2000s, more than one-third of school districts that offer "sex education" instruction "require that abstinence be taught as the only option outside of marriage." When contraception is mentioned in these programs, it "may only be discussed in a way that highlights its shortcomings."[77]

In 2004, a congressional study found that among the thirteen abstinence-only sex education programs that the federal government funds, eleven of them, used by "sixty-nine organizations in twenty-five states, contain unproved claims, subjective conclusions or outright falsehoods regarding reproductive health, gender traits and when life begins." For example, some programs teach that a girl can become pregnant by touching a boy's genitals. Programs also inaccurately teach high school-ers that AIDS can be transmitted by sweat and tears. They teach that half of the gay male teenagers in the United States have tested positive for AIDS, which is also untrue. Despite evidence to the contrary appearing in standard obstetric textbooks, one abstinence-only curriculum, called "Me, My World, My Future," teaches that "women who have an abortion 'are more prone to suicide' and that as many as ten percent of them become sterile."[78] When publicly funded (or privately funded) "educational" programs disregard the truth in order to control the behavior of young women, then young women are more likely to be harmed.

Indeed, one must ask, how have all these efforts to bolster traditional authority affected young women themselves? Might so much governmental emphasis on the importance of traditional, external authorities encourage young women to think of themselves as lacking authority and the personal resources we associate with autonomy? Today we have some evidence that huge numbers of young women do not possess sufficient power over their own lives to be safe from unwanted sexual relations. For example, 84 percent of high school girls believe that a girl is more likely to lose her boyfriend if she doesn't have sex with him. This is true even though most high school kids also believe that girls' "reputations" are harmed by having sex. Researchers generally agree that though teenage girls want to be powerful, they "often tell stories of powerlessness and difficulty controlling the progression and nature of their sexual encounters." Very young girls and teenagers with older boyfriends, especially, report high rates of involuntary or coerced first intercourse.[79]

One eighteen-year-old girl in this situation described how her reluctance to have sex was "broken down by an older boyfriend who said he wanted to see her in maternity clothes. 'He just pumped my head up. . . . He kept saying, "When you going to have my baby?" Then when I told him I was pregnant, it was like, "So?"'"[80] If government funds and programs were devoted to helping young women develop a sense of personal authority instead of to convincing them to bend to external authorities, perhaps this young woman would have responded differently to her boyfriend's manipulation.

When public policies prefer to supply funding for family planning organizations that promote adoption of babies born to teenagers, then the government and the law are taking this position: teenage mothers are basically unfit to be mothers.[81] The government is promoting the exclusion of any young woman from the dignified status of legitimate mother, as if age and wealth are the core characteristics of a legitimate mother—and as if biology has nothing to do with motherhood. And yet, most teenage girls who have babies keep and mother their children. If the government and the law supported the motherhood and mothering work of young women raising their children, perhaps millions of teenage mothers in the United States today could raise their children with the dignity and authority now denied them.

The law and public policy are today focused on implementing an ideology: that parents, the church, the school, and the state must hold authority over young women's reproductive capacity. Young women themselves cannot manage this authority, even though (or especially because) their own bodies are at stake. The outcomes of these laws and policies are apparently much less important than the ideology itself. A recent study of the experiences of young mothers receiving welfare found that despite the vivid and punitive language of welfare reform, which warns against reproduction and lays out the penalties, teen parents remain, years after the implementation of welfare reform, "undercounted, untracked, oversanctioned, underserved."[82]

Not surprisingly, the evidence mounts that many young people have internalized the government's message: teenage girls are not to be trusted with authority over their own bodies, even their own fertility. As this message becomes ever clearer and louder when it comes to abortion, larger numbers of young people find the fetus a more trustworthy and sympathetic subject than the pregnant girl. As a Minnesota teenager put it recently, "It's more about the baby's rights than the woman's rights."[83]

Is it possible to raise self-reliant girls on their way to self-possessed adulthood in the twenty-first century in a cultural context in which their own bodies, their sexuality, their fertility, their pregnancies, and their offspring are not their own business? The government prefers teenage girls not to have access to sex education or to birth control information and devices. The government promotes abstinence or, failing that, pregnancy and marriage, as if the culture has not budged one inch since the days of Postmaster Comstock.

PRISONERS AS "IDEAL" PREGNANT WOMEN

I have argued here that fetuses and teenage girls, like poor women, have become vehicles for rehabilitating traditional power relations. In different ways, each of these "emblems" has come to stand for—and to explain—why fertile females are not suited to exercise control over their own bodies. On the other hand, the female prisoner has emerged as the "ideal" pregnant woman.

The number of incarcerated women in the United States has increased fivefold since 1980, to about 150,000 today in federal, state, and local prisons and jails. About 80 percent are mothers of children under the age of eighteen. And mothers of young children are the fastest-growing population of incarcerated persons in the United States.[84] Political scientist Rachel Roth and others explain the enormous increase in the number of incarcerated women by pointing to two main factors: mandatory drug sentencing laws; and the huge and growing economic stake in mass imprisonment that local communities, state governments, and private corporations now have in the "prison industrial complex."[85]

About 10 percent of imprisoned women are pregnant at any given time. Like other prisoners, these women are resourceless and powerless, and live their days subjugated to institutional authority. Roth has shown us how hard this authority can come down on pregnant women. No laws exist that remove an imprisoned woman's reproductive rights as defined by *Roe v. Wade* because she is serving time, for example, for cocaine use. But in practice, she is typically choiceless. In some ways, state policies make the jobs of prison officials easier precisely because they are "unwritten and unregulated" and are wielded arbitrarily in "an arena fraught with allegations of race and class bias." Roth observes, "For every [imprisoned] woman who has to fight the authorities to exercise her abortion rights, there is another woman who feels pressured into having an abortion she does not really want." Officials in the criminal justice system impose these gendered punishments on women, coercing them to reproduce or not, as the officials decide.[86] Plus, under the Adoption and Safe Families Act, the state is negating their identities as mothers and subjecting these women to fast-track termination of their parental rights.[87] Incarcerated mothers resemble insubordinate mothers in the nineteenth century, vulnerable to losing custody of their children. Incarcerated mothers also resemble enslaved women, who, as a condition of their enslavement, had control over neither their own bodies nor their children.

This may be a particularly chilling comparison, since African American women, most of them mothers, are imprisoned at disproportionate rates in the United States. African Americans make up 12 percent of the U.S. population. But 46 percent of female inmates in state prisons are African American, and 39 percent of women in federal prisons are African American. As a result of law enforcement practices that target women of color, a disproportionate number of African American women are subjected to reproductive coercion and child loss.[88] Legal scholar Dorothy Roberts places policy outcomes like these squarely in the realm of racial domination: "Denying someone the right to bear children—or punishing her for exercising that right—deprives her of a basic part of her humanity." The use of this kind of control against disproportionately African American and other women of color, Roberts insists, functions "to preserve a racial hierarchy that essentially disregards Black humanity."[89]

But is this really a problem about race and gender? Or have incarcerated women simply forfeited whatever reproductive rights they may have had as "free women" when they broke the law? Isn't loss of freedom (that is, incarceration) simply incompatible with "reproductive freedom"? Put another way, one might think that the law that gives the government the right to take away the freedom of a law-breaking woman also gives the government the authority to punish this woman in whatever way the state decides is best.

We need only recall the images of American soldiers degrading the bodies and persons of prisoners at Abu Ghraib, the Baghdad jail, to understand the problem with the any-punishment-goes argument. And of course the Eighth Amendment to the Constitution prohibits the infliction on prisoners of "cruel and unusual punishments," a category that would surely include uniquely gendered and racialized punishments targeting reproductive capacity and maternal rights.

Federal courts have ruled that women, including pregnant women, do not lose their constitutional rights, including their reproductive rights, when they enter prison.[90] Yet prison regulations and practices often trample on women's reproductive rights as if these rights do not exist or apply inside the jailhouse. Under these circumstances, incarcerated pregnant women are living pre–*Roe v. Wade* lives, reproductively resourceless, choiceless, powerless, and dependent on the decisions of prison authorities. It may be that a prison official is a person interested in demonstrating how institutional or state or male power can be deployed to punish and humiliate women. A prison official may be more sympathetic to the "fetal person" than to the incarcerated woman. Or a prison official may have a strong commitment to an imprisoned woman's reproductive rights. In all of these scenarios, however, the woman is at the mercy of the official's preferences.

When we review the reproductive experiences of incarcerated women in the United States today, we end up recapitulating all of the themes at the center of this book. We end up recapitulating all the struggles women in the United States have waged, from 1776 to 2005, to gain and sustain rights over their own bodies against the determination of various power holders to deny women this basic human right.

Looking inside women's prisons, we can see policies and practices that reinforce enduring eugenic attitudes about women deemed unfit to bear children. When incarcerated pregnant women are denied prenatal health care, this is a sign that the system finds them unfit and doesn't care if they stay that way. The resulting high rates of miscarriage and stillbirth are signs that the prison authorities don't believe that incarcerated women are fit to be mothers, or that their babies ought to be born. (One California study indicates a rate of miscarriage and stillbirth fifty times higher for incarcerated women than for women outside.)[91]

Amnesty International considers the shackling of women during labor and delivery that occurs in prisons "a cruel and unusual practice." Shackling endangers the fetus and the woman as she tries to give birth. This practice surely constitutes another sign of disregard and degradation. It also functions as a punishment appropriate for reproductively insubordinate women—that is, women who should not be having babies, who do not deserve to be mothers, and yet they are.

On the one hand, prison policies and practices define incarcerated pregnant women as criminally dangerous and maternally irresponsible. In this scenario, attention is focused entirely on the woman. She looms large, justifying punishments such as coerced abortion. When prisons deal from this position, officials can, apparently, use abortion as an explicit weapon and a punishment. As Roth has found, "Some prisoners, especially those whose pregnancies are the result of sexual abuse by guards, are pressured to have abortions and then punished if they refuse, often placed in 23-hour lockdown."[92] In this sort of case, abortion effaces the crime.

On the other hand, the criminal justice system and prison practices are just as likely to efface the women and enlarge the fetus. Here, officials claim the power to "protect the child." As we saw earlier, officials can claim an interest in "protecting the child" when they punish a pregnant woman for using drugs. Sometimes a single positive drug test becomes the basis for finding a woman an unfit mother.[93] Or, claiming an interest in "the child," criminal justice officials may punish the pregnant woman for expressing her intention to have an abortion while she is in court for any infraction. Rachel Roth describes how an Ohio judge, Patricia Cleary, gave a young woman a six-month sentence for credit card forgery instead of the customary sentence of probation for that crime. The judge explained the basis of her decision: to prevent the woman from getting a second-trimester abortion. Judge Cleary later spoke in a church, rejoicing with the congregation that she had been "in the right place at the right time for the Lord to pick" her to save a baby.[94]

We see through Judge Cleary's words that the criminal justice system and the prison facility can become instruments in a religious crusade. The prison has also become an instrument of eugenic policy. The reproductive capacity of incarcerated women—mostly poor women and women of color—provides the occasion and the opportunity for these projects. Both projects violate Judge A. Leon Higginbotham's ringing words: "Prison walls do not form a barrier separating prison inmates from the protections of the Constitution."[95]

Prison policies and practices force pregnant prisoners to exercise their reproductive rights from what Roth calls "the far end of the continuum of 'reproductive freedom.'" Their experiences not only reflect a long history of women's struggle against reproductive coercion.[96] The experiences of pregnant prisoners also demonstrate how strongly some authorities are still committed to the idea—the ideal—that pregnant women are properly dominated by authorities they must obey in the name of the law. In prisons, even when officials lack explicit legal authority, pregnant women can still be made to obey because they face authorities who can extract obedience.

MOVING TARGETS

In the introduction I wrote that *Pregnancy and Power* is not a complete recounting of all the movements and events in the history of reproductive politics in the United States. Nor, I wrote, would the book incorporate histories of the reproductive experiences of all groups of women in this country. There are a number of pressing contemporary issues that I have not written about, such as the political battles surrounding the distribution and uses of "emergency contraception," and the problems associated with the dwindling number of abortion providers in the United States. I haven't laid out the debates over why drugs to enhance male sexual performance, such as Viagra, are covered by many health insurance programs that do not offer coverage for female contraception. I have not written about the politics of stem cell research, which, because the cells are often derived from fertility-clinic embryos no longer wanted by prospective parents, is an incendiary topic within the domain of reproductive politics. I have not written about current work exposing environmental impacts on reproductive health. All of these issues clarify how "reproductive politics" in the twenty-first century is a struggle between women claiming the right to make decisions about their own lives and their own bodies, against an increasingly demanding, intrusive central government that more and more frequently invokes religious and corporate language to justify power over women's bodies and their lives.

In response to these developments, scholars and activists have shown how various groups of women resist central control over their reproductive lives and have insisted on "reproductive health" and "reproductive justice" for themselves.[97] Many women-of-color organizations have been interested in bringing *reproductive health* and the *right to be a mother* and a broad concept of *reproductive justice* into the heart of our thinking about what it means to be a dignified fertile woman in the United States, particularly a woman of color.

Groups such as the National Black Women's Health Project (founded in 1984), the National Latina Health Organization (1986), and a number of other sister groups have stressed the need to break the silence surrounding the fact that reproductive capacity has been a site of exploitation, punishments, and other forms of oppression. Members of these groups have worked to create safe spaces for fertile women who are often reviled by the larger society. They have worked to articulate and meet the needs of women in their own communities.

In the 1980s and 1990s, women-of-color organizations developed this perspective: the elements of reproductive justice for some women may well constitute reproductive tyranny for others. For example, in the 1970s and beyond, legal contraception and accessible sterilization broadened the choices of middle-class women. But at the same time, public health officials drew coercively on these same methods to constrain the childbearing of women of color. Most fundamentally, the new women-of-color organizations have been clear about the dramatic limits of the mainstream pro-choice/pro-abortion rights agenda. Women of color have argued that "choice" masks the economic, political, and environmental context in which women live their reproductive lives. Choice, they argue, has masked the ways that laws, policies, and public officials punish or reward the reproductive activity of different groups of women differently. And choice has masked the equal importance of *access* to reproductive health services and the *right* to these services and has obscured the link between all forms of oppression. What, after all, does "choice" mean to a woman who doesn't have enough money to pay for the variety of options that are only available for a price?

Members of all of the relatively new women-of-color groups fighting for reproductive justice have faced and fought reproductive indignities. These women have all worked to end fertility-related oppression. They have built alliances and struggled to work with mainstream organizations like Planned Parenthood and the National Abortion and Reproductive Rights Action League (NARAL) at the same time that they have constructed a human rights framework claiming reproductive rights across communities of color. Because Native American women, Latinas, African American, and Asian–Pacific Islander women have all had distinct histories in the United States, each group—and women affiliating with other racially or ethnically specific groups—defines what it means by reproductive justice somewhat differently.

For example, Native Americans define the mother's body as "the first environment," inextricably related to the robust or diseased external environment. Given their specific history, Native American women believe that reproductive rights carries profound environmental meanings and often includes, as well, the right to be safe from domestic violence, the right to HIV/AIDS education and treatment, and the right to raise one's own children and to protect and pass on cultural legacies to the next generation.

Groups working to secure reproductive justice for Asian–Pacific Islander women have focused on the cultural value of producing male children—a mandate that pressures many women to have more pregnancies than they would like. These women have highlighted language and cultural impediments to reproductive health care services. Like Native American women, they have clarified the ways that poverty has interfered with reproductive rights and the right to raise one's children in a safe and healthy environment.

Over the past generation, millions of women in every demographic group in the United States have benefited from laws and policies that give women more control over their own bodies. Even women who themselves would not seek an abortion or use contraception have been the beneficiaries of reproductive rights. As a result of feminist claims for reproductive rights, the jobs of all women have been formally protected to various degrees by laws that secure the rights of pregnant or fertile women. Also, all American women now live in a society in which there is a critical mass of female doctors and lawyers and other professionals. This critical mass (and the next wave of young female professionals) could only emerge after women had the ability to control their fertility and could subordinate reproduction to training and career when necessary.

Women who believe in reproductive freedom as well as those who do not now live in a country that permits females to experience—to various degrees—the freedom of living as morally responsible agents, regarding reproduction. In chapter 1, I wrote about how enslaved women defined freedom for themselves. In the same way, if twenty-first-century women are to live as "morally responsible agents," they must own their own reproductive bodies and have the right to exercise their "moral and intellectual capacities"—self-determination.[98] This range of personal rights and responsibilities has contributed to elevating the status of women over the past two generations—as workers, as parents, and as citizens.

When we reflect on the persons women have become and on the range of their opportunities since the reproductive rights revolution, we may well wonder what will happen to these gains if the government removes women's reproductive rights. What would prosecutors do in response to the inevitably large number of college students and nurses and doctors and soldiers and other women they catch getting abortions? Some politicians, notably Senator (and gynecologist) Tom Coburn, Republican of Oklahoma, imagines a post-*Roe* America in which doctors who perform abortions are put to death. But what exactly are the proposals for constraining and punishing women who claim rights to manage their fertility when the law says that right is no longer theirs? As we've seen, before *Roe,* a woman put on the stand by a district attorney would often be forced to recount her sexual history in open court and explain to the jury why she was willing to have sex if she wasn't willing to become a mother.

Can we picture this post-*Roe* woman on the witness stand as a modern woman—a person whose reproductive rights have been canceled but who can, nevertheless, go right on working at her job, going to college, helping to pay the mortgage, supporting her children in the face of the overwhelming failure of separated, divorced, and never-married fathers to pay child support? Do the advocates of recriminalization think that reproductive rights are a "plug-in" that can be removed without changing anything else about a woman's life?

More than three decades after the *Roe v. Wade* decision, most women know that questions about contraception and abortion and other reproductive matters are not simply the concerns of individual women trying to deal with their reproductive problems. And most of us know that reproductive politics do not simply elevate or degrade an individual woman's life. Reproductive politics—*Who has power over matters of pregnancy and its consequences?*—shapes everybody's life in the United States. At the end of *Pregnancy and Power,* I can offer three foundational principles that illustrate why this is so.

REPRODUCTIVE RIGHTS AND FULL CITIZENSHIP

First, as I have suggested throughout this book, women cannot be full citizens in the United States (or in any other country) if they cannot control their own sexual and reproductive bodies. Wherever women are forbidden to manage their fertility, they do not share equal status with men. Having reproductive rights here and around the world is what can be called a necessary (if not sufficient) condition for gender equality. In countries where women do not have reproductive rights—where the state, through the law, forces women to have children—women are degraded by a number of aspects of this reproductive coercion. They are compelled to take medical risks that go with pregnancy and childbearing. They are required to bear discomfort and disability. They are forced to perform the uncompensated labor of pregnancy, childbearing, and motherhood whether they want to or not, whether they have the resources to take on these tasks or not. In millions of cases, they are also forced into positions of economic dependency because taking care of newborns and small children is often incompatible with earning money. For all these reasons and many others, state-enforced child-bearing cannot coexist with dignity and equality for women.

Women can be glorified, burdened, scorned, restricted, endangered, beloved, and martyred when they are forced to reproduce. But when they are forced, women end up enslaved by their reproductive capacity. They remain partial, not full, citizens. Under these conditions, full citizenship refers only to men.

REPRODUCTIVE RIGHTS AND WOMEN'S SAFETY

Second, as we've seen in all the chapters of *Pregnancy and Power*, reproductive capacity has been a site of various kinds of danger and degradation for women throughout American history. The slavery system in the United States depended on the master's control over the fertility of enslaved women. Slave masters stopped at little in their efforts to maximize their profits using the wombs of their female property. The definition of "whiteness" in the United States historically depended on policing sexual relations, particularly the sexual bodies of white women, and assigning value to babies depending on race. And the law itself has made reproductive capacity a dangerous attribute for women. As I've shown throughout *Pregnancy and Power*, when the law controls female fertility, women have felt a tremendous need to shape their own reproductive lives anyway. Doing what they felt they had to do, women have entered danger zones; many have been damaged or died in the process.

These and other manifestations of reproductive politics have stripped women of individual and collective power. During times when women have few reproductive rights, their bodies have become symbols and implements of large national projects that depend on women's dependency, hence their endangerment.

REPRODUCTIVE CAPACITY AND PRIVILEGE

The third principle I want to conclude with is this: throughout the history of reproductive politics in the United States, we have seen that when the state takes the right to decide which women are legitimate mothers, the state has, historically, also taken the right to treat different groups of women differently. On the one hand, across American history, we have the normative, properly married, white middle-class woman who gives birth to the valuable white child. The state has historically viewed this woman as a legitimate mother of her own precious baby, as long as she remains affiliated with this normative status. On the other hand, the state has constructed a constantly moving target of illegitimate mothers. The targets change from generation to generation. But the claims that some groups of women could make to be mothers of their own children have been severely—sometimes fatally—weakened by the mother's race or class or sexual orientation, sometimes by a woman's political views or disability or other "deviant" characteristics.

We've encountered the Indian woman whose children were dragged away to boarding schools in the 1870s. The poor Irish Catholic immigrant woman in New York in the mid-nineteenth century whose children were designated "orphans" and sent out West to be raised in good, Protestant farm families. The enslaved woman whose children were purchased as chattel and sold to other owners in the Lower South. The white unwed mother in the mid-twentieth century who, without a husband, had her child legally transferred to a properly married man and wife, no matter what she wanted. The coercively sterilized woman of color. The lesbian woman who had her children removed from her custody by a judge because she was a lesbian. The incarcerated woman today, in prison for a nonviolent crime unrelated to her mothering skills, whose children are permanently removed from her custody because the conditions of her incarceration make it impossible for her to meet the parenting conditions of the Adoption and Safe Families Act.

These are some examples of the many categories of women throughout American history who—because they lacked certain crucial resources, and because the state defined certain groups of women as illegitimate mothers—were horribly vulnerable in ways that women with resources have not been. When the state creates conditions for maternal legitimacy that give special treatment to white, middle-class women and threaten almost all other women, then reproductive capacity becomes a vehicle for institutionalizing racism and other forms of oppression. Reproductive politics becomes a powerful tool of privilege.

REPRODUCTIVE JUSTICE

In the introduction I showed how politicians and others have used reproduction across our history to mark and regret many different "problems" in American society: Foreign-born women give birth to too many children. Teenagers reproduce too young. Lesbian mothers are illegitimate mothers. Abortion is a sin. Poor women should not reproduce. Many Americans believe if we could only stamp out all of these female misbehaviors, by controlling who reproduces and under which circumstances, the United States would be a better country. As long as politicians and the law want to define reproduction as an arena for controlling women, female fertility will remain a dangerous site and a dangerous capacity for women to possess.

In a country committed to reproductive justice, the authorities and ordinary people together would agree that the right to reproduce safely and with dignity is a fundamental human right, as is the right *not* to reproduce. The authorities and ordinary people would reject ideas such as the very popular notion that motherhood should be a class privilege, an experience and a status reserved for women with "enough money." Those who believe in reproductive justice cannot accept motherhood as an economic status or a consumer status.

In the country of reproductive justice, the majority would argue that poverty generally happens to people because they were born poor. Most poor women in this country are not poor because of the number of children they give birth to but because their class status at birth, together with their race and gender, denies them the opportunities that enrich the lives of people who were born into the middle class. Poor women generally have the same number of babies as the number born to the average woman in the United States: 1.8. And yet in the United States, poor women are reviled and punished because of their alleged reproductive misbehavior.

In the country where reproductive justice prevails, the commitment to reproductive health for all women is strong. This combination of reproductive health and reproductive justice fundamentally refers to the right to lives of basic safety and decency. Reproductive capacity should not be the source of danger and degradation for a rich woman or a poor woman, a straight woman or a lesbian, a free woman or a woman behind bars, a disabled woman, an immigrant, a Native American woman, a Mexican American woman, or any woman.

We have a long way to go before we achieve the country of reproductive justice in the United States. I hope in the meantime that *Pregnancy and Power* has made clear that throughout the history of the
United States, the reproductive capacity of females has stimulated
power struggles. These struggles have usually focused on conserving
traditional power relations, often against women's claims to manage
their own bodies. As we've seen, reproductive conflicts have taken different forms across the history of this country. The struggles have had
content that depended on the historical moment and on the race, class,
and other attributes of the women whose reproductive capacity has
been at issue. But over time, authorities have exerted power—and
women have resisted—because, as *Pregnancy and Power* has shown,
women have always been determined to decide for themselves as best
they can when and whether or not to become mothers.

Notes

NOTES TO THE INTRODUCTION

1. Brenda Stevenson, "Distress and Discord in Virginia Slave Families," in Vicki L. Ruiz and Ellen Carol DuBois, eds., *Unequal Sisters: A Multicultural Reader in U.S. Women's History*, 3rd ed. (New York: Routledge, 2000), 51; also see Deborah Gray White, *Ar'n't I a Woman? Female Slaves in the Plantation South* (New York: Oxford University Press, 1985).

2. Adrienne Dale Davis, "Don't Let Nobody Bother Yo' Principle: The Sexual Economy of American Slavery," in Sharon Harley and the Black Women and Work Collective, eds., *Sister Circle: Black Women and Work* (New Brunswick, NJ: Rutgers University Press, 2002), 109–10.

3. Robert Coles, *Children of Crisis* (Boston: Little, Brown, 1964), 368–69.

4. Theodore Roosevelt, "Race Decadence," *Outlook*, April 8, 1911, 160–61.

5. Charlotte Perkins Gilman, quoted in Wendy Kline, *Building a Better Race: Gender, Sexuality, and Eugenics from the Turn of the Century to the Baby Boom* (Berkeley: University of California Press, 2001), 19.

6. Henry Goddard quoted in Kline, *Building a Better Race*, 27.

7. Helen Lefkowitz Horowitz, *Rereading Sex: Battles over Sexual Knowledge and Suppression in Nineteenth-Century America* (New York: Knopf, 2002) 206–7.

8. Daniel Patrick Moynihan, *The Negro Family: A Case for National Action* (Washington, DC: U.S. Government Printing Office, 1965).

9. Regarding the way that language has expressed changing ideas about what social problem needed fixing, historian Linda Gordon writes, "The purposes and meanings of . . . attempts to control reproduction were created and recreated differently in different contexts and historical periods. The languages of different reproductive control programs—neo-Malthusian, voluntary motherhood, planned parenthood, race suicide, birth control, population control, control over one's body, for example—were not merely different slogans for the same thing but helped to construct different activities, purposes, meanings: the language was itself inseparable from the creation of those different meanings and the political struggles that arose around them." *The Moral Property of Women: A History of Birth Control Politics in America* (Urbana: University of Illinois Press, 2002), 8–9.

10. Rosalind Pollack Petchesky, *Abortion and Women's Choice: The State, Sex-*

uality, and Reproductive Freedom (Boston: Northeastern University Press, 1990), 73.

11. Peggy Cooper-Davis, *Neglected Stories: The Constitution and Family Values* (New York: Hill and Wang, 1993), 372–75.

12. Dorothy Roberts, *Killing the Black Body: Race, Reproduction, and the Meaning of Liberty* (New York: Pantheon, 1997), 55.

13. See Carole Joffe, *Doctors of Conscience: The Struggle to Provide Abortion before and after* Roe v. Wade (Boston: Beacon Press, 1995), 211n1.

14. Hannah M. Adams and Ursula M. Gallagher, "Some Facts and Observations about Illegitimacy," *Children* 10 (March–April 1963): 43–48.

15. Martha Albertson Fineman, *The Neutered Mother, the Sexual Family and Other Twentieth Century Tragedies* (New York: Routledge, 1995), 125.

16. "Birth Rates by Marital Status," Child Trends, "Facts at a Glance," September 2002, 2. http://www.childtrends.org/Files/FAAG2002.pdf.

17. Reva Siegel, "Reasoning from the Body: A Historical Perspective on Abortion Regulation and Questions of Equal Protection," *Stanford Law Review* 44 (January 1992): 352–53.

18. Quoted in Carroll Smith-Rosenberg, "The Abortion Movement and the American Medical Association, 1859–1880," in *Disorderly Conduct: Visions of Gender in Victorian America* (New York: Oxford University Press, 1986), 236–37.

19. *Muller v. Oregon*, 208 U.S. 412, at 421 (1908).

20. Alice Kessler-Harris, *In Pursuit of Equity: Women, Men, and the Quest for Economic Citizenship in Twentieth-Century America* (New York: Oxford University Press, 2001), 99.

21. Siegel, "Reasoning from the Body," 270.

22. Abortion—Part II, Hearings before the Subcommittee on Constitutional Amendments of the Committee of the Judiciary, U.S. Senate, 93rd Cong., 2nd sess., S.J. Res. 119, Proposing an Amendment to the Constitution of the United States for the Protection of Unborn Children and other Persons, and S.J. Res. 130, Proposing an Amendment to the Constitution of the United States Guaranteeing the Right of Life to the Unborn, the Ill, the Aged, or the Incapacitated, 447.

23. Londa Schiebinger, "Exotic Abortifacients: The Global Politics of Plants in the Eighteenth Century," *Endeavour* 24 (2000): 118.

24. Coles, *Children of Crisis*, 368–69.

25. See Nancy Ehrenreich, "Surrogacy as Resistance? The Misplaced Focus on Choice in the Surrogacy and Abortion Funding Contexts," *DePaul Law Review* 41 (1992): 1369.

26. See Davis, "Don't Let Nobody Bother Yo' Principle."

27. Ehrenreich, "Surrogacy as Resistance," 1395.

28. Roberts, *Killing the Black Body*, 301.

29. Linda C. McClain, "Irresponsible Reproduction," *Hastings Law Journal* 47 (January 1996): 398–99.

30. Toni Cade, "The Pill: Genocide or Liberation?" in Toni Cade, ed., *The Black Woman: An Anthology* (New York: Vintage, 1970).

31. Siegel, "Reasoning from the Body," 274.

32. Laurel Thatcher Ulrich, *A Midwife's Tale: The Life of Martha Ballard Based on Her Diary, 1785–1812* (New York: Knopf, 1990), 158.

33. See Rickie Solinger, *Wake Up Little Susie: Single Pregnancy and Race before Roe v. Wade* (New York: Routledge, 2000).

34. *Griswold v. Connecticut,* 381 U.S. 479 (1965); *Eisenstadt v. Baird,* 405 U.S. 438 (1972).

35. Kristin Luker, *Taking Chances: Abortion and the Decision Not to Contracept* (Berkeley: University of California Press, 1975).

36. Cornelia Hughes Dayton, "Taking the Trade: Abortion and Gender Relations in an Eighteenth-Century Village," *William and Mary Quarterly* 48 (1991): 23.

37. Mary Ryan, *Womanhood in America: From Colonial Times to the Present,* 2nd ed. (New York: New Viewpoints, 1979), 98; White, *Ar'n't I a Woman?* 29.

38. White, *Ar'n't I a Woman?* 29.

39. Michael Sullivan DeFine, "A History of Governmentally Coerced Sterilization: The Plight of the Native American Woman," http://www.geocities.com/CapitolHill/9118/mike2.html, 2; Jennifer Nelson, *Women of Color and the Reproductive Rights Movement* (New York: New York University Press, 2003), chap. 2.

40. Stephen Trombley, "Sterilization and Informed Consent in the 1960s," in Stephen Trombley, ed., *The Right to Reproduce: A History of Coercive Sterilization* (London: Weidenfeld and Nicolson, 1988), 175–213.

41. Elena Rebecca Gutiérrez, "The Racial Politics of Reproduction: The Social Construction of Mexican-Origin Women's Fertility" (Ph.D. diss., University of Michigan, 1999), 204.

NOTES TO CHAPTER I

1. See, for example, Randall Kennedy, *Interracial Intimacies: Sex, Marriage, Identities, and Adoption* (New York: Pantheon, 2003).

2. Kristen Fischer, *Suspect Relations: Sex, Race, and Resistance in Colonial North Carolina* (Ithaca, NY: Cornell University Press, 2002), 193.

3. James H. Merrell, "Declarations of Independence: Indian-White Relations in the New Nation," in Jack Greene, ed., *The American Revolution: Its Character and Limits* (New York: New York University Press, 1987), 209.

4. Declaration of Sentiments 1833: "rooted in the violation of the slave's inalienable . . . right to his own body."

5. Dorothy Roberts, *Killing the Black Body: Race, Reproduction, and the Meaning of Liberty* (New York: Pantheon, 1997), 55.

6. Kathleen M. Brown, *Good Wives, Nasty Wenches, and Anxious Patriarchs* (Chapel Hill: University of North Carolina Press, 1996), 207.

7. Quoted in Carol Berkin and Leslie Horowitz, *Women's Voices, Women's Lives: Documents in Early American History*, (Boston: Northeastern University Press, 1998), 13.

8. Paul Finkelman, "Crimes of Love, Misdemeanors of Passion: The Regulation of Race and Sex in the Colonial South," in Catherine Clinton and Michele Gillespie, eds., *The Devil's Lane: Sex and Race in the Early South* (New York: Oxford University Press, 1997), 128.

9. Adrienne Dale Davis, "Don't Let Nobody Bother Yo' Principle: The Sexual Economy of American Slavery," in Sharon Harley and the Black Women and Work Collective, eds., *Sister Circle: Black Women and Work* (New Brunswick, NJ: Rutgers University Press, 2002), 111.

10. Berkin and Horowitz, *Women's Voices, Women's Lives*, 13.

11. Fischer, *Suspect Relations*, 124.

12. Brown, *Good Wives, Nasty Wenches*, 198.

13. Fischer, *Suspect Relations*, 101; Brown, *Good Wives, Nasty Wenches*, 211.

14. Fischer, *Suspect Relations*, 124

15. See Judith K. Schafer, *Slavery, the Civil Law, and the Supreme Court of Louisiana* (Baton Rouge: Louisiana State University Press, 1997).

16. Brenda Stevenson, "Distress and Discord in Virginia Slave Families, 1830–1860, in Carol Bleser, ed., *In Joy and Sorrow: Women, Family, and Marriage in the Victorian South* (New York: Oxford University Press, 1992), 46.

17. Roberts, *Killing the Black Body*, 29–30.

18. Brown, *Good Wives, Nasty Wenches*, 210.

19. Stevenson, "Distress and Discord," 53.

20. Marie Jenkins Schwartz, *Born in Bondage: Growing Up Enslaved in the Antebellum South* (Cambridge, MA: Harvard University Press, 2000), 18.

21. Fischer, *Suspect Relations*, 87; Jennifer M. Spear, "Colonial Intimacies: Legislating Sex in French Louisiana," *William and Mary Quarterly* 60 (2003): 95.

22. Wilma A. Dunaway, *The African-American Family in Slavery and Emancipation* (New York: Cambridge University Press, 2003), 54.

23. Ronald T. Takaki, *Iron Cages: Race and Culture in Nineteenth-Century America* (New York: Knopf, 1979), 44–45; Dunaway, *African-American Family*, 274.

24. Jacqueline Jones, "My Mother Was Much of a Woman: Black Women, Work, and the Family under Slavery," *Feminist Studies* 8 (1982): 238.

25. E. Franklin Frazier, "The Negro Slave Family," *Journal of Negro History* 15 (1930): 256.

26. Dunaway, *African-American Family*, 271.

27. Ibid., 129–30.

28. Ibid., 138–40. Dunaway writes that one-half of pregnant white wives received obstetric care but only 3 percent of pregnant slaves (131).

29. Richard Follett, "Heat, Sex, and Sugar: Pregnancy and Childbearing in the Slave Quarters," *Journal of Family History* 28 (2003): 510–39.

30. Dunaway, *African-American Family,* 138–40.

31. Follett, "Heat, Sex, and Sugar," 528.

32. Ibid., 527.

33. Ibid.

34. Frazier, "Negro Slave Family," 246.

35. Dunaway, *African-American Family,* 118–19.

36. Frazier, "Negro Slave Family," 246.

37. Stevenson, "Distress and Discord," 50.

38. Ibid., 49.

39. Ibid., 41.

40. Dunaway, *African-American Family,* 67–68.

41. Roberts, *Killing the Black Body,* 23.

42. Frazier, "Negro Slave Family," 240.

43. Dunaway, *African-American Family,* 136–38.

44. Ibid., 70.

45. Frazier, "Negro Slave Family," 222–23.

46. Ibid., 224.

47. Dunaway, *African-American Family,* 81.

48. Peggy Cooper-Davis, *Neglected Stories: The Constitution and Family Values* (New York: Hill and Wang, 1993), 373.

49. Darlene Clark Hine and Kathleen Thompson, *A Shining Thread of Hope: The History of Black Women in America* (New York: Broadway Books, 1998), 98–99; Deborah Gray White, *Ar'n't I a Woman? Female Slaves in the Plantation South* (New York: Oxford University Press, 1985), 84–89.

50. From Herbert G. Gutman, *The Black Family in Slavery and Freedom,* quoted in Janet Farrell Brodie, *Contraception and Abortion in Nineteenth-Century America* (Ithaca, NY: Cornell University Press, 1994), 52–53.

51. Stephanie Shaw, "Mothering under Slavery in the Antebellum South," in Janet Golden and Rima Apple, eds., *Mothers and Motherhood: Readings in American History* (Columbus: Ohio State University Press, 1997), 309.

52. Cooper-Davis, *Neglected Stories,* 392.

53. Ibid. 375.

54. Ibid., 375, 394.

55. Theda Perdue, *Cherokee Women: Gender and Cultural Change, 1700–1835* (Lincoln: University of Nebraska Press, 1998), 190.

56. Ibid., see chap. 1 generally, and 29–30, 34, 35, 36.

57. Ibid., 31–34.

58. Ibid., 161.

59. Ibid., 178.

60. Ibid.

61. Ibid., 186.

62. Ibid., 156; Theda Perdue, *Slavery and the Evolution of Cherokee Society, 1540–1866* (Knoxville: University of Tennessee Press, 1979), 96.

63. See, for example, Theda Perdue and Michael D. Green, *The Cherokee Removal: A Brief History with Documents* (New York: St. Martin's Press, 1995); John Ehle, *Trail of Tears: The Rise and Fall of the Cherokee Nation* (Garden City, NY: Doubleday, 1988).

64. Perdue, *Slavery and the Evolution of Cherokee Society,* 99–100.

65. Albert L. Hurtado, *Indian Survival on the California Frontier* (New Haven, CT: Yale University Press, 1988), 188–91.

66. David E. Stannard, *American Holocaust: The Conquest of the New World* (New York: Oxford University Press, 1992), 243–44.

67. Rebecca Tsosie, "Changing Women: The Crosscurrents of American Indian Feminine Identity," in Vicki L. Ruiz and Ellen Carol DuBois, eds., *Unequal Sisters: A Multicultural Reader in U.S. Women's History,* 3rd ed. (New York: Routledge, 2000), 565–86.

68. Nancy Shoemaker, "Introduction," in Nancy Shoemaker, ed., *Negotiators of Change: Historical Perspectives on Native American Women* (New York: Routledge, 1995), 9.

69. Ellen Carol DuBois and Linda Gordon, "Seeking Ecstasy on the Battlefield: Danger and Pleasure in Nineteenth-Century Feminist Sexual Thought," *Feminist Studies* 9 (1983): 7—25.

70. Susan M. Stabile, "A 'Doctrine of Signatures': The Epistolary Physicks of Esther Burr's Journal," in Janet Moore Lindman and Michele Lise Tartar, eds., *A Centre of Wonders: The Body in Early America* (Ithaca, NY: Cornell University Press, 2001), 120.

71. Ibid., 117.

72. Sally G. McMillen, *Motherhood in the Old South: Pregnancy, Childbirth, and Infant Rearing* (Baton Rouge: Louisiana State University Press, 1990), 6.

73. Linda K. Kerber, *Women of the Republic: Intellect and Ideology in Revolutionary America* (Chapel Hill: University of North Carolina Press, 1980); Mary Beth Norton, *Liberty's Daughters: The Revolutionary Experience of American Women, 1750–1800* (Ithaca, NY: Cornell University Press, 1980); and Ruth H. Bloch, "American Feminine Ideals in Transition: The Rise of the Moral Mother, 1785–1815," *Feminist Studies* 4 (1978): 101–26.

74. Fischer, *Suspect Relations,* 105–6.

75. Cornelia Hughes Dayton, *Women before the Bar: Gender, Law, and Society in Connecticut, 1639–1789* (Chapel Hill: University of North Carolina Press, 1995), 211.

76. Peter C. Hoffer and N. E. H. Hull, *Murdering Mothers: Infanticide in England and New England, 1558–1803* (New York: New York University Press, 1981), 47–48.

77. Ibid., 63–84; Merril D. Smith, "Unnatural Mothers: Infanticide, Child Abuse, and Motherhood in the Mid-Atlantic, 1973–1830," in Christine Daniels and Michael V. Kennedy, eds., *Over the Threshold: Intimate Violence in Early America* (New York: Routledge, 1999), 173–84.

78. Dayton, *Women before the Bar,* 160, 193.

79. Ibid., 60.

80. Ibid., 161.

81. Ibid., 212.

82. Ibid., 160.

83. Ibid., 160, 185–86.

84. Ibid., 226.

85. Catherine Clinton, "Wallowing in a Swamp of Sin: Parson Weems, Sex, and Murder in Early South Carolina," in Clinton and Gillespie, *Devil's Lane,* 29; Catherine E. Beecher, "Treatise on Domestic Economy," excerpted in Nancy Cott, Jeanne Boydston, Anne Braude, Lori D. Ginzberg, and Molly Ladd-Taylor, eds., *Root of Bitterness: Documents on the Social History of American Women,* 2nd ed. (Boston: Northeastern University Press, 1996), 132–37.

86. Sarah Grimké, "On the Condition of Women in the United States," in Cott et al., *Root of Bitterness,* 126–27.

87. Nancy Cott, "Passionlessness: An Interpretation of Victorian Sexual Ideology, 1790–1850," *Signs* 4 (1978): 219–36.

88. Ibid.

89. Fischer, *Suspect Relations,* 17.

90. Hannah More, *Strictures on the modern system of female education: with a view of the principles and conduct prevalent among women of rank and fortune* (London: T. Cadell Jun. and W. Davies, 1799).

91. Fischer, *Suspect Relations,* 64.

92. Ibid., 108.

93. John M. Riddle, *Eve's Herbs: A History of Contraception and Abortion in the West* (Cambridge, MA: Harvard University Press, 1997), 218.

94. Cornelia Hughes Dayton, "Taking the Trade: Abortion and Gender Relations in an Eighteenth Century New England Village," *William and Mary Quarterly* 48 (1991): 20.

95. Riddle, *Eve's Herbs,* 205.

96. James C. Mohr, *Abortion in America: The Origins and Evolution of National Policy, 1800–1900* (New York: Oxford University Press, 1978), 42.

97. Ibid., 46.

98. Jan Lewis and Kenneth A. Lockridge, "'Sally Has Been Sick': Pregnancy and Family Limitation among Virginia Gentry Women, 1780–1830," in Rima D. Apple and Janet Golden, eds., *Mothers and Motherhood: Readings in American History* (Columbus: Ohio State University Press, 1997), 204.

99. Horowitz, *Rereading Sex,* 68, 77.

100. Ibid., 149.

101. Ibid., 194–97.

102. James Mohr quoted in Rosalind Pollack Petchesky, *Abortion and Women's Choice: The State, Sexuality, and Reproductive Freedom* (Boston: Northeastern University Press, 1990), 52.

103. Lewis and Lockridge, "'Sally Has Been Sick,'" 207–8; also see Andrea Tone, ed., *Controlling Reproduction: An American History* (Wilmington, DE: Scholarly Resources, 1997), 80.

104. Brodie, *Contraception and Abortion*, 102.

105. Petchesky, *Abortion and Women's Choice*, 51–52.

106. Brodie, *Contraception and Abortion*, 154–55.

107. Linda Gordon, *The Moral Property of Women: A History of Birth Control Politics in America* (Urbana: University of Illinois Press, 2002), 74.

108. Brodie, *Contraception and Abortion*, 90–92.

109. Mohr, *Abortion in America*, 71.

110. Horowitz, *Rereading Sex*, 59.

111. Brodie, *Contraception and Abortion*, 89.

112. Ibid., 113–14.

113. Horowitz, *Rereading Sex*, 275.

114. Andrea Tone, *Devices and Desires: A History of Contraceptives in America* (New York: Hill and Wang, 2001), 17.

115. Mohr, *Abortion in America*, 110–11.

116. Ibid., 50.

117. Riddle, *Eve's Herbs*, 245.

118. Brodie, *Contraception and Abortion*, 107.

119. Mohr, *Abortion in America*, 108.

120. Ibid., 148–52; Petchesky, *Abortion and Women's Choice*, 81–83.

NOTES TO CHAPTER 2

1. See Joan Jacobs Brumberg, "'Ruined Girls': Changing Community Responses to Illegitimacy in Upstate New York, 1890–1920," *Journal of Social History* 18 (Winter 1984): 247–72.

2. Joanne Meyerowitz, *Women Adrift: Independent Wage Earners in Chicago, 1880–1930* (Chicago: University of Chicago Press, 1988), 8–9.

3. Alice Kessler-Harris, *Out to Work: A History of Wage-Earning Women in the United States* (New York: Oxford University Press, 1982), chap. 4.

4. Meyerowitz, *Women Adrift*, 4–5.

5. See Helen Lefkowitz Horowitz, *Rereading Sex: Battles over Sexual Knowledge and Suppression in Nineteenth-Century America* (New York: Knopf, 2002), 328.

6. Andrea Tone, *Devices and Desires: A History of Contraceptives in America* (New York: Hill and Wang, 2001), 15.

7. Janet Farrell Brodie, *Contraception and Abortion in Nineteenth-Century America* (Ithaca, NY: Cornell University Press, 1994), 192.

8. Carole McCann, *Birth Control Politics in the United States, 1916–1945* (Ithaca, NY: Cornell University Press, 1994), 7.

9. Tone, *Devices and Desires*, 20.

10. Meyerowitz, *Women Adrift*, 141.

11. Brodie, *Contraception and Abortion*, 204.

12. Robert Wiebe, *The Search for Order, 1877–1920* (New York: Hill and Wang, 1966), 51.

13. Brodie, *Contraception and Abortion*, 261.

14. James Mohr, *Abortion in America: The Origins and Evolution of National Policy, 1800–1900* (New York: Oxford University Press, 1979), 98.

15. Kessler-Harris, *Out to Work*, 102.

16. *Bradwell v. Illinois* 83 U.S. (16 Wall) 130 (1872) at 241.

17. Kessler-Harris, *Out to Work*, 98.

18. W. E. B. DuBois, *The Philadelphia Negro* (Philadelphia: University of Pennsylvania Press, 1998), 70–72.

19. Meyerowitz, *Women Adrift*, 50.

20. Ibid., 43.

21. Sherri Broder, *Tramps, Unfit Mothers and Neglected Children: Negotiating the Family in Late Nineteenth-Century Philadelphia* (Philadelphia: University of Pennsylvania Press, 2002), 199.

22. Ibid., 77, 79, 137.

23. Mohr, *Abortion in America*, 188–89.

24. Ibid., 167, 170.

25. Ibid., 186–87.

26. Rosalind Petchesky, *Abortion and Woman's Choice: The State, Sexuality and Reproductive Freedom* (Boston: Northeastern University Press, 1990), 53–55.

27. See Tone, *Devices and Desires*, chaps. 3 and 4.

28. Brodie, *Contraception and Abortion*, 77–79.

29. Carroll Smith-Rosenberg, *Disorderly Conduct: Visions of Gender in Victorian America* (New York: Oxford University Press, 1986), 238–39.

30. Mohr, *Abortion in America*, 162; Leslie J. Reagan, *When Abortion Was a Crime: Women, Medicine and Law in the United States, 1867–1973* (Berkeley: University of California Press, 1997), 49, 54.

31. Mohr, *Abortion in America*, 107.

32. Horowitz, *Rereading Sex*, chaps. 16 and 17.

33. Ibid., 403, 441.

34. Constance M. Chen, *"The Sex Side of Life": Mary Ware Dennett's Pioneering Battle for Birth Control and Sex Education* (New York: New Press, 1996), xx.

35. Quoted in Horowitz, *Rereading Sex*, 395.

36. Quoted in Tone, *Devices and Desires*, 22–23.

37. Chen, *"The Sex Side of Life,"* xxiii.

38. Reva Siegel, "Reasoning from the Body: A Historical Perspective on Abortion Regulation and Questions of Equal Protection," *Stanford Law Review* 44 (January 1992): 261–381.

39. Linda Gordon, *The Moral Property of Women: A History of Birth Control Politics in America* (Urbana: University of Illinois Press, 2002), 66.

40. Ibid., 61.

41. Siegel, "Reasoning from the Body," 307.

42. Ibid., 313.

43. Brodie, *Contraception and Abortion*, 218–19.

44. Gordon, *Moral Property of Women*, 62–63.

45. Ibid., 62.

46. Brodie, *Contraception and Abortion*, 227.

47. Mohr, *Abortion in America*, 58.

48. Gordon, *Moral Property of Women*, 25; Mohr, *Abortion in America*, 161.

49. Smith-Rosenberg, *Disorderly Women*, 221.

50. Brodie, *Abortion and Contraception*, 281.

51. Tone, *Devices and Desires*, 41–42.

52. Horowitz, *Rereading Sex*, 274–77.

53. Angela Davis, "Racism, Birth Control, and Reproductive Rights," in Marlene Gerber Fried, ed., *From Abortion to Reproductive Freedom: Transforming a Movement* (Boston: South End Press, 1990), 18.

54. Kessler-Harris, *Out to Work*, 101.

55. See Kathy Peiss, *Cheap Amusements: Working Women and Leisure in Turn-of-the-Century New York* (Philadelphia: Temple University Press, 1987).

56. Broder, *Tramps, Unfit Mothers*, 130, 134–35, 169.

57. Ibid., 188.

58. Ibid., 160.

59. Brodie, *Contraception and Abortion*, 287.

60. Mari Jo Buhle, *Feminism and Its Discontents: A Century of Struggle with Psychoanalysis* (Cambridge, MA: Harvard University Press, 1998); Gordon, *Moral Property*, 120–21.

61. Ruth M. Alexander, *The "Girl Problem": Female Sexual Delinquency in New York, 1900–1930* (Ithaca, NY: Cornell University Press, 1995); Karen W. Tice, *Tales of Wayward Girls and Immoral Women: Case Records and the Professionalization of Social Work* (Urbana: University of Illinois Press, 1998).

62. Reagan, *When Abortion Was a Crime*, 114–15.

63. Ibid., 44–45.

64. Gordon, *Moral Property of Women*, 156–59.

65. Ellen Chesler, *Woman of Valor: Margaret Sanger and the Birth Control Movement in America* (New York: Simon and Shuster, 1992), 3.

66. Chen, *"The Sex Side of Life,"* 206.

67. Wendy Kline, *Building a Better Race: Gender, Sexuality, and Eugenics from the Turn of the Century to the Baby Boom* (Berkeley: University of California Press, 2001), 66.

68. Leslie J. Reagan, "'About to Meet Her Maker': The State's Investigation of Abortion in Chicago, 1867–1940," in Andrea Tone, ed., *Controlling Reproduction: An American History* (Wilmington, DE: Scholarly Resources, 1997), 123.

69. Reagan, *When Abortion Was a Crime*, 89.

70. Quoted in Regina Kunzel, *Fallen Women, Problem Girls: Unmarried Mothers and the Professionalization of Social Work, 1890–1945* (New Haven, CT: Yale University Press, 1993), 68.

71. James F. Cooper, M.D., *Technique of Contraception: The Principles and Practice of Anti-conceptional Methods* (New York: Day-Nichols, 1928), 255.

72. Chesler, *Woman of Valor*, 280.

73. Cooper, *Technique of Contraception*, 10–11.

74. Kline, *Building a Better Race*, 63–64.

75. Dorothy Roberts, *Killing the Black Body: Race, Reproduction and the Meaning of Liberty* (New York: Pantheon, 1997), chap. 2; McCann, *Birth Control Politics*, 19, 25.

76. McCann, *Birth Control Politics*, 38.

77. Tone, *Devices and Desires*, 29, 32, 35, 45.

78. David J. Garrow, *Liberty and Sexuality: The Right to Privacy and the Making of* Roe v. Wade (New York: Macmillan, 1994), chap. 1.

79. Chen, *"The Sex Side of Life,"* 334.

80. Reagan, *When Abortion Was a Crime*, 127.

81. Reagan, "'About to Meet Her Maker,'" 118–21.

82. Ibid., 119.

83. Thomas J. Morgan, "Supplemental Report on Indian Education," Department of the Interior, Office of Indian Affairs, December 1, 1889, in Nancy Shoemaker, ed., *American Indians* (Malden, MA.: Blackwell, 2001), 235–40.

84. David E. Stannard, *American Holocaust: The Conquest of the New World* (New York: Oxford University Press, 1992), 245.

85. David Wallace Adams, *Education for Extinction: American Indians and the Boarding School Experience, 1875–1928* (Lawrence: University Press of Kansas, 1995), 18.

86. Ibid., 10, 18.

87. Julie Davis, "American Indian Boarding School Experiences: Recent Studies from Native Perspectives," *Organization of American Historians Magazine of History* 15 (Winter 2001): 20–22.

88. Adams, *Education for Extinction*, 210, 211.

89. "Convention on the Prevention and Punishment of the Crime of Genocide," adopted by Resolution 260 (III) A of the U.N. General Assembly on December 9, 1948, Art. II(e).

90. Adams, *Education for Extinction*, 215.

91. Ibid., 65.

92. Ibid., 108, 141.

93. Carolyn Marr, "Assimilation through Education: Indian Boarding Schools in the Pacific Northwest," http://content.lib.washington.edu/aipnw/marr.html.

94. See, for example, Christine Stansell, "Women, Children, and the Uses of the Streets: Class and Gender Conflict in New York City, 1850–1860," *Feminist Studies* 8 (1982): 309–35; and Linda Gordon, *The Great Arizona Orphan Abduction* (Cambridge, MA: Harvard University Press, 1999).

95. *Muller v. Oregon*, 208 U.S. 412 (1908); Alice Kessler-Harris, *In Pursuit of Equity: Women, Men, and the Quest for Economic Citizenship in Twentieth-Century America* (New York: Oxford University Press, 1981) 31; Rachel Roth, *Making Women Pay: The Hidden Costs of Fetal Rights* (Ithaca, NY: Cornell University Press, 2003), 104.

96. See Paul Popenoe and Roswell Johnson, *Applied Eugenics* (New York: Macmillan, 1926).

97. Gordon, *Moral Property of Women,* 102, 189–90.

98. Glenda Gilmore, *Gender and Jim Crow: Women and the Politics of White Supremacy in North Carolina, 1896–1920* (Chapel Hill: University of North Carolina Press, 1996), 171; Greg Dorr, "Assuring America's Place in the Sun: Ivey Foreman Lewis and the Teaching of Eugenics at the University of Virginia, 1915–1953," *Journal of Southern History* 56 (Spring 2000): 261.

99. George J. Sanchez, "Go After the Women: Americanization and the Mexican Immigrant Woman, 1915–1929," in Janet Golden and Rima Apple, eds., *Mothers and Motherhood: Readings in American History* (Columbus: Ohio State University Press, 1997), 486.

100. Edwin Black, *War against the Weak: Eugenics and America's Campaign to Create a Master Race* (New York: Four Walls Eight Windows, 2003), 192, 202

101. Ian Haney Lopez, *White by Law: The Legal Construction of Race* (New York: New York University Press, 1998), 121.

102. Ibid., 59.

103. Cooper, *Technique of Contraception,* 2.

104. Daniel J. Kevles, *In the Name of Eugenics: Genetics and the Uses of Human Heredity* (Cambridge, MA: Harvard University Press, 1985); Black, *War against the Weak,* chap. 5.

105. Dorr, "Assuring America's Place in the Sun," 260.

106. Joan Didion, *Where I Was From* (New York: Random House, 2003).

107. Kline, *Building a Better Race,* 60. Regina Kunzel points out that when social workers replaced "the melodramatic story of seduction and abandonment with feeblemindedness and sex delinquency" as causes for "promiscuity" or "lost virtue," then "the emotional, moralistic world of old-fashioned benevo-

lence" was replaced with "the objective, empirical realm of science." *Fallen Women, Problem Girls*, 62.

108. Black, *War against the Weak*, 119–23.

109. *Buck v. Bell*, 274 U.S. 200 (1927).

110. See, for example, Brumberg, "'Ruined Girls'"; Kunzel, *Fallen Women, Problem Girls*; Alexander, *The "Girl Problem"*; Mary Odem, *Delinquent Daughters: Protecting and Policing Adolescent Female Sexuality in the United States, 1885–1920* (Chapel Hill: University of North Carolina Press, 1995).

111. W. E. B. DuBois, "The Damnation of Women," in *Darkwater: Voices from within the Veil* (New York: Dover, 1999).

112. Elsie Johnson McDougald, "The Double Task: The Struggle of Negro Women for Sex and Race Emancipation" (1925), in Gerda Lerner, ed., *Black Women in White America* (New York: Vintage, 1973), 170–71.

113. Tone, *Devices and Desires*, 85.

114. Jesse M. Rodrique, "The Black Community and the Birth Control Movement," in Darlene Clark Hine, Wilma King, and Linda Reed, eds., *We Specialize in the Wholly Impossible: A Reader in Black Women's History* (New York: Carlson, 1995), 511.

115. Tone, *Devices and Desires*, 86.

116. Rodrique, "The Black Community and the Birth Control Movement," 516.

117. Roberts, *Killing the Black Body*, 87.

118. Molly Ladd-Taylor, ed., *Raising a Baby the Government Way: Mothers' Letters to the Children's Bureau, 1915–1932* (New Brunswick, NJ: Rutgers University Press, 1985), letter dated January 13, 1928.

119. Gordon, *Moral Property of Women*, 155.

120. Ladd-Taylor, *Raising a Baby*, 180–82.

121. Reagan, *When Abortion Was a Crime*, 29.

122. Ibid., 40–42.

123. Gordon, *Moral Property of Women*, 127.

124. Alexander, *The "Girl Problem,"* 18–20.

125. Tone, *Devices and Desires*, 106–10.

126. Gordon, *Moral Property of Women*, 130–33.

127. Chen, *"The Sex Side of Life,"* 237.

128. Ibid., 183; McCann, *Birth Control Politics*, 15; Gwendolyn Mink, *Wages of Motherhood: Inequality in the Welfare State, 1917–1942* (Ithaca, NY: Cornell University Press, 1995).

129. Leta Hollingworth, "Social Devices for Impelling Women to Bear and Raise Children," *American Journal of Sociology* 22 (1916): 22.

130. Chen, *"The Sex Side of Life,"* 223–24.

131. Cooper, *Technique of Contraception*, 197; Reagan, *When Abortion Was a Crime*, 23; Reagan, "'About to Meet Her Maker,'" 114.

132. Tone, *Devices and Desires,* 118.

133. McCann, *Birth Control Politics,* 30–36.

134. Gordon, *Moral Property of Women,* 174.

135. Cooper, *Technique of Contraception,* 138, 223.

136. Tone, *Devices and Desires,* 108.

137. McCann, *Birth Control Politics,* 128.

138. Cooper, *Technique of Contraception,* 143.

139. Kline, *Building a Better Race,* 88.

140. Chesler, *Woman of Valor,* 318–20.

141. Hollingworth, "Social Devices for Impelling Women to Bear and Raise Children," 19–29.

142. Chen, *"The Sex Side of Life,"* 206.

NOTES TO CHAPTER 3

1. Wendy Kline, *Building a Better Race: Gender, Sexuality, and Eugenics from the Turn of the Century to the Baby Boom* (Berkeley: University of California Press, 2001), 96–97.

2. Ellen Chesler, *Woman of Valor: Margaret Sanger and the Birth Control Movement in America* (New York: Simon and Shuster, 1992), 325.

3. Linda Gordon, *The Moral Property of Women: A History of Birth Control Politics in America* (Urbana: University of Illinois Press, 2002), 226.

4. Laura Briggs, *Reproducing Empire: Race, Sex, Science and U.S. Imperialism in Puerto Rico* (Berkeley: University of California Press, 2002), 83.

5. Constance Chen, *"The Sex Side of Life": Mary Ware Dennett's Pioneering Battle for Birth Control and Sex Education* (New York: New Press, 1996), 301.

6. Chesler, *Woman of Valor,* 331.

7. *United States v. One Package of Japanese Pessaries,* 13 F. Supp. 334 (E.D.N.Y. 1936), aff'd 86 F. 2d 737 (2d Cir. 1936, the United States Court of Appeals); Carole McCann, *Birth Control Politics in the United States, 1916–1945* (Ithaca, NY: Cornell University Press, 1994), 75; Gordon, *Moral Property of Women,* 226.

8. Andrea Tone, *Devices and Desires: A History of Contraceptives in America* (New York: Hill and Wang, 2001), 113.

9. Chesler, *Woman of Valor,* 320–41; McCann, *Birth Control Politics,* 199.

10. Sucheng Chan, "Race, Ethnic Culture, and Gender in the Construction of Identities among Second-Generation Chinese Americans, 1880s to 1930s," in K. Scott Wong and Sucheng Chan, eds., *Claiming America: Constructing Chinese American Identities during the Exclusion Era* (Philadelphia: Temple University Press, 1998), 127.

11. Sucheta Mazumdar, "What Happened to the Women? Chinese and Indian Male Migration to the United States in Global Perspective," in Shirley

Hune and Gail M. Nomura, eds., *Asian/Pacific Islander American Women: A Historical Anthology* (New York: New York University Press, 2003), 60.

12. Sucheng Chan, "The Exclusion of Chinese Women, 1870–1943," in Sucheng Chan, ed., *Entry Denied: Exclusion and the Chinese Community in America, 1882–1943* (Philadelphia: Temple University Press, 1991), 138–39.

13. Neil Betten and Raymond A. Mohl, "From Discrimination to Repatriation: Mexican Life in Gary, Indiana, during the Great Depression," *Pacific Historical Review* 42 (1973): 377; Raymond G. Carroll, "The Alien on Relief," *Saturday Evening Post,* January 11, 1936, 16–17; Handbook of Texas Online, "Mexican Americans and Repatriation," a joint project of the General Libraries at the University of Texas at Austin and the Texas State Historical Association, http://www.tsha.utexas.edu/handbook/online/articles/print/mm/pqmyk.html, 2.

14. Abraham Hoffman, "Stimulus to Repatriation: The 1931 Federal Deportation Drive and the Los Angeles Mexican Community," *Pacific Historical Review* 42 (May 1973): 208.

15. Handbook of Texas, "Mexican Americans and Repatriation," 4.

16. Jorge L. Chinea, "Ethnic Prejudice and Anti-immigration Policies in Times of Economic Stress: Mexican Repatriation from the United States, 1929–1939," *East Wind/West Wind* (Winter 1996): 9–13.

17. Camille Guerin-Gonzalez, *Mexican Workers and American Dreams: Immigration, Repatriation, and California Farm Labor, 1900–1939* (New Brunswick, NJ: Rutgers University Press, 1994), 111.

18. Hoffman, "Stimulus to Repatriation," 218–19; Handbook of Texas, "Mexican Americans and Repatriation," 2.

19. Chinea, "Ethnic Prejudice," 12. See, for example, "Measure Shedding Light on Shameful 1930s 'Repatriation' Program Approved by Legislature; MALDEF Urges Governor to Sign Bill," August 26, 2004, Mexican American Legal Defense and Education Fund, http://www.maldef.org/news/press.cfm?ID=230.

20. Quoted in R. Reynolds McKay, "The Impact of the Great Depression on Immigrant Mexican Labor: Repatriation of the Bridgeport, Texas, Coal Miners," *Social Science Quarterly* 65 (June 1984): 361; Emma R. Stevenson, "The Emigrant Comes Home, *Survey,* May 1, 1931, 177.

21. Mary S. Melcher, "Tending Children, Chickens, and Cattle: Southern Arizona Ranch and Farm Women, 1910–1940" (Ph.D. diss., Arizona State University, 1994), 157–61.

22. Fran Leeper Buss, *La Partera: Story of a Midwife* (Ann Arbor: University of Michigan Press, 1980), 115–16.

23. Melcher, "Tending Children, Chickens, and Cattle," 147.

24. A good place to begin researching this topic is "Reproductive Health in

the Context of Forced Migration: An Annotated Bibliography" (2001), prepared by Christopher Haskew, United Nations Population Fund, International Centre for Migration and Health, http://www.icmh.ch/.

25. Daniel J. Kevles, *In the Name of Eugenics: Genetics and the Uses of Human Heredity*, rev. ed. (Cambridge, MA: Harvard University Press, 1995), ix.

26. Dorothy Roberts, *Killing the Black Body: Race, Reproduction, and the Meaning of Liberty* (New York: Pantheon, 1997), 71, 216.

27. Johanna Schoen, "Fighting for Child Health: Race, Birth Control, and the State in the Jim Crow South," *Social Politics* 4 (1997): 90–113.

28. Roberts, *Killing the Black Body*, 72.

29. Kline, *Building a Better Race*, 105.

30. Wendy Kline found thousands of letters written to Ezra S. Gasney, the author of a eugenics textbook, *Human Sterilization Today*, from "students, professors, ministers, rabbis, social workers, public health and welfare workers, Rotary Club members, physicians, librarians, birth control advocates, PTA members," praising sterilization as the "'only logical and humane method of protecting ourselves' from the rising tide of degeneracy." Ibid., 80.

31. Ibid., 97.

32. Gordon, *Moral Property of Women*, 214.

33. Schoen, "Fighting for Child Health."

34. Kline, *Building a Better Race*, 106.

35. Chesler, *Woman of Valor*, 344.

36. Ibid., 300.

37. Jesse M. Rodrique, "The Black Community and the Birth Control Movement," in Darlene Clark Hine, Wilma King, and Linda Reed, eds., *We Specialize in the Wholly Impossible: A Reader in Black Women's History* (New York: Carlson, 1995), 507.

38. Leslie J. Reagan, *When Abortion Was a Crime: Women, Medicine and Law in the United States, 1867–1973* (Berkeley: University of California Press, 1997), 49, 54.

39. Ruth Barnett, *They Weep on My Doorstep* (Beaverton, OR: Halo, 1969), 43.

40. Reagan, *When Abortion Was a Crime*, 22.

41. Gordon, *Moral Property of Women*, 273. Ellen Chesler writes that this kind of referral for "therapeutic abortion" may have "been a standard practice" at the clinics in the 1930s (*Woman of Valor*, 302).

42. Reagan, *When Abortion Was a Crime*, 148, 159; also see Dr. X as told to Lucy Freeman, *The Abortionist* (Garden City, NY: Doubleday, 1962).

43. Reagan, *When Abortion Was a Crime*, 138.

44. Ibid., 133–34.

45. Edward Keemer, *Confessions of a Pro-Life Abortionist* (Detroit: Velco Press, 1980), 63–64.

46. Reagan, *When Abortion Was a Crime*, 137.

47. Ibid., 138.

48. Debbie Nathan, *Women and Other Aliens: Essays from the Mexico Border* (El Paso, TX: Cinco Puntos Press, 1991), 37.

49. McCann, *Birth Control Politics*, 198–99.

50. Reagan, *When Abortion Was a Crime*, 146–47.

51. Ibid., 135.

52. Keemer, *Confessions*, 74.

53. *Chinese Digest,* January 10, 1936, quoted in Judy Yung, *Unbound Voices: A Documentary History of Chinese Women in San Francisco* (Berkeley: University of California Press, 1999), 10, 15.

54. Jane Kwong Lee, "A Richer Life for All," in Yung, *Unbound Voices,* 352–53.

55. Sandy Polishuk, *Sticking to the Union: An Oral History of the Life and Times of Julia Ruuttila* (New York: Palgrave, 2003), 66.

56. Yung, *Unbound Voices,* 353.

57. Schoen, "Fighting for Child Health"; Rodrique, "The Black Community and the Birth Control Movement," 334, 337–38; Lucien Brown, "Keeping Fit," *New York Amsterdam News,* November 28, 1932.

58. "The Lend A Hand Club, Washington, D.C., August 28, 1931," and "Robert S. Barrett to Mrs. Harriet Wilson Taylor, Nashville, March 23, 1936," two documents in the author's files, from the National Archives.

59. Schoen, "Fighting for Child Health."

60. Chesler, *Woman of Valor,* 294–95; Tone, *Devices and Desires,* 152; Rodrique, "The Black Community and the Birth Control Movement," 512.

61. Maxine Davis, *Women's Medical Problems* (New York: Pocket Books, 1953), 90.

62. Tone, *Devices and Desires,* 160.

63. Ibid., 156–57, 299.

64. "Esperanza Salcido," in Nan Elasser, Kyle MacKenzie, and Yvonne Tixier y Vigil, eds., *Las Mujeres: Conversations from a Hispanic Community* (Old Westbury, NY: Feminist Press, 1979), 64.

65. See, for example, Helene Deutsch, *The Psychology of Women* (New York: Grune and Stratton, 1944).

66. See Mari Jo Buhle, *Feminism and Its Discontents: A Century of Struggle with Psychoanalysis* (Cambridge, MA: Harvard University Press, 1998).

67. Kline, *Building a Better Race,* 68.

68. Reagan, *When Abortion Was a Crime,* 133.

69. McCann, *Birth Control Politics,* 92–93.

70. Regina Kunzel, *Fallen Women, Problem Girls: Unmarried Mothers and the Professionalization of Social Work, 1890–1945* (New Haven, CT: Yale University Press, 1993), 101.

71. Keemer, *Confessions,* 87.

NOTES TO CHAPTER 4

1. "A Social Security Program Must Include All Those Who Need Its Protection," radio address on the third anniversary of the Social Security Act, Franklin D. Roosevelt, August 15, 1938, from *FDR Statements on Social Security*, http://www.ssa.gov/history/fdrstmts.html; Anne O'Hare McCormick, "Vast Tides That Stir the Capital," *New York Times Magazine*, May 7, 1933, 1–2, 9.

2. "Message to Congress on Social Security," Franklin D. Roosevelt, January 17, 1935, from *FDR Statements on Social Security*.

3. Joanne Goodwin, *Gender and the Politics of Welfare Reform: Mothers' Pensions in Chicago, 1911–1929* (Chicago: University of Chicago Press, 1997); Gwendolyn Mink, *The Wages of Motherhood: Inequality in the Welfare State, 1917–1942* (Ithaca, NY: Cornell University Press, 1995).

4. Alice Kessler-Harris, *Out to Work: A History of Wage-Earning Women in the United States* (New York: Oxford University Press, 1982), 277, 289–91, 301, 309–10; Richard A. Easterlin, "The Impact of Demographic Factors on the Family Environment of Children, 1940–1995," in Richard R. Nelson and Felicity Skidmore, eds., *American Families and the Economy: The High Cost of Living* (Washington, DC: National Academy Press, 1983), 260–97.

5. Johanna Schoen, "Fighting for Child Health: Race, Birth Control, and the State in the Jim Crow South," *Social Politics* 4 (1997): 90–113. Schoen found this story of a determined woman, probably typical of many: a woman in North Carolina "told her husband that she would simply catch a hen and take it to the store and sell it in order to get money to buy some Trojans." A public health official observed, "It is true that a lot of our mothers are not financially able to pay fifty cents for three Trojans. Yet, it is encouraging to see that some will be willing to sacrifice their chickens and eggs in order to stop babies from coming."

6. Andrea Tone, *Devices and Desires: A History of Contraceptives in America* (New York: Hill and Wang, 2001), 135.

7. Quoted in Linda Gordon, *The Moral Property of Women: A History of Birth Control Politics in America* (Urbana: University of Illinois Press, 2002), 247.

8. David Garrow, *Liberty and Sexuality: The Right to Privacy and the Making of Roe v. Wade* (New York: Macmillan, 1994), 106–7.

9. Lucinda Cicler, "Birth Control," in Robin Morgan, ed., *Sisterhood Is Powerful: An Anthology of Writings from the Women's Liberation Movement* (New York: Vintage, 1970), 246.

10. Marynia Farnham and Ferdinand Lundberg, *Modern Woman: The Lost Sex* (New York: Harper and Brothers, 1947), 235.

11. Ibid., 235–40.

12. Ibid., 124, 295, 395–96.

13. See, for example, Juan Williams, *Thurgood Marshall: American Revolutionary* (New York: Three Rivers Press, 2000); Mark V. Tushnet, *Making Civil Rights*

Law: Thurgood Marshall and the Supreme Court, 1936–1961 (New York: Oxford University Press, 1994); Richard Kluger, *Simple Justice* (New York: Vintage, 1977); Mary Dudziak, *Cold War Civil Rights: Race and the Image of American Democracy* (Princeton, NJ: Princeton University Press, 2000).

14. Tushnet, *Making Civil Rights Law,* 97.

15. Ibid., 70.

16. Ibid., 99.

17. Ibid., 136.

18. "Third Parties," *Time,* October 11, 1948, 24–27.

19. A. Delafield Smith, "Public Assistance as a Social Obligation," *Harvard Law Review* 63 (1949): 266–88.

20. *Skinner v. Oklahoma ex rel. Williamson,* 316 U.S. 535 (1942); see Peggy Cooper-Davis, *Neglected Stories: The Constitution and Family Values* (New York: Hill and Wang, 1997).

21. See Lizabeth Cohen, *A Consumers' Republic: The Politics of Mass Consumption in Postwar America* (New York: Knopf, 2003).

22. See Linda K. Kerber, *Women of the Republic: Intellect and Ideology in Revolutionary America* (Chapel Hill: University of North Carolina Press, 1980); and Mary Beth Norton, *Liberty's Daughters: The Revolutionary Experience of American Women, 1750–1800* (Ithaca, NY: Cornell University Press, 1980).

23. See, for example, Rickie Solinger, *The Abortionist: A Woman against the Law* (New York: Free Press, 1994), for a glimpse of widespread disobedience of abortion laws in the postwar era. Also Leslie J. Reagan, *When Abortion Was a Crime: Women, Medicine, and the Law in the United States, 1867–1973* (Berkeley: University of California Press, 1997); and Carole Joffe, *Doctors of Conscience: The Struggle to Provide Abortions before and after* Roe v. Wade (Boston: Beacon Press, 1994).

24. Nell Irvin Painter, *Southern History across the Color Line* (Chapel Hill: University of North Carolina Press, 2002), 186; Wilber Cash, *The Mind of the South* (New York: Vintage, 1941).

25. Quoted in Gordon, *Moral Property of Women,* 250.

26. Quoted in Donald Critchlow, *Intended Consequences: Birth Control, Abortion, and the Federal Government in Modern America* (New York: Oxford University Press, 1999), 19.

27. See Kluger, *Simple Justice.*

28. Jesse M. Rodrique, "Black Women and the Birth Control Movement" in Darlene Clark Hine, Wilma King, and Linda Reed, eds., *We Specialize in the Wholly Impossible: A Reader in Black Women's History* (New York: Carlson, 1995), 515; Dorothy Boulding Ferebee, "Planned Parenthood as a Public Health Measure for the Negro Race," *Human Fertility* 7 (January 1942): 7–10.

29. E. Franklin Frazier, "Birth Control for More Negro Babies," *Negro Digest,* July 1945, 41–44.

30. Dr. Julian Lewis, "Can the Negro Afford Birth Control," *Negro Digest,* July 1945, 19–22.

31. For a journalistic treatment of these matters, see A. J. Liebling, "Horsefeathers Swathed in Mink," in A. J. Liebling, *The Press* (New York: Ballantine, 1961), 79–89.

32. Franklin Delano Roosevelt, State of the Union address, January 11, 1944, http://www.presidency.ucsb.edu/.

33. See "Families Receiving Aid to Dependent Children," Federal Security Agency, Social Security Board, Bureau of Public Assistance, Public Assistance Report no. 7 (1942).

34. See Winifred Bell, *ADC* (New York: Columbia University Press, 1965).

35. Ibid., 6; "Families Receiving Aid to Dependent Children."

36. Bell, *ADC,* 87–89.

37. Ibid., Chapter 3.

38. Gordon, *The Moral Property of Women,* 251.

39. Johanna Schoen, "Between Choice and Coercion: Women and the Politics of Sterilization in North Carolina, 1929–75," *Journal of Women's History* 13 (Spring 2001): 135–36.

40. See, for example, *Congressional Record,* 82nd Cong., 1st sess., September 26, 1951, 97, pt. 9, "Fraud and Waste in Public Welfare Programs."

41. Bell, *ADC,* 97–99; Rickie Solinger, *Wake Up Little Susie: Single Pregnancy and Race before* Roe v. Wade (New York: Routledge, 2000), chaps. 1 and 2.

42. Critchlow, *Intended Consequences,* 32.

43. Quoted in Solinger, *Wake Up Little Susie,* 50.

44. This section is drawn from my book-length study of these matters, *Wake Up Little Susie.*

45. See Rickie Solinger, "Race and 'Value': Black and White Illegitimate Babies in the U.S.A.," *Gender and History* 4 (1992): 343–63.

46. This section is a distillation of four of my publications dealing with abortion in the middle of the twentieth century in the United States: my book-length treatment of criminal abortion before and after World War II, *The Abortionist;* "Justifying Choice: The Back Alley Butcher as Spectral Icon," chap. 2 of *Beggars and Choosers: How the Politics of Choice Shapes Adoption, Abortion, and Welfare in the United States* (New York: Hill and Wang, 2001); "'Extreme Danger': Women Abortionists and Their Clients before *Roe v. Wade,*" in Joanne Meyerowitz, ed., *Not June Cleaver: Women and Gender in Postwar America* (Philadelphia: Temple University Press, 1994), 335–57; and "'A Complete Disaster': Abortion and the Politics of Hospital Abortion Committees," *Feminist Studies* 19 (1993): 241–68. Each of these publications provides extensive guides to sources and further reading on this topic.

NOTES TO CHAPTER 5

1. *New York Times,* September 4, 1959, 23; December 3, 1959, 1; December 4, 1959, 16; December 27, 1959, 44. Also see Donald T. Critchlow, *Intended Consequences: Birth Control, Abortion, and the Federal Government in Modern America* (New York: Oxford University Press, 1999).

2. James Reston, "Washington: The Politics of Birth Control," *New York Times,* June 10, 1966, 44.

3. Steven M. Spencer, "The Birth Control Revolution," *Saturday Evening Post,* January 15, 1966, 22.

4. Critchlow, *Intended Consequences,* 56.

5. Ibid., 75.

6. U.S. Congress, Senate, Committee on Government Operations, Subcommittee on Foreign Aid Expenditures; Population Crisis: Hearings on S. 1676, A Bill to Reorganize the Department of State and the Department of Health, Education, and Welfare, 89th Cong., 1st sess. (Washington, DC: U.S. Government Printing Office, 1966), pt. 3-A, 1540–41.

7. Lizabeth Cohen, *A Consumers' Republic: The Politics of Mass Consumption in Postwar America* (New York: Knopf, 2003); Elaine Tyler May, *Homeward Bound: American Families in the Cold War Era* (New York: Basic Books, 1988).

8. John F. Kennedy, *Let the World Go Forth: The Speeches, Statements, and Writings of John F. Kennedy* (New York: Delacourt Press, 1988), 131.

9. *New York Times,* November 10, 1960, 39.

10. Nicole J. Grant, *The Selling of Contraception: The Dalkon Shield Case, Sexuality, and Women's Autonomy* (Columbus: Ohio State University Press, 1992), 103.

11. Spencer, "Birth Control Revolution," 21.

12. Andrew Hacker, "The Pill and Morality," *New York Times Magazine,* November 21, 1965, 138.

13. Spencer, "Birth Control Revolution," 22.

14. Critchlow, *Intended Consequences,* 79.

15. Gloria Steinem, "The Moral Disarmament of Betty Coed," *Esquire,* September 1962, 92; Spencer, "Birth Control Revolution," 67.

16. Grant, *Selling of Contraception,* 19; Lawrence Lader, "Why Birth Control Fails," *McCall's,* October 1969, 163.

17. Spencer, "Birth Control Revolution," 22, 66.

18. DELFEN ad, *True Story,* January 1967, 22; Spencer, "Birth Control Revolution," 22.

19. Elizabeth Siegel Watkins, *On the Pill: A Social History of Oral Contraceptives, 1950–1970* (Baltimore: Johns Hopkins University Press, 1998), 70.

20. Julius Horowitz, "The Arithmetic of Delinquency," *New York Times Magazine,* January 31, 1965, 12.

21. Arthur Campbell, "The Role of Family Planning in the Reduction of Poverty," *Journal of Marriage and the Family* 30 (May 1968): 236–45.

22. Watkins, *On the Pill*, 62; Andrea Tone, *Devices and Desires: A History of Contraceptives in America* (New York: Hill and Wang, 2001), 236–56.

23. Howard Osofsky, *The Pregnant Teenager: A Medical, Educational and Social Analysis* (Springfield, IL: Thomas, 1966), 88.

24. Donald Bogue, "Family Planning in the Negro Ghettos of Chicago," *Milbank Memorial Fund Quarterly* 48 (April 1970, pt. 2): 283–99.

25. Joyce A. Ladner, *Tomorrow's Tomorrow: The Black Woman* (New York: Anchor Books, 1972), 213, 223.

26. M. Rivka Polatnick, "How a Black and a White Group of the 1960s Viewed Motherhood," *Signs* 21 (1996): 679–706.

27. Betty Friedan, *The Feminine Mystique* (New York: Norton, 1963), 45.

28. Tone, *Devices and Desires*, 241.

29. Watkins, *On the Pill*, 36–39.

30. Ibid., 88–89; Spencer, "Birth Control Revolution," 24.

31. U.S. Food and Drug Administration, Advisory Committee on Obstetrics and Gynecology, Second Report on Intrauterine Devices (1968 [document no. 290-137 0-68-3]), 1.

32. Tone, *Devices and Desires*, 280.

33. Ibid., 266.

34. U.S. Congress, House of Representatives, Committee on Population, The Depo-Provera Debate, 95th Cong., 2nd sess., 1978; Grant, *Selling of Contraception*, esp. 68–69, 150.

35. Grant, *Selling of Contraception*, 31, 129–30.

36. Watkins, *On the Pill*, 3, 109, 124–27.

37. Barbara Seaman, *The Doctors' Case against the Pill* (New York: Dolphin, 1969); Boston Women's Health Collective, *Our Bodies Ourselves* (Boston: Boston Women's Health Collective, 1970).

38. Grant, *Selling of Contraception*, 72, 135.

39. *Griswold v. Connecticut*, 381 U.S. 479 (1965); *Eisenstadt v. Baird*, 405 U.S. 438 (1972).

40. Steinem, "Moral Disarmament," 155.

41. Constance Nathanson, *Dangerous Passage: The Social Control of Sexuality in Women's Adolescence* (Philadelphia: Temple University Press, 1991), 29–30.

42. Ladner, *Tomorrow's Tomorrow*, 232–33.

43. This discussion of the Sherri Finkbine ordeal is drawn from Rickie Solinger, "Sherri Finkbine and the Origins of *Roe v. Wade*," in William Graebner, ed., *True Stories from the American Past*, vol. 2, *Since 1865*, 3rd ed. (New York: McGraw Hill, 2003), 226–45.

44. Jack Gould, "TV Drama Used as Editorial Protest," *New York Times*, April

30, 1962; Val Adams, "Disputed Drama," *New York Times,* April 9, 1962; Val Adams, "Ten Stations Shun Show on Abortion," *New York Times,* April 27, 1962.

45. Christopher Tietze, "Two Years' Experience with a Liberal Abortion Law: Its Impact on Fertility Trends in New York City," *Family Planning Perspectives* 5 (1973): 36–41.

46. Lucinda Cisler, "Unfinished Business: Birth Control and Women's Liberation," in Robin Morgan, ed., *Sisterhood Is Powerful: An Anthology of Writings from the Women's Liberation Movement* (New York: Vintage, 1970), 245–88.

47. Ellen Willis, "Up from Radicalism: A Feminist Journal," *US Magazine,* October 1969.

48. Critchlow, *Intended Consequences,* 151.

49. See Jennifer Nelson, *Women of Color and the Reproductive Rights Movement* (New York: New York University Press, 2003).

50. Rosalind Pollack Petchesky, *Abortion and Women's Choice: The State, Sexuality, and Reproductive Freedom,* rev. ed. (Boston: Northeastern University Press, 1990), 129.

51. Quoted in James Mohr, "Iowa's Abortion Battles of the Late 1960s and Early 1970s: Long-Term Perspectives and Short-Term Analysis," *Annals of Iowa* 50 (1989): 82.

52. Carole Joffe, *Doctors of Conscience: The Struggle to Provide Abortion before and after* Roe v. Wade (Boston: Beacon Press, 1996)

53. Critchlow, *Intended Consequences,* 91–92, 157.

54. See Nelson, *Women of Color,* chap. 1.

55. Amy Kesselman, "Women v. Connecticut: Conducting a Statewide Hearing on Abortion," in Rickie Solinger, ed., *Abortion Wars: A Half-Century of Struggle, 1950–2000* (Berkeley: University of California Press, 1998), 42–67.

56. *Griswold v. Connecticut,* 381 U.S. 479 (1965).

57. Reva Siegel, "Reasoning from the Body: A Historical Perspective on Abortion Regulation and Questions of Equal Protection," *Stanford Law Review* 44 (January 1992): 261–381.

58. "Letter to State Agencies Administering Approved Public Assistance Plans," Bureau of Public Assistance, State Letter No. 452, January 17, 1961, reprinted in Gwendolyn Mink and Rickie Solinger, eds., *Welfare: A Documentary History of U.S. Policy and Politics* (New York: New York University Press, 2003), 204.

59. Martin Gilens, *Why Americans Hate Welfare: Race, Media, and the Politics of Antipoverty Policy* (Chicago: University of Chicago Press, 2000), 105, 114, 129.

60. In 1968, a University of Michigan economist, James N. Morgan, testified before Congress regarding Americans' general—if mistaken—belief that "natural mothers" were the best caretakers of their children. He said, "Our society has never had the courage to suggest that if children are not being properly

raised, they ought to be separated from their parents. . . . The [poor] mother has been used as a cheap source of taking care of her own children. I happen to think this may be a big mistake." Michigan representative Martha Griffin agreed, reminding the speaker: "But this is what the $600 million is in the welfare amendment for, setting up day care centers, trying to withdraw the children away from their homes as quickly as you can." "Income Maintenance Programs," Hearings before the Subcommittee on Fiscal Policy of the Joint Economic Committee, Congress of the United States, 90th Cong., 2nd sess., June 1968 (Washington, DC: U.S. Government Printing Office, 1968), vol. 1, 178–80.

61. Phillips Cutright and John Scanzoni, "Income Supplements and the American Family," in *The Family, Poverty, and Welfare Programs: Factors Influencing Family Stability*, paper no. 12, part I, A Volume of Studies Prepared for the Use of the Subcommittee on Fiscal Policy of the Joint Economic Committee, U.S. Congress, November 4, 1973 (Washington, DC: U.S. Government Printing Office, 1973), 91.

62. Edward C. Banfield, "The Cities: Babies for Sale," *New York Times*, October 13, 1970, 45.

63. See Thomas Sugrue, *The Origins of the Urban Crisis: Race and Inequality in Postwar Detroit* (Princeton, N.J.: Princeton University Press, 1998).

64. Quoted in Critchlow, *Intended Consequences*, 61.

65. Dick Gregory, "My Answer to Genocide," *Ebony*, October 1971, 66.

66. Toni Cade, "The Pill: Genocide or Liberation?" in Toni Cade, ed., *The Black Woman: An Anthology* (New York: Vintage, 1970), 167.

67. Ibid.; Dorothy Roberts, *Killing the Black Body: Race, Reproduction, and the Meaning of Liberty* (New York: Pantheon, 1996), 98–99.

68. "Statement on Birth Control," Black Women's Liberation Group, Mount Vernon, New York, in Morgan, *Sisterhood Is Powerful*, 361.

69. "Poem," by Kay Lindsey in Cade, *The Black Woman*, 17.

70. Mary Crow Dog and Richard Erdoes, *Lakota Woman* (New York: Grove Weidenfeld, 1990); Angela Y. Davis, "Outcast Mothers and Surrogates: Racism and Reproductive Health in the Nineties," in Linda S. Kauffman, ed., *American Feminist Thought at Century's End: A Reader* (Cambridge, MA: Blackwell, 1993).

71. Johnnie Tillmon, "Welfare Is a Women's Issue," *Ms.*, Spring 1972, 111–16.

72. Ibid.

73. Shirley Chisholm, *Unbought and Unbossed* (New York: Houghton Mifflin, 1970), 113–22.

74. Iris Lopez, "Agency and Constraint: Sterilization and Reproductive Freedom among Puerto Rican Women in New York City," in Louise Lamphere, Helena Ragone, and Patricia Zavellas, eds., *Situated Lives: Gender and Culture in Everyday Lives* (New York: Routledge, 1997), 157–74.

75. Ibid.

76. Elena R. Gutierrez, "Policing 'Pregnant Pilgrims': Situating Abuse of

Mexican-Origin Women in L.A. County," in Georgina Feldberg, Molly Ladd-Taylor, Alison Li, and Kathryn McPherson, eds., *Women, Health, and Nation: Canada and the United States since 1945* (Ithaca, NY: McGill-Queen's University Press, 2003), 380.

77. Gerhard Gessell, *Relf v. Weinberger et al.*, U.S. District Court of D.C., March 15, 1974.

78. U.S. Congress, Senate Committee on Labor and Public Welfare, Subcommittee on Health, Quality of Health Care—Human Experimentation: Hearings before the Subcommittee on Health, 93rd Cong., 1st sess., April 30, June 28–29, July 10, 1973 (Washington, DC: U.S. Government Printing Office, 1973), pt. 4, 1586.

79. Gutiérrez, "Policing 'Pregnant Pilgrims,'" 395.

80. Ibid., 396.

81. Ibid., 384.

82. Ibid., 385.

83. Ibid., 386.

84. Ibid., 387.

85. Ibid., 390–91.

86. Ibid., 393–94.

87. Jane Lawrence, "The Indian Health Service and the Sterilization of Native American Women," *American Indian Quarterly* 24 (Summer 2000): 400–419; Bernard Rosenfeld, Sidney M. Wolfe, and Robert E. McGarrah Jr., "A Health Research Group Study on Surgical Sterilization: Present Abuses and Proposed Regulations" (Washington, DC: Health Research Group, October 29, 1973), 2–7.

88. *Congressional Record*, Senate, vol. 124, pt. 14, September 27, 1978, 31917.

89. *Congressional Record*, House, vol. 123, pt. 16, June 17, 1977, 19698–19715.

90. Lawrence Berger, M.D., "Abortions in America: The Effects of Restrictive Funding," *New England Journal of Medicine* 298 (June 1978): 1474–77.

91. Remarks of Charles Grassley ("Medicaid for Abortions?"), reprint from the *Des Moines Register, Congressional Record*, Senate, vol. 123, pt. 25, September 29, 1973, 31673.

92. *Congressional Record*, Senate, vol. 124, pt. 14, September 27, 1978, 31900.

93. Richard Lincoln, Brigitte Doring-Bradley, Barbara L. Lindheimand, Maureen A. Cotterill, "The Court, the Congress, and the President: Turning Back the Clock on the Pregnant Poor," *Family Planning Perspectives* 9 (September–October 1977): 211. The authors point out that in the mid-1970s, in Mississippi, the average cost of an abortion was ten times higher than the monthly AFDC check and that thirty-seven states had lower AFDC payments than the cost of an abortion.

94. *Maher v. Roe*, 432 U.S. 494 (1977); *Harris v. McCrae*, 448 U.S. 297 (1980).

95. George Cameron Nixon, "*Harris v. McRae*: Cutting Back Abortion Rights," *Columbia Human Rights Law Review* 12 (Spring–Summer 1980): 115.

96. James Trussell, Jann Menken, Barbara L. Lindheim, and Barbara Vaughan, "The Impact of Restricting Medicaid Financing for Abortion," *Family Planning Perspectives* 12 (May–June 1980): 120.

97. Ibid.; also see *Abortions and the Poor: Private Morality, Public Responsibility* (New York: Alan Guttmacher Institute, 1979); Rachel Benson Gold, "After the Hyde Amendment: Public Funding for Abortion in FY 1978," *Family Planning Perspectives* 12 (May–June 1980): 134.

98. Trussell et al., "Impact of Restricting Medicaid Financing," 129.

99. Sharon Gold-Steinberg and Abigail J. Stewart, "Psychologies of Abortion: Implications of a Changing Context," in Solinger, *Abortion Wars*, 364.

100. Petchesky, *Abortion and Women's Choice*, 245, 256, 273; see chap. 7, generally.

101. Abortion—Part 2, Hearings before the Subcommittee on Constitutional Amendments of the Committee on the Judiciary, U.S. Senate, 93rd Cong., 2nd sess., S.J. Res. 119, Proposing an Amendment to the Constitution of the United States for the Protection of Unborn Children and Other Persons, and S.J. Res. 130, Proposing an Amendment to the Constitution of the United States Guaranteeing the Right to Life to the Unborn, the Ill, the Aged, or the Incapacitated (Washington, DC: U.S. Government Printing Office, 1974), 487.

102. Ibid., 463.

103. Quoted in Nelson, *Women of Color*, chap. 5.

104. Abortion—Part 2, 593.

105. Siegel, "Reasoning from the Body," 365.

106. Critchlow, *Intended Consequences*, 200.

107. Carole Mason, *Killing for Life: The Apocalyptic Narrative of Pro-life Politics* (Ithaca, NY: Cornell University Press, 2002), 10–11.

NOTES TO CHAPTER 6

1. Lynn Paltrow, "Amicus Brief: Richard Thornburgh v. American College of Obstetricians and Gynecologists," *Women's Rights Law Reporter* 9 (Winter 1986): 20.

2. Ibid., 23.

3. Christopher Tietze, "Two Years' Experience with a Liberal Abortion Law: Its Impact on Fertility Trends in New York City," *Family Planning Perspectives* 5 (1973): 36.

4. Stanley Henshaw, "Unintended Pregnancies in the United States, 1987–1994," *Family Planning Perspectives* 30 (1998): 24–29, 46; S. S. Brown and L. Eisenberg, eds., *The Best Intentions: Unintended Pregnancy and the Well-Being of Children and Families* (Washington, DC: Institute of Medicine and National Academic Press, 1995), 3.

5. Loretta Ross, Sherrilyn Ifill, and Sabrae Jenkins, "Emergency Memoran-

dum to Women of Color," in Marlene G. Fried, ed., *From Abortion to Reproductive Freedom: Transforming a Movement* (Boston: South End Press, 1990), 147–49.

6. Linda Gordon, *The Moral Property of Women: A History of Birth Control Politics in America* (Urbana: University of Illinois Press, 2002), 25.

7. Phillip B. Levine, Douglas Staiger, Thomas J. Kane, and David J. Zimmerman, "*Roe v. Wade* and American Fertility," *American Journal of Public Health* 89 (1999): 199–203.

8. Elizabeth Terry-Humen, Jennifer Manlove, and Kristin A. Moore, "Births Outside of Marriage: Perceptions vs. Reality," A Child Trends Research Brief (Washington, D.C., April 2001).

9. Ibid.

10. See Rickie Solinger, *Wake Up Little Susie: Single Pregnancy and Race before Roe v. Wade* (New York: Routledge, 2000).

11. "Divorce, Child Custody and Child Support," U.S. Department of Commerce, Bureau of the Census, June 1979, table 8, 14.

12. Barbara Seaman, "Pelvic Autonomy: Four Proposals," *Social Policy* 6 (September–October 1975): 43–47. Seaman first presented these demands at a women's health conference—another expression of post-*Roe* women's activism—in Boston in April 1975.

13. The American Civil Liberties Union established its Reproductive Freedom Project in 1974. Historian Jennifer Nelson treats the successes and frustrations of post-*Roe* coalition-building in "Race, Class, and Sexuality: Reproductive Rights and the Campaign for an Inclusive Feminism," chap. 5 of her *Women of Color and the Reproductive Rights Movement* (New York: New York University Press, 2003).

14. *Congressional Record*, Senate, May 21, 1981, 10684.

15. Mildred Hanson, "Reflections of a Provider before and since *Roe*," *Perspectives on Sexual and Reproductive Health* 35 (January–February 2003): 34–36.

16. Maureen Bitler and Madeline Zavodny, "Did Abortion Legalization Reduce the Number of Unwanted Children? Evidence from Adoptions," *Perspectives on Sexual and Reproductive Health* 34 (January–February 2002): 27.

17. Karin Evans, *The Lost Daughters of China: Abandoned Girls, Their Journey to America, and the Search for a Missing Past* (New York: Tarcher, 2000), 244.

18. Anjani Chandra, Joyce Abma, Penelope Maza, and Christine Bachrach, "Adoption, Adoption Seeking and Relinquishment for Adoption in the United States," Advance Data, No. 306. National Center for Health Statistics, U.S. Department of Health and Human Services (May 1999), 5.

19. George A. Akerlof, Janet L. Yellen, and Michael L. Katz, "An Analysis of Out-of-Wedlock Childbearing in the United States," *Quarterly Journal of Economics* 111 (1996): 277–318.

20. Pamela Black, "Abortion Affects Men, Too," *New York Times Magazine*, March 28, 1982, 83, 94.

21. Linda Greenhouse, "New Poll Finds Wide Support for Abortion Rights," *New York Times,* January 21, 1988, 18.

22. Hanson, "Reflections of a Provider," 36.

23. Susan Bordo, *Unbearable Weight: Feminism, Western Culture, and the Body* (Berkeley: University of California Press, 1993).

24. See Reva Siegel, "Reasoning from the Body: A Historical Perspective on Abortion Regulation and Questions of Equal Protection," *Stanford Law Review* 44 (1993): 331.

25. Rosalind Pollack Petchesky, *Abortion and Woman's Choice: The State, Sexuality and Reproductive Freedom* (Boston: Northeastern University Press, 1990), xviii. Feminist leader Eleanor Smeal defined abortion violence this way in 1995: "The violence must be understood in the context of trying to destroy the feminist movement. . . . To call us Nazis is an attempt to destroy the intellectual and moral underpinnings of the movement. We used to say we would know the movement had power when they started shooting us. . . . The good part is we're nearer to power, and the bad part is they're shooting us." "Where Do We Go from Here?" *Ms.,* May–June 1995, 58.

26. Jane Mauldon and Suzanne Delbanco, "Public Perceptions about Unplanned Pregnancy," *Family Planning Perspectives* 29 (January–February 1997): 29.

27. Rachel K. Jones, Jacqueline E. Darroch, and Stanley K. Henshaw, "Patterns in the Socioeconomic Characteristics of Women Obtaining Abortions in 2000–2001," *Perspectives on Sexual and Reproductive Health* 34 (September 2002): 231–34.

28. William D. Mosher and Christine A. Bachrach, "Understanding U.S. Fertility: Continuity and Change in the National Survey of Family Growth, 1988–1995," *Family Planning Perspectives* 28 (January–February 1996): 5.

29. Charles Murray, "The Coming White Underclass," *Wall Street Journal,* October 29, 1993, 14.

30. "The America We Seek: A Statement of Pro-Life Principles and Concerns" (1996), firstthings.com.

31. "Woman Hopes for Marriage, More Children," *Visalia Times-Delta,* January 11, 1991, 3A; "Legal Interventions during Pregnancy: Court-Ordered Medical Treatments and Legal Penalties for Potentially Harmful Behavior by Pregnant Women," Board of Trustees Report, *Journal of the American Medical Association* 264 (November 28, 1990): 2663–70.

32. Tamar Lewin, "A Plan to Pay Welfare Mothers for Birth Control," *New York Times,* February 9, 1991, A11.

33. Linda McClain, "'Irresponsible' Reproduction," *Hastings Law Journal* 47 (1996): 415.

34. Dorothy Roberts, *Killing the Black Body: Race, Reproduction, and the Meaning of Liberty* (New York: Pantheon, 1997).

35. Charles Murray, "Stop Favoring Unwed Mothers," *New York Times*, January 16, 1992, 23.

36. "Serving the Term," *New York Times*, October 26, 1982, 28.

37. Katha Pollitt, "Subject to Debate," *Nation*, December 12, 1994, 717.

38. Dallas A. Blanchard, *The Anti-abortion Movement and the Rise of the Religious Right: From Polite to Fiery Protest* (New York: Twayne, 1994), 40.

39. Siegel, "Reasoning from the Body," 379.

40. See Blanchard, *Anti-abortion Movement*; and Patricia Baird-Windle and Eleanor J. Bader, *Targets of Hatred: Anti-abortion Terrorism* (New York: Palgrave, 2001); Marlene Gerber Fried, ed., *From Abortion to Reproductive Freedom: Transforming a Movement* (Boston: South End Press, 1990), 145.

41. Tamar Lewin, "Hurdles Increase for Many Women Seeking Abortions," *New York Times*, March 15, 1992, A1.

42. Joseph Berger, "Centers' Abortion Ads Called 'Bogus,'" *New York Times*, July 16, 1986, II, 2.

43. *Webster v. Reproductive Health Services*, 492 U.S. 490 (1989).

44. *Rust v. Sullivan*, 500 U.S. 173 (1991).

45. *Planned Parenthood of Southeastern Pa. v. Casey*, 505 U.S. 833 (1992).

46. Ronald Reagan, "Abortion and the Conscience of the Nation," *Human Life Review*, Spring 1983.

47. Neil A. Lewis, "Selection of Conservative Judges Insures a President's Legacy," *New York Times*, July 1, 1992, A13.

48. Nadine Brozan, "Abortion Ruling: Ten Years of Bitter Conflict," *New York Times*, November 15, 1983, 17.

49. See Will Saletan, *Bearing Right: How Conservatives Won the Abortion War* (Berkeley: University of California Press, 2003).

50. Jacqueline E. Darroch, David J. Landry, and Susheela Singh, "Changing Emphases in Sexual Education in U.S. Public Secondary Schools, 1988–1999," *Family Planning Perspectives* 32 (September–October 2000): 204–12.

51. *Committee to Defend Reproductive Rights v. Myers*, Cal., 625 P.2d 799.

52. "Where Do We Go from Here?" 60.

53. See, for example, Stephen Matthews, David Ribar, and Mark Wilhelm, "The Effects of Economic Conditions and Access to Reproductive Health Services on State Abortion Rates and Birthrates," *Family Planning Perspectives* 2 (March–April 1997): 52–60.

54. Siegel, "Reasoning from the Body," 360–63.

55. Rachel Roth, *Making Women Pay: The Hidden Costs of Fetal Rights* (Ithaca, NY: Cornell University Press, 2000), 194.

56. See, for example, Amy Harmon, "As Gene Test Menu Grows, Who Gets to Choose?" *New York Times*, July 21, 2004, A1, A15.

57. Bioethicist Ruth Hubbard has written: "As far as a fetus's medical and legal rights are concerned, I insist that it does not have any. My criteria rely on

simple geography: as long as one cannot get at the fetus without manipulating the woman, she is the only one with the right to make decisions. Once the baby is outside and its well-being no longer impacts her physical autonomy, then others can begin to speak for it, provided they take responsibility for what they say or do." *Profitable Promises: Essays on Women, Science and Health* (Monroe, ME: Common Courage Press, 1995), 146.

58. Roth, *Making Women Pay*, 117; Bordo, *Unbearable Weight*, 88.

59. Carol Mason, *Killing for Life: The Apocalyptic Narrative of Pro-life Politics* (Ithaca, NY: Cornell University Press, 2002), 38–39.

60. Bordo, *Unbearable Weight*, 85.

61. See Ruth Hubbard, *The Politics of Women's Biology* (New Brunswick, NJ: Rutgers University Press, 1990), 192.

62. Roth, *Making Women Pay*, 47–48.

63. Ibid., 97.

64. Roberts, *Killing the Black Body*, 175, 178, 181.

65. Siegel, "Reasoning from the Body," 366–67. When we review what the government has been doing lately for the "fetal person," we see that its activities focus on neither the well-being of the woman nor the health of the fetus. I am thinking of the Unborn Victims of Violence Act, George W. Bush's initiative to provide Medicaid for the unborn, and recent interest in appointing attorneys for fetuses. See Jean Reith Schroedel, *Is the Fetus a Person? A Comparison of Policies across the Fifty States* (Ithaca, NY: Cornell University Press, 2000).

66. Howard J. Osofky, *The Pregnant Teenager: A Medical, Educational and Social Analysis* (Springfield, IL: Thomas, 1966), 104–5.

67. *Ordway v. Hargraves*, 323 F. Supp. 1155 (D. Mass. 1971). A pregnant, unmarried high school student excluded from regular school classes and given home instruction sued for readmission. The court ordered immediate readmission of the student on an equal basis with other students because (1) there was no showing of danger to her physical or mental health resultant from her attending classes during regular school hours; (2) nor was there any valid educational reason, or any other reason, that would justify her receiving educational treatment which was not equal to that given all other students in her class.

68. *Eisenstadt v. Baird*, 405 U.S. 438 (1972). Justice Brennan's words in this decision made the legalization of abortion inevitable. He wrote, "If the right to privacy means anything, it is the right of the individual . . . to be free from unwarranted governmental intrusion into matters so fundamentally affecting a person as the decision whether to bear or beget a child."

69. *Danforth v. Missouri*, 428 U.S. 52 (1976).

70. Between 1960 and 1986, the proportion of teenage mothers who were unmarried rose from 15 percent to 61 percent, while the total number of children growing up with only one parent doubled to a full quarter of all children under

eighteen. Stephanie Coontz, *The Way We Never Were: American Families and the Nostalgia Trap* (New York: Basic Books, 2000), 3.

71. See the "Introduction" of the Personal Responsibility and Work Opportunity Act (PRWOA) regarding the "negative consequences" for a child born to a single mother. In response to these charges, Dorothy Roberts observes that the new federal welfare program, described in this document, "does not simply exclude Black women; it penalizes their reproduction. The law not only cuts off Black children from benefits needed to survive but it blames their very birth for their disadvantaged status." *Killing the Black Body*, 86.

72. William J. Bennett, "Illegitimacy and Welfare: Hearings on H.R. 4 before the Subcommittee on Human Resources, 104th Cong., 1st sess., January 20, 1995 (Washington, DC: U.S. Government Printing Office, 1995).

73. "A National Strategy to Prevent Teen Pregnancy," 1997–1998 Annual Report, U.S. Department of Health and Human Services, June 1998; Laura Meckler, "Teen Pregnancy Rate Continues to Fall," Associated Press, April 23, 1997.

74. Steven A. Holmes, "Study of Teenagers Hints Gains for Those Having Abortions," *New York Times*, January 25, 1990, A21; "Parental Notice Laws: Their Catastrophic Impact on Teenagers' Right to Abortion," ACLU Foundation (1986); "Battle on Abortion Turns to Rights of Teenagers," *New York Times*, July 6, 1989, A1, A23.

75. Bob Reeg, Christine Grisham, and Annie Shepard, "Families on the Edge: Homeless Young Parents and Their Welfare Experiences: A Survey of Homeless Youth and Service Providers," Center for Law and Social Policy and National Network for Youth, 2002, 8; Richard Wertheimer and Kristin Anderson Moore, "Childbearing by Teens: Links to Welfare Reform," publication no. 308015, August 1998, Urban Institute.

76. Naomi Seiler, "Is Teen Marriage a Solution?" Center for Law and Social Policy, April 2002, 9.

77. David J. Landry, Lisa Kaeser, and Cory L. Richards, "Abstinence Promotion and the Provision of Information about Contraception in Public School District Sexuality Education Policies," *Family Planning Perspectives* 31 (1999): 280–86.

78. Ceci Connolly, "Some Abstinence Programs Mislead Teens, Report Says," *Washington Post*, December 2, 2004, A1.

79. "Sex Smarts Survey: Gender Roles" (Menlo Park, CA: Kaiser Family Foundation, 2002); "Fact Sheet—Sex Education and Teenage Sexuality," prepared by Lisa D. Wade for Sociologists for Women in Society; "A National Strategy to Prevent Teenage Pregnancy."

80. Kate Shatzkin, "A Better Mess on Teen Pregnancy," *Baltimore Sun*, November 9, 1999.

81. P. Donovan, "The Adolescent Family Life Act," *Family Planning Perspectives* 16 (September–October 1984): 227.

82. Janellen Dufy and Jodie Levin Epstein, "Adding It Up: Teenage Parents and Welfare . . . Uncounted, Oversanctioned, Underserved," Center for Law and Social Policy, 2002.

83. Scott Boggess and Carolyn Bradner, "Trends in Adolescent Males' Abortion Attitudes, 1988–1995: Differences by Race and Ethnicity," *Family Planning Perspectives* 32 (May–June 2000): 118–23; Elizabeth Hayt, "Surprise, Mom: I'm against Abortion," *New York Times,* March 30, 2003, IX, 1.

84. Rachel Roth, "The Reproductive Rights of Prisoners: Between a Rock and a Hard Place," *Sojourner: The Women's Forum,* July 31, 1999, 11.

85. See Rachel Roth, "Do Prisoners Have Abortion Rights?" *Feminist Studies* 30 (Summer 2004): 353–81.

86. Roth, "Reproductive Rights of Prisoners."

87. Adoption and Safe Families Act of 1997 (ASFA–Public Law 105-89) (1997).

88. Joan Callahan, "Contraception or Incarceration: What's Wrong with This Picture?" *Stanford Law and Policy Review* 7 (1996): 67–82.

89. Roberts, *Killing the Black Body,* 305.

90. *Monmouth County Correctional Institute Inmates v. Lanzaro,* 834 F.2d 326, 347 (3d Cir. 1987).

91. Roth, "Reproductive Rights of Prisoners."

92. Roth, "Do Prisoners Have Abortion Rights?"

93. Lynn Paltrow, "The War on Drugs and the War on Abortion: Some Initial Thoughts on the Connections, Intersections and the Effects," 28 *Southern University Law Review* 28 (2001): 201.

94. Roth, "Reproductive Rights of Prisoners."

95. *Monmouth County Correctional Institution Inmates v. Lanzaro.*

96. Roth, "Do Prisoners Have Abortion Rights?"

97. The following six paragraphs are based on Jael Silliman, Marlene Gerber Fried, Loretta Ross, and Elena R. Gutierrez, *Undivided Rights: Women of Color Organize for Reproductive Justice* (Boston: South End Press, 2004).

98. Ibid., 375, 394.

Acknowledgments

IN THESE VERY TOUGH TIMES, when the political party in power wants to roll back the human rights achievements of the last generation and more, I am very grateful to be a historian. Historians insist on the long view. They are dedicated to understanding change over time. The historians I've always relied on are dedicated to studying the ways that social justice movements live on, sometimes quietly, in difficult historical eras, and flourish again. These perspectives, so important to my work and my life, make me want to thank my teachers all over again, starting with the late Herbert Gutman and the very much living Eric Foner. Equally important, I want to thank in a very heartfelt if general way the scores of historians and others whose work is incorporated in this book. Writing a synthetic volume has been an unexpected pleasure and a wonderful intellectual journey because of the contours and content of this body of work.

Several scholars have read all or parts of the book at various stages. Thanks to the mid-Hudson contingent: Miriam Cohen, Molly Shanley, and Amy Kesselman, for very important readings of a somewhat ragged manuscript. I am very grateful to Laura Briggs and Rachel Roth and Eric Zinner for extremely careful and helpful readings of the penultimate version. Rachel Roth devoted extraordinary care to everything from sentence structure to factual accuracy to conceptual cogency. She saved me from dozens of mistakes. I am particularly grateful that all of the readers urged me to broaden the scope of the book at crucial places. Until now, I don't think I've ever really fully understood the public acknowledgement to one's readers that excludes them from responsibility for the final product while honoring their contribution. This time I understand. These readers were brilliant and cannot be held responsible for how far I fell from using all the riches they offered.

Thanks are due to Eric Zinner, who invited me to write this volume some years ago and who nicely waited while I whittled away the pile of

287

other projects I kept concocting. He even published another volume of mine while waiting for this one. That was gracious.

Thanks to Ruby Tapia, Maurice Stevens, Katie Stewart, Maddy Fox, Dennis O'Keefe, Joe Stoeckert, and Russ Howitt. Thank you very much to Katherine Arnoldi. And thanks to Patti Gassaway because I always thank her.

Finally, deep into middle age, I am still finding out about being a mother, and about the blessings of having been able to have the right number of children for me. (And exactly the right children.) Thanks to Nell Geiser, who read a couple of chapters of the manuscript and incisively pointed out all the things I needed to fix, while encouraging me to believe this book is important. Thanks to Zachary Leeds, who provided me with some Supreme Court briefs and access to other legal materials just when I needed them and who challenges me intellectually and makes me laugh all the time. And thanks to Jim Geiser, my husband.

Index

A. H. Robbins Co., 175, 177

Abbey, Dr. Charlotte, 78

Abele v. Markle, (1972), 185

Abortion, 153–161; and adoption, 204, 216; "back-alley," 119; and the Catholic Church, 69, 183; changing meanings of, 20–21; and common ground, 206; and community control, 198; cost of, 118–119, 202; as crime against chastity, 55–56, 62; criminalization, 10, 55, 69; delay and risk, 202; experiences, post-*Roe*, 203–204; and female frivolity, 69; and feminism, 181, 185; and the Great Depression, 118–122; and hospital exemptions, 207; insurance, 120; and lack of prosecution before *Roe*, 100, 218; and lack of religious objection to, 183; and the law, 157–158; legalization, 178–186; "license," 222; and mandatory counseling, 230; in New York City, 181, 210; and Medicaid, 203; and nineteenth-century feminists, 60; outcomes, 120; and overpopulation, 184; and post-*Roe* deathrate, 211; and privacy, 186; and promiscuity, 54; prosecution and race, 122; and prostitution, 74; and psychiatrists, 158; and public funding restrictions, 200; as public health issue, 118; and public opinion, 81; and quickening, 54; and race, 62, 69; and racialized death rates, 193; and rape and incest, 207, 224; rates, 57, 61, 76, 100, 118, 203, 210, 239; recriminalization of, 249–250; rights and Young Lords, 183; and reform, 184–185; in rural South, 124; and safety, 157; self-induced, 105, 120–122, 157; self-induced and race, 211; and sexuality, 216–217; and slavery, 229; therapeutic and race, 211; and third-party consent, 207; underground, 183; as women-centered practice, 55; and women's emancipation, 61–62; and women's resistance, 157

"Abortion and the Conscience of the Nation," 229

Abortion clinic, as symbol and target, 219, 225

Abortion funding cases, 201–203

Abortion "trauma," 204

Abortionists, 76, 104–105; arrests of, 154–155; "back-alley," 157; Chinese, 123; and personal danger, 154; in postwar era, 153–161; proficiency of, 118; protection of, 118, 154; as public health asset, 154; and race, 122; trials, 155–158

Abstinence education, 230, 238, 240–241; and misinformation, 240–241

Abu Ghraib prison, 244

May 14, 2004 - Approx. 7:30pm

— Dad gave me 2 letters from
Equifax. They were wrinkled
and appeared to be have been
Steamed open. They were
dated mid-April + confirmed
my Security freeze +
NY address.

↓

Odd, among other things,
b/c he's been here since Tues

About the Author

Rickie Solinger is a historian and a curator. She is the author of *Wake Up Little Susie: Single Pregnancy and Race before Roe v. Wade* (1992, 2000); *The Abortionist: A Woman against the Law* (1994); and *Beggars and Choosers: How the Politics of Choice Shapes Adoption, Abortion, and Welfare in the United States* (2001). She is the editor of *Abortion Wars: A Half Century of Struggle, 1950–2000* (1998) and, with Gwendolyn Mink, *Welfare: A Documentary History of U.S. Policy and Politics* (2003). Solinger has curated art and photography exhibitions associated with her work on reproductive politics, welfare politics, and the politics of motherhood, race, and class in the United States. These shows have traveled to more than seventy college and university galleries around the country since 1992.